"I can assure you that death is another beginning, and that when you are dead, you are not silenced. For is this voice that you hear now, silence? Is the presence that you sense within this room, death? . . ."

Late in 1963, Jane Roberts and her husband were experimenting with a Ouija board when a personality calling himself "Seth" began forming messages. Soon, Miss Roberts began passing easily into trance—her gestures, her eyes, her voice "borrowed" by Seth himself.

THE SETH MATERIAL is the documented story of how a woman who balked at the idea of life after death was confronted with overwhelming proof. Seth has diagnosed illnesses, correctly described the contents of sealed envelopes (and buildings thousands of miles away), and given life readings. He has materialized apparitions in a well-lit living room, and continues to amaze students of the occult and professionals alike. And from the very beginning, the text of each semi-weekly session has been recorded in full.

Here is the best from an ongoing series of remarkable "lectures" on health, dreams, astral projection, God, reincarnation, and the mechanisms of man's subconscious. As Raymond Van Over says in his Introduction, "Seth, I believe, has a great talent for introducing complex and often difficult subjects simply and clearly. . . . Philosophically, the Seth material is some of the best of its type I have ever read." Often picking up a topic exactly where he left off six months before, Seth brilliantly explains many of the problems and paradoxes of the occult, and gives numerous instructions for developing ESP that any reader can test for himself. Illustrated with striking photographs taken during an actual session, THE SETH MATERIAL offers absorbing and convincing evidence of one of the most extraordinary psychic "teachers" of the century.

Jane Roberts grew up in Saratoga Springs, N.Y., and attended Skidmore College. Before her work led her into psychic exploration, she published a number of short stories and poems in national magazines and quarterlies; and two novels: *The Rebellers* and *Bundu*. Her HOW TO DEVELOP YOUR ESP POWER was published by Frederick Fell. She now lives in Elmira with her husband, Robert Butts, and has compiled a new book dictated entirely in trance— *SETH SPEAKS: The Eternal Vitality of The Soul*, now also available from Prentice-Hall.

W9-AYX-026

Books by Jane Roberts

HOW TO DEVELOP YOUR ESP POWER
*THE SETH MATERIAL
*SETH SPEAKS: The Eternal Validity of the Soul
*THE NATURE OF PERSONAL REALITY: A Seth Book

Novels:

THE REBELLERS
BUNDU
*THE EDUCATION OF OVERSOUL 7

* Available from Prentice-Hall, Inc.

THE SETH MATERIAL

by

Jane Roberts

PRENTICE-HALL, Inc., Englewood Cliffs, New Jersey

*This book is dedicated to Seth,
and to Rob, my husband*

The Seth Material by Jane Roberts
© 1970 by Jane Roberts
Copyright under International and Pan American
Copyright Conventions

ISBN 0–13–807180–2
Paperback 0–13–807198–5
Library of Congress Catalog Card Number: 75–112971
Printed in the United States of America   T
Prentice-Hall International, Inc., London
Prentice-Hall of Australia, Pty. Ltd., Sydney
Prentice-Hall of Canada, Ltd., Toronto
Prentice-Hall of India Private Ltd., New Delhi
Prentice-Hall of Japan, Inc., Tokyo

20 19 18 17 16 15 14 13 12 11

INTRODUCTION

Mediumship is a fascinating and provocative subject for it touches upon essential questions about the mind of man, the nature of his consciousness, and even his ultimate destiny. A medium is normally defined as "a person supposed to be susceptible to supernormal agencies and able to impart knowledge derived from them, or to perform actions impossible without their aid." Most people picture a medium as a lady bedecked in exotic clothing, skulking in dark corners, waiting to bilk her clients of their hard-earned money. While I have no doubt that such mediums still do exist—and have even run across some—this is hardly a complete picture.

It was just before the turn of the century that mediumship became popular and Spiritualism developed as its religion. Séances were then held in semidarkness in a small, well-designed room, often resembling a small theater whose set was a chapel or had some other religious overtones. The sitters, usually emotionally overwrought by some recent tragedy in their family, were further brought to a point of hysteria by hymn singing and organ music. It was, overall, a well-staged production. The medium went into a trance and through the help of her spirit "control," communicated messages from departed loved ones in the "spirit world." Most often these messages were trivial and even foolish, but the bereaved went home comforted that their loved ones still existed "somewhere" and were "happy."

Sometimes the medium exhibited knowledge that appeared to be some form of extrasensory perception. It was this aspect of mediumship that gave rise to parapsychology, or the controlled, scientific investigation of ESP. There is no doubt that mediumship and Spiritualism were, and still are, excessively open to fraud. In the subtler realms of perception, objective evidence is hard to come by and almost impossible to place under effectively controlled conditions. In most such investigations, facts are often accepted not on evidence, of which there is little, but on faith, of which there is always an abundance. Perhaps the well-known psychical researcher Harry Price put it best when he observed that "Spiritualism is, at its best, a religion; at its worst, a 'racket'."

But since investigation of mediumistic trances began, it has become clear that they are a complex experience and part of a larger phenomenon now designated as "altered states of consciousness." Pathological conditions often predominate among the other types of trance states such as comas, catalepsy, syncope, and suspended animation. All these are associated with unconsciousness, as are a number of other states resulting from certain drugs or the effects of disease upon the body chemistry; and these are all more intense than other altered states such as normal sleep, hypnosis, or somnambulism.

Of the many types of altered states of consciousness, mediumship is among the most valuable, for it is in mediumship that the subjective realm of man's mind may be investigated most conveniently. Many who have studied mediumship have written that in effect it is a method for expanding awareness. British physicist Raynor Johnson has observed that there are many states "in which consciousness is withdrawn from the normal waking level—which collectively we may call trance states. Some can be created by hypnosis . . . by drugs like mescaline or by anaesthetics, and others can be entered by certain yogic practices. . . . A medium, or a sensitive, can pass voluntarily into one of these states, in which consciousness is withdrawn to an interim level of the self, and can at the same time maintain a 'communication line' to the external world." Because it is the *self*-induction of a trance state and is relatively free of pathological conditions, mediumship affords a greater element of control over the experience, just as in the case of hypnosis.

Jane Roberts shares a unique characteristic with a few other outstanding mediums such as Eileen Garrett and Mrs. Osborne Leonard. Many mediums react to their own trance material with an almost religious credulity, and indeed religious convictions frequently grow out of their mediumistic experience. But in spite of their fascination with the subliminal world they have made contact with, some mediums resist the temptation to believe immediately and to depend upon the communications of a trance personality. Mrs. Garrett, for instance, has dedicated her life to investigating the meaning of mediumship, her own unconscious world, and parapsychological phenomena in general. Mrs. Leonard also dedicated herself to probing the questions of her own mediumship, and allowed herself to be the subject of numerous tests.

Great mediums are as rare as great musicians or great artists. Their characteristics include a peculiar mixture of susceptibility to trance states and a strong personality that is at once curious, objective, and honestly self-critical. Of course, many earmarks of the exceptional medium's character cannot be so easily characterized, but it seems clear to me that Jane Roberts is an exceptional medium.

To experiment boldly with one's own subjective experience—to examine the sources of inspiration, imagination or creativity—has always been characteristic of the exceptional personality. André Breton, author of the *Surrealist Manifesto,* was obsessed with the idea of combining the real and unreal in art, perhaps because like the Japanese sumi artist, he was unsure of the distinctions between the two. He conducted a series of experiments in automatic writing in an attempt to discover the arcane aspects of what we know as "real." The result, Breton argued, was a purer expression of the inner man, and this wedding of the unconscious world with objective or conscious awareness is not dissimilar to the trek Jane Roberts has undertaken. For a young woman who has not spent many years in mediumship, she has come a remarkably long way toward the open, self-critical analysis necessary to truly understanding her mediumship and its broader implications. Already she has become deeply committed to the practical application of what are, basically, philosophical questions. Some of this drive, however, must be attributed to the nature of Seth, the trance personality that has developed from her mediumship.

A trance personality is usually called a "control" because it supposedly manipulates the physical body of the entranced medium, often taking on unique and individualized characteristics. Originally, the medium's control was of course believed to be a spirit or discarnate entity who took over the medium as a means of communicating with the living. But in *The World of Psychic Phenomena*, F. S. Edsall points out that the development of trance personalities or controls seems to depend on subconscious experiences related to the medium's background or environment. The questions of what a "control" personality is and how it communicates are extremely difficult ones that have been studied for decades by parapsychologists and depth analysts. (Seth, incidentally—with common sense and honesty, it seems to me—discusses the difficult problem of distortion of fact in material coming through a medium. Because they are closely associated with supposedly supernormal powers, mediums are also expected to be absolutely one hundred percent accurate. This, of course, is not the case, but the attitude popularly prevails and can be seen in the public attitude toward Cayce or Dixon.) Some believe that man has talents that can transcend the senses, and quite possibly influence the unconscious without seeming to affect the conscious mind at all. Edsall writes that experiences related to a medium's "environment might play a part in the formation of these extraordinary secondary personalities that, in the case of certain outstanding mediums, seem so uncannily all-knowing."

Many psychological theories have been put forward to explain the existence of trance personalities, such as New York analyst Ira Progoff's theory of the "dynatype." After extensive research with Eileen Garrett, Progoff concluded that the "presence of the various control figures is essential to maintaining a . . . balance in Mrs. Garrett's psyche." Dr. Progoff views control figures in mediumship "not as spirit entities, but as symbolic forms of dramatization by which larger principles of life are made articulate in human experience." Similarly,

Socrates had his personal "daimon," Graves his White Goddess of Poetry, and Noah in drunken dreams perceived himself as the incarnation of his own ancestors, first Adam, then Jeremiah. Each man—so the theory relates—personifies in such a way what he *is*, subliminally. Psychics such as Mrs. Garrett have speculated that perhaps they create their own alternative selves, only in a more recognizable and reasonable form—as such daimons or "spirit" controls.

W. H. Salter, a well-known and objective psychical researcher, made another point, however: if the trance personality continues to communicate year after year, "never puts the mental or emotional emphasis wrong, and never speaks out of character, it is hard to construct a plausible explanation out of subconscious inference and dramatization on the medium's part."

The final, definitive answers lie somewhere in the future. And while it is important to ask questions, such inquiries should not supersede other equally important aspects of mediumship. The *content* of a medium's trance communications are often overlooked, undoubtedly because most of the time, they are somewhat foolish and incoherent statements. But again in those rare instances—such as the trance utterances of Edgar Cayce—there appear important and provocative ideas that demand consideration. And communications through Jane Roberts "trance" personality, Seth, deserve such attention.

The best trance material shows good psychological insight communicated through a compassionate, strong personality; and the Seth material conveys all of these qualities. Seth, however, adds one ingredient that most trance material lacks: clarity of thought and presentation. Most trance material, from ancient as well as modern mediumistic controls, couches itself not only in jumbled syntax but confused thought; however, Seth, I believe, has a great talent for introducing complex and often difficult subjects simply and clearly. To the practiced eye, the professional philosopher, and the academic parapsychologist, he will sometimes seem to deal with the familiar. (His feeling that one's mind leaves the body during sleep, for instance, is classical and hearkens back to primitive times.) But to those just beginning their acquaintance with the fascinating world of dreams, ESP and the other phenomenal aspects of the unconscious, Seth will be a crystal-sighted teacher.

And it is to these, the seeker, the questioner, that Seth continually addresses himself. The stated purpose of his communications is to provide a "means by which people can understand themselves better, reevaluate their reality, and change it." In the chapter on inner sensing, Seth offers clear and sound advice on how to go about expanding one's awareness and developing meditational techniques and ESP. Again unique to Seth and a few others, such as Edgar Cayce's trance communications, is a large dose of common-sense advice and sympathetic concern for individual problems that heavily dilute the philosophical and metaphysical speculations. These elements seem one of the prime characteristics of the Seth material, and are surely the ones I personally find most attractive.

Interestingly, Seth's personality and presentation are so individualistic that after a short period of familiarization one tends to regard them as coming from a trained modern intellect rather than from the opposite side of Isis' veil. The material also covers a surprisingly broad range of ideas, which are often intriguing and original. I am particularly interested in Seth's treatment of "personality fragment projection," which is strongly in the tradition of the Teutonic *doppleganger* and the Slavic *Vardoger*. (This is a very widespread phenomenon: even Freud, for instance, saw his *doppleganger,* fleetingly, in a mirror. De Maupassant once saw his "double" walk into a room, sit down in front of him, and dictate part of a book that had been giving the French author particular trouble. When finished, it stood up and vanished. I only wish Seth would more clearly describe the *mechanics* of the thing as opposed to the *theory*.) There is also, of course, the occult tradition of thought-form projection as described by Mrs. David-Neel when she created her Tibetan "tulpa."

Indeed, "an idea *is* an event," according to Seth. It is therefore logical that any idea—in whatever sphere of activity, whether physically materialized or not—would have an impact upon our lives. The "idea as reality" is another ancient concept which was formalized early in Western civilization by Plato and which has been retained by many philosophers down through the ages. But rather than discuss this concept in abstract terms only, Seth develops it to its logical conclusion. All ideas, thoughts, and areas of concentration help create a dynamic and continually interrelating universe with the *idea* playing as important and as tangible a role as any physical event.

Seth's theory on the Crucifixion is an ideal example. According to Seth, the Crucifixion originated in the "universe of dreams," occurring within another reality, and "emerged into history as an *idea*." Seth is not saying that the Crucifixion was just a "dream" rising from a common need within man, but an idea being actualized in another realm of time and space that affected our temporal world and changed our civilization. This is, of course, interesting speculation; but consider for a minute how readily we accept the simple philosophical dictum that "an idea can change the world." There are many examples: "Man cannot live by bread alone," "Love thy neighbor as thyself." In our daily lives we do try to manifest these ideas into reality, to make them move from the abstract world into the temporal one of cause and effect. Seth, in effect, is turning the tables on us by suggesting that reality can perhaps function in the *other* direction as well: the idea *is* reality which has a profound effect upon the temporal world all the time. The problem is to broaden our perceptual base and awareness so that temporal consciousness can manifest itself in this world of ideas, so we can become aware of the impact of this world of ideas upon our civilization and our personal lives. Seth says that "the dream universe possesses concepts which will some day completely transform the history of the physical world, but a denial of such concepts as possibilities delays their emergence." Kant, much of whose philosophy rests on the concept that "mind imposes" reality on the "data of sense," would have probably agreed with Seth that the senses "create the material world," rather than simply perceiving it.

Also within Seth's comments are passing glimpses of material that is so thought-provoking that it deserves considerably more attention that it receives. Seth mentions, for example, the existence of symbolic figures which assume identifiable forms within the unconscious in order to communicate more effectively. This is an area of research devoid of hard facts, but rich in speculation and experiental reports. The great Swiss psychoanalyst Carl Jung noted the existence of what he called archetypal figures in the unconscious who often communicate to the conscious mind through the symbolic garb of mythical, religious or great historical figures. (Jung himself spent years communicating with Philemon, an archetypal figure in his own unconscious.) Masters and Huston, after extensive research into the effects of LSD, classified the drug-induced expansion of consciousness into four categories; in the third or symbolic level, they reported the consistent manifestation of historical or legendary persons and an abundance of mythical symbols.

Philosophically, the Seth material is some of the best of its type I have ever read. A comparative study of Seth's thought should prove very interesting. His material is complex enough so that even the confines of this large book are not adequate. Naturally, it is therefore impossible to summarize it all in this short introduction. Many questions came to mind during the reading; many have remained unresolved; but to my mind, this is not a bad thing. After all, if we are mentally, emotionally, or spiritually stimulated to ask questions, probe our standardized attitudes and press beyond the limits of our prejudices into ever widening areas of thought, we can accomplish much. This, I believe, is the greatest value of the Seth personality and his communications. As he himself has indicated, he is a communicator and a stimulator of thought—as too few temporal teachers are.

No one can possibly know where this search is going to lead, but of one thing we can be sure: records of trance communications like the Seth material are of inestimable value, for they afford the rare opportunity of delving into the subjective mind of man. This is not a casual or passing benefit, for it is a glimpse into the headwaters of a river that is at once mysterious, provocative, and vitally important for humanity's well-being. This is the spring where inspiration drinks, where intuition sparks the scientific mind, where poets' dreams burst forth, and where a major portion of our lives, in terms of both time and energy, are spent.

Raymond Van Over
New York, New York

CONTENTS

Author's Introduction

It was February 29, 1968. I was holding one of my twice-weekly ESP classes. The large bay window was open, letting in the unusually warm night air. The lights were normally lit in my living room where classes are held. Suddenly I felt that we had a visitor. As always I went into trance easily, without preamble.

This class was composed of college girls. They had read my first book, knew about Seth, and had attended a few classes, but they had never witnessed a Seth session. My eyes closed. When they opened a few moments later, they were much darker. I began to speak for Seth. He had thrown my glasses to the floor in a quick characteristic gesture, yet now I scrutinized each student with sharp, clear focus. The voice that spoke was deep, quite loud, more masculine than feminine.

We were having a spontaneous Seth session. It served to introduce the students to Seth, and I will let a few excerpts from it serve the same purpose now, introducing Seth to those readers who have not heard of him:

1

"According to what you have been taught, you are composed of physical matter and cannot escape it, and this is not so. The physical matter will disintegrate, but you will not. Though you cannot find me, know that I am here. Your own parents seem to disappear before your eyes and vanish into nothingness forever. I can assure you that they will continue to live. I can assure you that death is another beginning, and that when you are dead, you are not silenced. For is this voice that you hear now, silence? Is this presence that you sense within this room, death?

"I am here to tell you that your joy is not dependent upon your youth, for I am hardly young. I am here to tell you that your joy is not dependent upon your physical body, for in your terms I have none. I have what I have always had, the identity that is mine. It is never diminished. It grows and develops.

"You are what you are, and you will be more. Do not be afraid of change, for you are change, and you change as you sit before me. All action is change, for otherwise there would be a static universe, and then indeed death would be the end. What I am is also what you are: individualized consciousness.

"Change with the seasons, for you are more than the seasons. You form the seasons. They are the reflections of your inner psychic climate. I came for one purpose this evening: so that you could sense my vitality, and sensing it, know that I speak to you from dimensions beyond those with which you are acquainted. The grave is not the end, for such a noisy one as I never spoke with the lips of death.

"I am in this room, although there is no object within which you can place me. You are as disembodied as I. You have a vehicle to use, a body that you call your own, and that is all. I borrow Ruburt's [Seth's name for me; in addition, Seth always speaks of me as male] with his consent, but what I am is not dependent upon atoms and molecules and what you are is not dependent upon physical matter. You have lived before and will live again, and when you are done with physical existence, you will still live.

"I come here as though I appeared through a hole in space and time. There are walks in space and time through which you can travel, and in dreams you have been where I am. I want you to feel your own vitality. Feel it travel through the universe and know that it is not dependent upon your physical image. In reality you project your own energy out to form the physical world. Therefore, to change your world, it is yourself you must change. You must change what you project.

"You always were and you always will be. This is the meaning of existence and joy. The God that is, is within you, for you are a part of all that is."

Seth spoke through me for over two hours, so quickly that the students had trouble taking notes. His joy and vitality were obvious. The personality was not mine. Seth's dry, sardonic humor shone from my eyes. The muscles of my face rearranged themselves into different patterns. My normally feminine gestures were replaced by his. Seth was enjoying himself in the guise of an old man, shrewd, lively, quite human. When he spoke of the joy of existence, ringing even through such a voice as his, that deep voice boomed. Later one of the students, Carol, told me that although she knew the words were coming from my mouth, still she felt that they were coming from all over, from the walls themselves.

During a break, Carol read the notes that she had taken. Suddenly, without transition, I was Seth again, leaning forward, joking:

"If you are to be my stenographer, you must do better than that. You are a mad scribbler."

Then a give-and-take period began in which Seth corrected Carol's notes as she read them, added several remarks to clear certain sentences, and bantered back and forth with her. The students asked questions, and Seth answered them.

This was a very simple session. Seth addressed himself to the students for the first time, yet he touched upon several issues that appear often in the Seth Material: The personality is multidimensional. The individual is basically free of space and time. The fate of each of us is in our own hands. Problems not faced in this life will be faced in another. We cannot blame God, society, or our parents for misfortunes, since before this physical life we chose the circumstances into which we would be born and the challenges that could best bring about our development. We form physical matter as effortlessly and unselfconsciously as we breathe. Telepathically, we are all aware of the mass ideas from which we form our overall conception of physical reality.

As of December 1969, my husband, Rob, and I have held over 500 Seth sessions, over a period of five years. My first book in this field, *How to Develop Your ESP Power*, briefly explained the circumstances leading to my interest in ESP, and the experiments that led to my introduction to Seth. Since then, Seth has demonstrated telepathic and clairvoyant abilities on occasions too frequent to mention. Through sessions he has helped friends, strangers, and students, and by following his instructions my husband and I are learning to develop our own psychic potentials.

Yet I was not a "born psychic" with a background of paranormal experience. Neither Rob nor I had any knowledge of such matters. Even after my first enthusiasm, I didn't accept these developments without serious self-questioning and intellectual analysis. I wanted to keep my experiences on as scientific a basis as possible.

"Yes," I said in effect. "I do speak in trance for a personality who claims to have survived death. Yes, you can develop your own extrasensory abilities. Yes, Seth does insist that reincarnation is a fact. But . . . but . . . but." I found the ideas presented in the Seth Material fascinating, but I was not about to accept them as the same kind of solid fact with which I accepted, say, the bacon I eat for breakfast. Now I know they are far more important.

To me it was tantamount to intellectual suicide to even admit the possibility that Seth actually was a personality who had survived death. Nowhere in my first book did I say that I thought Seth was exactly what he said he was: "an energy personality essence no longer focused in physical reality." Instead I studied the various explanations for such personalities given by psychologists and parapsychologists on the one hand, and by spiritualists on the other. Nowhere did I find an explanation as logical and consistent as that given in the Seth Material itself.

I was so used to thinking of myself as a physical creature, bound to space and time, that I almost refused to accept the evidence of my own experience. While involved in the most intuitive work in the

4

world, I tried to become more and more objective. I tried to step back into a world I had really left forever—a universe in which nothing existed except in physical terms, a world in which communications from any other realities or dimensions were impossible. Yet, we continued to have Seth sessions twice a week.

I began to have out-of-body experiences (astral projections) as I sat in the living room, speaking for Seth. Seth described what I saw while my own consciousness was miles away, perceiving locations and events in another town or state. Our files contain statements from two brothers in California, for example, asserting that Seth correctly described their home and neighborhood while I spoke for him in Elmira, New York, some three thousand miles away. I could hardly deny those facts.

Following publication of my earlier book, letters came from strangers asking for help or advice. Finally I agreed to hold a few sessions for those most in need, though the responsibility frightened me. The people involved didn't attend the sessions since they lived in other parts of the country, yet they said the advice helped them; information given concerning individual backgrounds was correct. Seth often explained problems as the result of unresolved stresses in past reincarnational lives, and gave specific advice as to how the individuals could use their abilities now to meet these challenges.

Before this I had suspected that the reincarnational data was a delightful dish of fantasy cooked up by my own subconscious. When all this began, in fact, I wasn't at all sure that we survived death once, much less over and over again.

Rob and I were hardly religious in conventional terms. We haven't been to a church in years, except to attend weddings or funerals. I was brought up a Catholic, but as I grew older I found it more and more difficult to accept the God of my ancestors. Irony whispered that He was as dead as they were. The heaven that had sustained me as a child seemed in my teens to be a shallow mockery of meaningful existence. Who wanted to sit around singing hymns to a father-God, even if He *did* exist, and what sort of intelligent God would require such constant adoration? A very insecure, appallingly human kind of God indeed.

The alternative, that of hellfire, was equally unbelievable. Yet the conventional God of our fathers apparently sat without a qualm with the blessed in heaven, while the devil tortured the rest of the unlucky dead. That God, I decided, was out. I would not tolerate Him as a friend. For that matter He didn't treat His son too well either, as the story goes. But Christ you could at least respect, I thought. He'd been here; he knew how it was.

Before I was twenty, then, I'd left behind me that archaic God, the Virgin, and the communion of saints. Heaven and hell, angels and devils, were dismissed. This particular group of chemicals and atoms I called "me" would fall into no such traps—at least none that I could recognize.

Rob's background was different. His parents' brand of religion was a sort of social Protestantism, rather delightfully innocent of dogma. In general, God loved little boys and girls with starched shirts, acceptable addresses, polished shoes, and fathers who made good money—it also helped if their mothers baked cookies for the PTA.

Neither of us was bitter about such a God's apparent injustices— we didn't pay Him that much attention. I had my poetry; Rob, who is an artist, had his painting. Each of us felt a strong sense of contact with nature. No one was more surprised than I was, then, to find myself quite abruptly speaking for someone who was supposed to have survived death. I berated myself at times, thinking that even my Irish grandmother would have found spirits in the living room rather hard to take—and I used to think *she* was superstitious! A surviving soul seemed part and parcel of the adults' nonsense I'd thought I'd escaped, thanks to a college education, a quick mind, and a fine dose of native rebelliousness. It took me a while to discover that I was being as prejudiced against the idea of survival as some others were for it. Now I realize that while I was priding myself on my open-mindedness, my mental flexibility extended only to ideas that fit in with my own preconceptions. Now I know that human personality has a far greater reality than we are usually prepared to give it. *Someone* has produced over fifty notebooks of fascinating material, and even at my most skeptical moments I have to accept the reality of the sessions and the material. The scope, quality, and theories of the material "hooked" us almost at once.

Rob and I are both convinced that the Seth Material springs from sources beyond my self, and that it is much less distorted by pat, conventionalized symbolism than are other paranormal scripts we have encountered. Seth says this material has been given by himself and others in other times and places, but that it is given again, in new ways, for each succeeding generation through the centuries. The reader will have to make his own judgments, but personally I do accept his theories as valid and significant.

Moreover, the riddle of such personalities as Seth—call it "spirit possession," a "daemon" (as Socrates did)—has concerned mankind through the ages. The phenomenon is hardly new. Through telling my own story and presenting the material, I hope to throw some light upon the nature of such experiences and to show that human personality has abilities still to be tapped, and other ways to receive knowledge than those it usually employs.

The Seth Material has completely changed my ideas of the nature of reality, and reinforced my sense of identity. No longer do I feel as I did before, that man is the slave of time, illness, decay, and at the mercy of built-in destructive tendencies over which he has no control. I feel in control of my own destiny as never before, and no longer ruled by patterns subconsciously set during my childhood.

I don't mean to imply that I feel myself entirely released from every worry and fear, only that I now know we do have the freedom to change ourselves and our environment, and that in a very basic manner, we ourselves form the environment to which we then react. I believe that we form our own reality—now, and after death.

The purpose of this book is to introduce you to Seth and the Seth Material. Though Seth has appeared only once in a physical materialization, Rob has seen him clearly enough to paint a portrait of him that hangs in our living room (see the illustrated section). Through me, Seth has produced a continuing manuscript that runs well over five thousand double-spaced typewritten pages, in not quite five years' time. I know many "living" persons who haven't produced that much in a lifetime. Yet my own work continues: since the sessions began, I've written two books of nonfiction (not counting this one), two of poetry, and a dozen short stories. Seth certainly hasn't "stolen" any of my own creative energy for his own purposes.

The first chapters of this book will deal with the emergence of

Seth's personality and the impact he had on our lives as we tried to understand what was happening. Out of nowhere it seemed, I found myself having experiences that I considered nearly impossible. Never in our lives had we found ourselves so caught between curiosity and caution, so fascinated and baffled.

Excerpts from some of the early sessions will also be included in the first chapters, since Seth's ideas were then as new and strange to us as the sessions themselves. But the main emphasis will be on the story itself, from the first Ouija board experiment through the first instance when I startled Rob and myself by speaking for Seth; and the changes in our attitudes as further developments occurred. I'll also include examples of Seth's clairvoyant abilities.

The bulk of the book will deal with Seth's ideas on various subjects, such as life after death, reincarnation, health, the nature of physical reality, the God concept, dreams, time, identity, and perception. I'm sure that these excerpts from the material itself and some sample reincarnational readings will give most readers greater insights into their own personalities and the situations in which they find themselves. I hope that Seth's theories on health will benefit all my readers, and that the material on personality will help each discover for himself the multidimensional reality that is his heritage.

The philosophical and psychological implications of mediumship and ESP phenomena and the possible origins of the Seth Material, along with several questions concerning Seth's independent reality, will be considered. I'll also give Seth's advice as to the development of psychic abilities.

Someone who was familiar with psychic literature and paranormal experiences would have been better prepared for these events than I was, but I would not have missed them for the world.

CHAPTER
ONE:

We Meet Seth

———◦●◦———

The circumstances leading up to the Seth sessions still surprise me. I wasn't drifting, looking for a sense of purpose, for example. My first novel had just been published in paperback, and all my energies were channeled into becoming a good novelist and poet. I considered nonfiction the field of journalists, not creative writers. I thought my life and work were planned, my course set. Yet here I am, writing my third book of nonfiction.

The year 1963 had been a poor one for us, though. Rob had severe back trouble, and hardly felt well enough to paint when he came home from work. I was having difficulties settling on another book idea. Our old pet dog, Mischa, had died. Perhaps these circumstances made me more aware than usual of our human vulnerability, but certainly many people have had difficult years with no resulting emergence of psychic phenomena. Perhaps, all unknowing, I had reached a crisis and my psychic abilities awoke as the result of inner need.

Certainly such matters were far from my mind. To my knowledge, I'd never had a psychic experience in my life, and I didn't know anyone who had. Nothing in my background prepared me for the astonishing evening of September 9, 1963, yet it was this event, I'm sure, that initiated the sessions and my introduction to Seth.

It was a lovely autumn evening. After supper I sat down at my old table in the living room, as I always did, to work on my poetry. Rob was painting in the back studio, three rooms away. I took out my pen and paper and settled down with my ninth or tenth cup of coffee for the day, and my cigarettes. Willie, our cat, dozed on the blue rug.

What happened next was like a "trip" without drugs. If someone had slipped me an LSD cube on the sly, the experience couldn't have been more bizarre. Between one normal minute and the next, a fantastic avalanche of radical, new ideas burst into my head with tremendous force, as if my skull were some sort of receiving station, turned up to unbearable volume. Not only ideas came through this channel, but sensations, intensified and pulsating. I was tuned in, turned on—whatever you want to call it—*connected* to some incredible sorce of energy. I didn't even have time to call out to Rob.

It was as if the physical world were really tissue-paper thin, hiding infinite dimensions of reality, and I was suddenly flung through the tissue paper with a huge ripping sound. My body sat at the table, my hands furiously scribbling down the words and ideas that flashed through my head. Yet I seemed to be somewhere else, at the same time, traveling through things. I went plummeting through a leaf, to find a whole universe open up; and then out again, drawn into new perspectives.

I felt as if knowledge was being implanted in the very cells of my body so that I couldn't forget it—a gut knowing, a biological spirituality. It was feeling and knowing, rather than intellectual knowledge. At the same time I remembered having a dream the night before, which I had forgotten, in which this same sort of experience had occurred. And I knew the two were connected.

When I came to, I found myself scrawling what was obviously meant as the title of that odd batch of notes: *The Physical Universe As Idea Construction.* Later the Seth Material would develop those ideas,

10

but I didn't know that at the time. In one of the early sessions Seth said that this had been his first attempt to contact me. I only know that if I'd begun speaking for Seth that night, I would have been terrified.

As it was, I didn't know what had happened, yet even then I felt that my life had suddenly changed. The word "revelation" came to mind and I tried to dismiss it, yet the word was apt. I was simply afraid of the term with its mystical implications. I was familiar with inspiration in my own work, but this was as different from ordinary inspiration as a bird is from a worm!

The ideas that I "received" were just as startling. They turned all my ideas of reality upside down. That morning and each morning until that time, I'd been sure of one thing: you could trust physical reality. You might not like it at times, but you could depend on it. You could change your ideas toward it if you chose, but this would in no way change what reality was. Now I could never feel that way again.

During that experience I knew that we formed physical matter, not the other way around; that our senses showed us only one three-dimensional reality out of an infinite number that we couldn't ordinarily perceive; that we could trust our senses only so far and only so long as we did not ask questions that were beyond their limited scope of knowledge.

But more: I just didn't know, for example, that everything had its own consciousness. Now I suddenly *felt* the fantastic vitality present even in things I'd previously considered inanimate. A nail was sticking in the windowsill, and I experienced ever so briefly the consciousness of the atoms and molecules that composed it.

Despite all my previous ideas and common sense, I knew that time wasn't a series of moments one before the other, each one like a clothespin stuck on a line, but that all experience existed in some kind of eternal now. All of this was scribbled down so fast—and I still have that manuscript. Even now it fills me with that sense of discovery and revelation:

Here are a few quotes from that manuscript:

"We are individualized portions of energy, materialized within physical existence, to learn to form ideas from energy, and make

11

them physical (this is idea construction). We project ideas into an object, so that we can deal with it. But the object is the thought, materialized. This physical representation of idea permits us to learn the difference between the 'I' who thinks and the thought. Idea construction teaches the 'I' what it is, by showing it its own products in a physical manner. We learn by viewing our own creations, in other words. We learn the power and effects of ideas by changing them into physical realities; and we learn responsibility in the use of creative energy. . . .

"The entity is the basic self, immortal, nonphysical. It communicates on an energy level with other entities, and has an almost inexhaustible supply of energy at its command. The individual is the portion of the whole self that we manage to express physically. . . .

"The eye projects and focuses the inner image (idea) onto the physical world in the same manner that a motion-picture camera transfers an image onto a screen. The mouth creates words. The ears create sound. The difficulty in understanding this principle is due to the fact that we've taken it for granted that the image and sound already exist for the senses to interpret. Actually the senses are the channels of creation by which idea is projected into material expression.

"The basic idea is that the senses are developed, not to permit awareness of an already existing material world, but to create it. . . ."

Those ideas were only a touchstone for what would come later. The manuscript finally consisted of about a hundred pages, including new definitions of old terms. For example: "The subconscious is the threshold of idea's emergence into the individual conscious mind. It connects the entity and the individual. . . . The physical body is the material construction of the entity's idea of itself under the properties of matter. . . . Instinct is the minimum ability for idea construction necessary for physical survival. . . . The present is the apparent point of any idea's emergence into physical matter."

I think that this experience and the manuscript were *extensions* of the creative subconscious processes that are behind each creative act: normal creativity suddenly "turned on" or stepped up to an almost

12

incredible degree. Enough energy was generated in that evening to change the direction of my life and my husband's. For this reason I believe such experiences to be of utmost importance psychologically. I'm certain that the affair set off the emergence of my own unsuspected "psychic" abilities and acted as a trigger for the production of the Seth Material.

Apparently I'd reached a point where these abilities were ready to show themselves, so they did. Because of my early training as a writer, they emerged through words, rather than, say, visions, and in an experience that wouldn't frighten me too much.

I'd also like to mention here that I believe psychic ability itself is an outcropping or extension of creative abilities, inherent in each of us, and therefore normal rather than supranormal. As you'll see later, however, I do think that these abilities are attributes of another portion of our personalities with which we're relatively unfamiliar. I think, then, that normal creative abilities, stepped up, tune us into other dimensions of reality.

Following this episode, even my ordinary subjective experiences began to change. Very shortly afterward I began to recall my dreams —suddenly, and for no apparent reason. It was like discovering a second life. Not only that, but in the next two months I had two vivid precognitive dreams, the first, to my knowledge, that I ever had.

Our curiosity was aroused, to say the least. At a newsstand we noticed a book on ESP. The words "Clairvoyant Dreams" popped up from the cover, and we bought it. About this time I was also looking for a new book idea, and Rob made the suggestion that was to lead us further and further away from the way of life we'd always known.

The paperback we'd just purchased was on the coffee table between us as we sat talking. "I've got outlines for three novels, and none of them really please me," I said.

Rob picked up the book and said jokingly, "Why don't you do a do-it-yourself book on ESP?"

"Hon, you're out of your mind. I don't know a thing about ESP, that's why not. Besides, that's nonfiction. I've never done anything but fiction and poetry in my life."

13

"I know," Rob said. "But you're interested in dreams, certainly after those two particular ones you had. And what do you call that experience you had last month? Besides, the books we've seen have dealt only with well-known mediums. But what about ordinary people? What if everyone has those abilities?" I stared at him. He'd turned quite serious. "Couldn't you work out a series of experiments and try them out? Use yourself as a guinea pig."

Put that way, Rob's idea made sense. I could investigate a subject that now intrigued me, and do a book at the same time.

The very next day I began. Within a week I'd developed a group of experiments designed to discover whether or not the ordinary person could develop extrasensory abilities. I did an outline for the book and shipped it off to my publisher, but without any great hopes.

Somewhat to my surprise he answered quickly, and he was quite enthusiastic. What he wanted was three or four sample chapters. Rob and I were delighted, but somewhat appalled too, as we looked over the chapter headings I'd listed for the book: "A Do-It-Yourself Séance," "Telepathy, Fact or Fiction?", "How to Work the Ouija."

"Well, get to it," Rob said, laughing.

"You and your suggestions," I countered. By now I was really having second thoughts. We'd never been to a medium. We'd never had a telepathic experience in our lives, never even seen a Ouija board. On the other hand, I thought, what did I have to lose? (It wasn't until much later that I remembered that another of Rob's suggestions had launched me into fiction in the first place.)

So we began. We settled on the Ouija board first, because it seemed the least complicated of our various experiments. Our land-lady found a board in the attic and we borrowed it. Actually both of us were a little embarrassed the first few times we tried the board. My attitude was, "Well, let's get this out of the way so we can really get down to the things we're interested in, like telepathy and clairvoyance." No wonder our first attempts were failures.

The third time we tried it, the little pointer finally began to move beneath our fingertips. It spelled out messages supposedly coming from a Frank Withers (not the real name) who had lived in Elmira and died during the 1940's.

Here are a few examples. Rob asked the questions. The pointer spelled out the answers.

"Can you give us the year of your death?"
1942

"Did you know either of us?"
NO

"Were you married?"
YES

"Is your wife alive or dead?"
DEAD

"What was her first name?"
URSULA

"What was her last name?"
ALTERI

"What was your nationality?"
ENGLISH

"What was her nationality?"
ITALIAN

"In what year were you born?"
1885

We were surprised that the board worked for us. I thought it was a riot, two adults watching the pointer go scurrying across the board, and we didn't take it too seriously. For one thing, of course, neither of us particularly believed in life after death—certainly not conscious life, capable of communicating. Later on, we did learn that a man with the communicator's name was known to have lived in Elmira, and died in the 1940's—that took me back a bit. But we were much more interested in finding out what made the pointer move than in the messages it gave.

The next time we tried a few days later, Frank Withers said that he had been a soldier in Turkey during one life, and insisted (through the board) that he had known Rob and me in a city called Triev, in Denmark, in still another life. Dates and locations were given, though it was made clear that Triev no longer exists.

Then, on December 8, 1963, we sat at the board again, wondering whether or not it would work. It was a comfortable evening, warm in the room. Snow fell past the windows. Then suddenly the pointer began to move so quickly that we could hardly keep up with it.

Rob asked the questions, then we paused while he wrote out the answers the pointer spelled. Frank Withers had given simple one- or two-word responses in previous sessions. Now the answers became longer, and their character seemed to change. The atmosphere of the room was somehow different.

"Do you have a message for us?" Rob asked.

CONSCIOUSNESS IS LIKE A FLOWER WITH MANY PETALS, replied the pointer.

From the first few messages, Frank Withers had insisted upon the validity of reincarnation, so Rob said, "What do you think of your various reincarnations?"

THEY ARE WHAT I AM, BUT I WILL BE MORE. PUN: THE WHOLE IS THE SUM OF ITS HEARTS.

This was the first time the pointer spelled complete sentences. I laughed.

"Is all of this Jane's subconscious talking?" Rob asked.

SUBCONSCIOUS IS A CORRIDOR. WHAT DIFERENCE DOES IT MAKE WHICH DOOR YOU TRAVEL THROUGH?

"Maybe it's *your* subconscious," I said to Rob, but he was already asking another question:

"Frank Withers, can we refer back to you on any specific question in the future?"

YES. I PREFER NOT TO BE CALLED FRANK WITHERS. THAT PERSONALITY WAS RATHER COLORLESS.

Rob and I shrugged at each other: this was really wild, and the pointer was speeding faster and faster. Rob waited a moment, then asked, "What would you prefer to be called?"

TO GOD, ALL NAMES ARE HIS NAME, the pointer spelled.

Now Withers was getting religious! I rolled my eyes and pretended to stare out the window.

"But we still need some kind of name to use in talking to you," Rob said.

YOU MAY CALL ME WHATEVER YOU CHOOSE. I CALL MYSELF SETH. IT FITS THE ME OF ME, THE PERSONALITY MORE CLEARLY APPROXIMATING THE WHOLE SELF I AM, OR AM TRYING TO BE. JOSEPH IS YOUR WHOLE SELF, MORE OR LESS, THE IMAGE OF THE SUM OF YOUR VARIOUS PERSONALITIES IN THE PAST AND FUTURE.

All this was spelled out so quickly that we could hardly keep our hands on the pointer. Despite myself, I leaned closer. The back of my neck prickled. What was going on?

"Can you tell us more?" Rob asked. "If you call me Joseph, what do you call Jane?"

RUBURT.

We looked at each other again. I grimaced. "Would you clear that up a bit?" Rob said.

WHAT'S TO CLEAR? replied the pointer.

"Well, it seems like a strange name to us. I don't think Jane likes it either."

STRANGE TO THE STRANGE.

There was a pause. We didn't know what to ask or how to proceed. Finally Rob said, "Could you tell me why I had all that back trouble earlier this year?

VERTEBRA 1 DIDN'T CHANNEL VITAL FORCE THROUGH ORGANISM. RESTRAINED BY FEARS PINCHING NERVES. EXPANSION OF SPIRIT ALLOWS PHYSICAL ORGANISM TO EXPAND, RELEASES PRESSURES.

These are only a few excerpts from that first session with Seth. (A few weeks later, though, Rob had some more difficulty with his back and went to a chiropractor who told him that his first vertebra was out of alignment.) The session lasted until after midnight, and after that we sat up talking about it.

"Maybe he's a part of *both* of our subconscious minds in a way we don't understand," I said.

"Maybe," Rob said, then added with a grin, "Maybe he actually *is* someone who survived death."

"Oh, hon," I said, rather disgusted. "Besides, what purpose would he have? If there are spirits, they must have better things to do than going around moving Ouija boards."

"What did you say, Ruburt?" Rob asked. I could have crowned him.

Seth had a purpose, all right: to deliver the material he's been giving us twice a week, now, like clockwork for the past five years. But we didn't know that then. While this was already our fourth session at the board, it was really our first Seth session.

The next two were much the same, except for one bewildering element: I began to anticipate the board's replies. This bothered me no end, and I grew uneasy. At the next session—our fourth with Seth—I heard the words in my head at a faster and faster rate, and not only sentences but whole paragraphs before they were spelled out.

The next session started like the others. I was working afternoons at an art gallery, and after the dishes were done and Rob was through with painting for the day, we got out the board.

"Why is Jane rather reserved about our contacts with you?" Rob asked, when we were set up. "I can tell she isn't too enthusiastic."

SHE IS CONCERNED BECAUSE SHE RECEIVES MY MESSAGES BEFORE THEY ARE SPELLED OUT. IT WOULD MAKE YOU CAUTIOUS, TOO.

"But why is this cause for concern?" Rob asked, with, I thought at the time, a marvelously faked innocence.

IT IS MORE UNSETTLING.

"Why?" Rob persisted.

A BOARD IS NEUTRAL. MESSAGES IN THE MIND ARE NOT.

In the meantime we had told a friend of ours, Bill Macdonell, what we were doing. Bill in turn had told us about an apparition he'd

18

seen a few years earlier when he was an art student. He'd never mentioned such a thing before. Now Rob asked what Bill had seen.

A FRAGMENT OF HIS OWN ENTITY, A PAST PERSONALITY REGAINING MOMENTARY INDEPENDENCE ON VISUAL PLANE. SOMETIMES A LAPSE OCCURS OF THIS TYPE.

"Was the image conscious of Bill's presence?"

I hardly heard Rob ask the question. Through the whole session I'd been hearing the words in my head before they were spelled, and I'd felt the impulse to speak them. Now the impulse grew stronger and I grew more determined to fight it. Yet I was terribly curious. And what could happen, after all? I didn't know—and this made me even more curious.

The pointer began to spell out the answer to Rob's question.

IN SOME SUBMERGED MANNER, ALL FRAGMENTS OF A PERSONALITY EXIST WITHIN AN ENTITY, WITH THEIR OWN INDIVIDUAL CONSCIOUSNESS . . .

The pointer paused. I felt as if I were standing, shivering, on the top of a high diving board, trying to make myself jump while all kinds of people were waiting impatiently behind me. Actually it was the words that pushed at me—they seemed to rush through my mind. In some crazy fashion I felt as if they'd back up, piles of nouns and verbs in my head until they closed everything else off if I didn't speak them. And without really knowing how or why, I opened up my mouth and let them out. For the first time I began to speak for Seth, continuing the sentences the board had spelled out only a moment before.

"When Bill saw the image and recognized its presence, the fragment itself seemed to have a dream. The entity operates its fragments in what you would call a subconscious manner, that is, without conscious direction. The entity gives the fragment independent life, then the entity more or less forgets the fragment. When a momentary lapse of control occurs, they both come face to face. It's as impossible for the entity to control fragment personalities as for the conscious mind to control the body's heartbeat."

Suddenly the words stopped. I stared at Rob.

19

"Could you hear yourself?" he asked.

I nodded, bewildered. "Dimly, as if a radio program was going on in my head from some other station." I paused and put my hands back on the pointer, thinking that I'd had enough of this speaking—or whatever it was—for one night.

"Seth, would you verify Jane's reception of the above message?" Rob asked.

YES. IT SHOULD MAKE HER FEEL BETTER.

I relaxed a little; the pointer was taking over the messages again. But Rob asked another question.

"Then it's possible to walk down a street and meet a fragment of yourself?"

The pointer began the answer.

OF COURSE. I WILL TRY TO THINK OF A GOOD ANAL-OGY TO MAKE THE POINT CLEARER. EVEN THOUGHTS, FOR INSTANCE, ARE FRAGMENTS, THOUGH ON A DIF-FERENT PLANE . . . .

Again the words were speeding through my head while the little pointer spelled them out slowly and methodically. I remember a terrific impatience, and then I was finishing the message aloud: "They have to be translated into physical reality. Fragments of another sort, called personality fragments, operate independently, though under the auspices of the entity."

Once more the words just stopped. This time I was determined not to let the same thing happen again until I had time to think it over, and I told Rob. Still we agreed to check with the board. "Was Jane's answer right, Seth?" Rob asked.

YES, replied the pointer. IT PERKS HER UP NOT TO HAVE TO WAIT AROUND FOR THE BOARD TO SPELL OUT THE ANSWERS.

"I'm glad somebody thinks so," I said to Rob, but now that things were safely back with the board, my curiosity was at me again. I told Rob to ask if one of us alone could work the pointer, and the pointer suggested that we try. Rob put his hands on the pointer and asked a question, but it barely moved.

Then we both put our hands back on it. "What did you think of that, Seth?" Rob asked.

NOT VERY GOOD. ANY CONTACTS ON YOUR PART WILL PROBABLY INCLUDE INTERNAL VISUAL DATA. JANE WILL PROBABLY BE ABLE TO RECEIVE ME DIRECT. IN EITHER CASE, CONTACT IS NOT POSSIBLE AT ALL TIMES. YOU WOULD FIND THIS MORE EMBARRASSING THAN I WOULD.

"Hmm," Rob said. We laughed and finally ended the session.

I don't know what Rob would have thought then if he'd realized what Seth meant by "internal visual data," though; and writing this now I just remembered that he was pretty surprised when his first few internal visions appeared with extraordinary vividness. I'll describe these later. That night, of course, we were primarily concerned with my speaking experience. If I'd known how this was to be expanded in the next session, I probably would have been a nervous wreck.

In fact, the next month waited for us with experiences so startling that we nearly called the whole thing to a halt. Yet we felt lighthearted at the same time. If there was more to this world and reality than we suspected, we certainly wanted to find out. And we still are finding out, for new elements appear in the sessions even now. The Seth Material continues, and we still have countless questions we want answered.

On December 8, then, Seth introduced himself. On the 15th I spoke for him for the first time. Soon, freed completely from the board, his personality began to express itself with much greater freedom. The process is fascinating to watch. For this reason I'll devote some space to the early sessions so that you can become acquainted with the material as Seth gave it, and see him emerge as a personality in his own right.

CHAPTER TWO:

The York Beach Images— "Fragment" Personalities

------◆------

I was quite nervous before the next session. I'd had a particularly trying day at the gallery, and Rob was tired, too. Yet Rob woke up quickly enough, for I was to speak for Seth for over two hours. This session was quite startling for another reason also—the information itself was quite as surprising as the way I was saying it.

Almost immediately I heard the words in my head, as before, but I insisted on starting with the board. The pointer moved before either of us said a thing. YES. GOOD EVENING.

Rob yawned, and the pointer spelled out: I HOPE IT'S NOT THE COMPANY.

Rob laughed, and said, "Seth, are plants and trees fragments?"

The pointer began to dash across the board. IN A SENSE, ALL THINGS COULD BE CALLED FRAGMENTS . . . but the words were piling up in my head, and after the first few sentences were spelled out, I felt that sense of diving down into the unknown, of letting go. Then I began speaking for Seth again. "But there are different kinds. Personality fragments differ from others in that they can cause other fragments to form from themselves . . ."

Rob said it was as if I were reading from some invisible manuscript. My eyes were wide open. At that point I utterly refused to close them, nor would I sit down. Whatever was happening, I was going to be on my feet so I could have a good running start for the door in case I got worried.

This was a rather hilarious attitude, come to think of it. Actually, as I spoke for Seth I paced the room constantly, yet was hardly aware of doing so. Rob took notes as quickly as he could. He didn't know shorthand or speedwriting, so he took everything down in longhand and then typed it up the following day. He soon began to develop his own system of symbols and abbreviations, however.

"The present individual in any given life could be called a fragment of his entire entity, having all the properties of the original entity, though they remain latent or unused. The image that your friend saw was a personality fragment of his own. It contained all the abilities of your friend, whether latent or not I do not know. This type of personality fragment is of different origin than your friend, who is himself a fragment of his own entity. We call this type a split personality fragment or a personality image fragment. Usually it cannot operate on all levels of your physical plane.

"An individual may send a personality fragment image into another level of existence entirely, even without his own conscious knowledge. It may gain valuable information on this other level, and then return. Sometimes the individual is not capable of assimilating this knowledge, or even of recognizing his own returning personality image. The type of fragment your friend saw was of this type, but so disconnected from your friend, and so absentmindedly was it sent upon its travels, that its information was probably passed directly to the entity which your friend represents. . . ."

Later Rob told me that he had all kinds of questions, but he didn't want to interrupt, and his hand was already tired from taking notes. All the while I kept pacing up and down the room, eyes half open, delivering this monologue without a trace of hesitation.

"Increased concentration of the conscious individual is the trend.

24

Then these split personality fragments or images can be kept under scrutiny without taxing the present ego to distraction. Now, what you would call the subconscious performs this task; not too well, since it was never meant to focus clear attention. Consciousness will expand within your plane. The scope of consciousness will be so broadened that all personality fragments, split personality images, and individual fragments in succeeding incarnations will be held in clear focus without strain. It is toward this that evolution is headed, though of course, at its usual donkey-slow rate."

I continued giving this material from 9:00 on, steadily, until Rob had writer's cramp at 9:50. I've only given excerpts. Both of us were amazed that I'd spoken for so long, and delivered such involved sentences without corrections or hesitations of any kind. Then, ten minutes later while we were resting, Rob said that he was going to ask if we'd ever seen such "personality fragment" images. At once, the words started up in my head again, and I began to dictate. While speaking I had no idea of the meaning of the words, so it wasn't until our next rest period that I knew what Seth had been saying. It was this following passage that both of us, later, found so disquieting.

"The man and woman in the York Beach dancing establishment . . . were fragments of your selves, thrown-off materializations of your own negative and aggressive feelings . . . the images were formed by the culminating energy of your destructive energies at the time. While you did not recognize them consciously, unconsciously you knew them well. Unconsciously you saw the image of your destructive tendencies, and these images themselves roused you to combat them."

Rob knew instantly the episode to which Seth was referring. How he managed to sit there calmly taking notes while Seth went on, is more than I know.

In late 1963, some months before our sessions began, we'd taken a vacation in York Beach, Maine, hoping that a change of environment would improve Rob's health. The doctor didn't know what was wrong with his back and suggested that he spend some time under traction in the hospital. Instead we decided that his reaction to stress was at least partially responsible, hence the trip.

On the night in question we went to a nightclub in search of a festive atmosphere. Rob was in constant pain, and though he didn't complain, he couldn't hide the sudden spasms. Then I noticed an older couple sitting across the room from us. They really frightened me by their uncanny resemblance to Rob and myself. Did we look like that—aloof, bitter—only younger? I couldn't take my eyes off them, and finally I pointed them out to Rob.

Rob looked over at the couple and groaned with another back spasm. Then something happened that neither of us had been able to explain. To my complete amazement Rob stood up, grabbed my arm, and insisted that we dance. A minute earlier, he'd hardly been able to walk.

I just stared at him. We hadn't danced together in the eight years of our marriage, and the band was playing a twist, with which we were entirely unfamiliar at the time. Moreover, Rob wouldn't take no for an answer. I was afraid of making a fool of myself, but Rob dragged me out on the dance floor. We danced for the rest of the evening, and from that point on his physical condition improved remarkably. His whole outlook on life seemed brighter as of that moment.

Now Seth was saying, "Looking back, you can say that the effect was therapeutic, but if you had subconsciously accepted the images, it would have marked the beginning of a severe deterioration for you both, personally and creatively. Again, the images marked the critical culmination of your destructive energies. The fact that the images were of yourselves shows that your destructive energies were turned inward, even though materialized in physical form.

"Your dancing represented the first move away from what those images meant, and violent action was the best thing under the circumstances . . . a subtle transformation could have taken place in which you and Jane transferred the bulk of your personalities into the fragments you had yourselves created . . . and from their eyes watched yourselves across the room. In this case your present dominant personalities would no longer be dominant."

During a break Rob told me what Seth had said about the images. Neither of us had ever heard about thought-forms then, and the whole thing sounded incredible to me. And yet, I thought, psychologists talk about projection and transference by which we project our fears outward to another person or object and then react to them.

"Maybe Seth means a symbolic creation?" I said. But soon the words started coming again, and it became obvious that Seth was insisting upon a literal materialization.

"Who left the room first, Jane and I or the images?" Rob asked.

Again I was speaking for Seth. "The projected fragments disappeared. They stood up, walked across the floor, and disappeared in the crowd. They had no power to leave the place where they were born unless you gave it to them. Remember that they did exist . . . by the same token your triumph reinforced the healthy aspects of your present egos."

The evening grew late, but Seth showed no signs of wearing out. Just before midnight, Rob and I took another rest period, and decided to end the session. (It was Seth, incidentally, who suggested we take a five-to-ten-minute break every half hour or so.) Rob and I didn't know what to make of this session. It was the first time I'd spoken for so long at a time, for one thing. For another, we didn't know how to evaluate what was said.

Seth's explanation of the York Beach affair made intuitive sense to us. Certainly something significant had happened that night, but had we actually materialized the physical images of our hidden fears? Did people do this often? If so, the implications were staggering. Or was the explanation psychologically and symbolically valid, but *practically* a lot of nonsense?

Should we continue with the sessions? I was somewhat more reluctant than Rob, being so directly involved, but what an opportunity, I thought! We decided to hold at least a few more sessions to see what might develop. Rob had some questions about fragment personalities he wanted to ask: What did Seth mean when he said we could have turned into those images? Rob wrote the questions down so he wouldn't forget them, and two nights later we sat down at the board once more. At this point, of course, we had no idea whether or not each session would be our last, regardless of our conscious decisions. For all we knew, Seth might vanish as Frank Withers had. Rob had his list of questions ready so we could get some answers while we still had the opportunity.

But in this next session, I spoke for Seth for a longer time than I had before. Seth gave us a detailed account of two past lives and began a reincarnational history of Rob's family. The material contained some excellent psychological insights; using them, we found ourselves getting along much better with our relatives. But I didn't like this insistence upon reincarnation at all. "The psychological insights are great," I said to Rob at break. "But the reincarnational part is probably fantasy. Delightful, but fantasy."

"You don't have to make your mind up one way or the other tonight, do you?" Rob asked. "What's the rush? See what else he has to say. Besides, I've learned as much about my family tonight as I have all my life. That's worth something."

Then when the session resumed, Rob asked the question that had been on our minds since Seth first mentioned the York Beach images. "If Jane and I had subconsciously accepted those images, would we have been able to return home, where we're known? The images were older."

Instantly the words tumbled through my head and out my mouth. I was out and Seth was on. "The images represented a culmination of many years' experience of a negative trend. If you had accepted them, you would have ended up as replicas as you transferred into the images. Yet, what creativity and constructiveness you possessed would have softened the faces. You would be recognizable to friends but changes would be noted. The remark would be made that perhaps you didn't seem the same, and with good reason."

"Have either of us had other similar experiences?" Rob asked.

"There was an afternoon in a small park when you were a child about eleven. You thought you were alone. It was close to five, September 17, on a day when there was no school. Another boy appeared. You had not seen him approach and took it for granted that he came by way of a walk that wound around a bandstand. He had jacks in his hand. You looked at each other and were about to speak, when a squirrel ran up a nearby tree.

"You turned to watch and when you turned back, the boy was

28

gone. For a short time you wondered, and then the incident was forgotten. As a matter of fact, at the same time your brother, Loren, was looking out the window of your father's shop [across the way] and saw nothing."

"Was the boy real or what?" Rob asked.

"It was a personality fragment of your own. You were wishing for a playmate, and were jealous because your brother stayed so long with your father. Quite without knowing it, you materialized a personality fragment as a playmate. You had no way of knowing what had happened at the time, and could not give any permanence to the image.

"Occasionally a personality will astound itself by such an image production. Usually this type vanishes by the time the personality reaches adulthood. In childhood, however, such instances are frequent. Often when a child cries about a bogeyman, what he has seen is such an image production or fibrous projection, formed by vivid desire on the part of the subconscious."

"I love the way he ties all this in with subconscious motivation," I said later.

Rob grinned, "Would you rather he didn't?"

"But reincarnation—and kids forming fragment personalities or whatever as playmates?" I frowned. "Still, it's fascinating as the dickens. And think what it means if it's true!"

"And think of the people we've known who suddenly seem entirely different than they used to be, in ways we can't fathom," Rob said. "If Seth's right, they actually became the destructive images they had of themselves."

I shivered uneasily. "But it wouldn't always be destructive, would it? Couldn't it work the other way around?"

"Worried?" Rob asked. He was teasing me.

"Not at all," I said loftily, but I could see the faces of that couple in my mind still, and there were so many questions left up in the air. Some were answered in following sessions, and this explanation from a session some three years later is particularly interesting:

"Now as to the York Beach images. Here aggressive and destructive energies were unconsciously projected outward, given a pseudo-reality and temporary physical validity. The emotional charge provides the pattern and impetus for such creations. According to the extent of physical reality to be achieved, the physical body of the originator transfers or transposes portions of its own chemical structure. Proteins are used, and there is a high carbohydrate loss.

"In the same way that the body's proteins and chemicals can be used to form various kinds of images, they may also be utilized to form an ulcer, goiter, or to affect other changes [in the body itself]. Here particular emotions are denied, dissociated. The individual does not want to accept them as a part of the self. Instead of projecting them outward as you did in the York Beach images, they are directed to a specific area of the body, or in other cases allowed to wander, traveling troublemakers, so to speak, through the body's physical system."

By the time Seth gave us this information, we had the background to understand it. In his discussions on health, Seth has always maintained that illness is often the result of dissociated and inhibited emotions. The psyche attempts to get rid of them by projecting them into a specific area of the body; in the case of ulcers, the diverted energy goes into the actual production of the ulcer itself. If really large areas of the self are inhibited, a secondary personality can be formed, grouped about those qualities distrusted and denied by the primary ego, and usually opposed to it. In other instances, the inhibited emotions can be projected outward into other persons, or as in the case of the York Beach images, very charged repressed energy can actually form pseudophysical images which present the personality with the physically materialized image of his fears.

Then, however, all of this was new to us. For all I knew, Seth was a secondary personality himself, and at this point we could have dropped the sessions. Though we found them intriguing, we certainly weren't convinced that Seth was someone who had survived death. Most likely, we thought, he was a very lively portion of my own subconscious. By now we'd done enough reading to worry about the secondary personality angle. There was no evidence of excessive emotionalism in the material, though: no repressed hates, prejudices, or desires. Seth made no demands of any kind upon either of us.

30

In the meantime, the Christmas holidays came along. We had no sessions for two weeks. Both of us wondered what would happen when—and if—we tried again. But the next episode so upset our ideas of what was possible, so outraged our conventional theories, that we very nearly quit the whole thing. Obviously we didn't—yet our reactions were to color our activities for the next several years, and greatly influence the direction in which I would allow my own psychic abilities to operate.

CHAPTER
THREE:

Seth Comes to a Seance—
A "New" Set of Fingers

An experimental séance was the next on the list of experiments for my book. We had only the foggiest idea of what a séance was, never having attended one. We did think that more than two people should be involved, though, so we decided to ask Bill Macdonell to join us, since he was the only one who knew of our experiments. Bill dropped by on the evening of January 2, 1964, and on the spur of the moment I suggested that the three of us give it a try.

The results were so surprising that rather than paraphrase Rob's notes, I'm going to include them exactly as he wrote them. For one thing, he was a more objective observer than I was. The very way his notes are written also shows his state of mind, his careful attitude and critical manner. Bill Macdonell read the notes and agrees with them.

"We began by sitting at a small table in our living room. We covered the table with a piece of dark material. The kitchen opens off the living room, so we closed the blinds in both rooms and pulled the curtains over them.

"Not knowing just how to go about having a séance, we plugged in a small red electric Christmas candle. Our walls are white, so we could see fairly well once our eyes were adjusted.

"I asked Jane to lay her wedding ring on the table. The three of us joined hands around it. Sitting quietly in the dim light, staring at the ring, I realized that the unwary observer might not have too much trouble seeing whatever he wanted to see.

"A tiny point of light grew on the edge of the ring, but by moving my arm, I discovered I could make the light wink off and on. It was simply the red reflection from the candle, so I placed the candle behind the curtains where the light was diffused. Nothing happened as we stared at the ring again. I began to ask questions out loud, at random, but I did not address them to Seth.

"Then suddenly Jane announced in a firm clear voice, 'Watch the hand.' It was a command, and I knew that Seth was with us. Jane felt her hand grow cold. With considerable relish Seth, through Jane's voice, described in detail each effect that followed—so that, he said, there would be no doubt as to what happened.

"He began by telling us to watch Jane's thumb. The tip of it began to glow. It seemed to be an internal suffusing of the flesh with a cold white light. There was no radiant effect, merely the changing color of the flesh itself. Since the hand was in shadow, there was no mistaking the change.

"The glow spread up the length of the thumb to the mound of flesh at its base, next to the palm. 'Watch the mound,' Seth said, with more than a little satisfaction. 'See the color change and the shadows in the palm disappear? If you want a demonstration, then you shall have it, silly as it is . . . And now the wrist. See it thicken and turn white?'

"Jane's wrist did thicken. She sat with the wrist of her left hand pressed to the tabletop. She wore a black sweater with the sleeves half pushed up and the cold white light spread up over the thickening wrist, up her forearm, to the sweater.

"Then the hand began to change its general proportions and resembled a pawlike shape. I had the eerie feeling of an animal's forepaw. Jane's fingers, normally long and graceful, had shrunken to stubby appendages, or so it appeared. The glow suffused the palm, eliminating the shadows normally to be seen there, so that it did not seem that the fingers were merely folded over.

"Slowly the hand regained normal shape. Jane still sat with her palm up. Now Seth really extended himself. The fingers began to elongate noticeably and to whiten. Then a second set of fingers began to rise up over Jane's own fingers. Now it could have been easy enough for Jane to bend her own fingers into this position, but here the three of us now saw the second set rising up long and white. Moreover, this second set had the fingernails *on top.* Had they been Jane's own fingers, the nails would have been on the undersides and invisible.

" 'For a first attempt, I'm doing beautifully,' Seth said. 'What do you think of that? Take a good look.' For some minutes we studied the effect before us. To me the extra fingers bent so grotesquely looked waxen, almost wet, as though freshly molded. Jane did not appear to be frightened. Then, gradually, the extra set of fingers disappeared.

" 'Now the hand changes again,' Seth said. 'It becomes a stubby fat one. Frank Withers had a hand like that, just like that. Frank Withers was a fathead,' he said, with great satisfaction, even though Frank was, according to Seth, a personality fragment of his own entity.

"The hand did become stubby and fat for a moment. Then it resumed the pawlike shape. 'Now,' Seth said to me, 'very carefully reach out and touch the hand. I want you to touch it, so that you can feel what it is like.' Gingerly, I touched my fingertips to Jane's palm. The pawlike hand felt very cold, wet and clammy, and the skin had a bumpy feeling that I wasn't used to in Jane's hand.

"Seth now had this cold inner light suffuse Jane's wrist and palm to an even more remarkable degree. At the joining of hand and wrist, the flesh rose up in an egglike lump. The white crept up Jane's arm to the sweater, and bled down her fingers, until all semblance of shadow was gone from the arm and palm. Then to end this part of the demonstration, Seth had Jane place her hands side by side on the table, so that we could plainly see the difference between the two. Gradually the hand returned to normal, and Seth instructed us to take a rest period.

"After the break, Seth told us to shut the door leading to the bath.

The living room side of the door holds a full-length mirror, and Seth told us to look into it. Since the mirror is tall and narrow, we had to crowd in close on three sides of the little table, in order to see our reflections. Jane sat in the middle. Her lips were very close to my ear as she talked. I could hear and feel each breath, each swallow she took. Her voice dropped considerably in volume and I really had the sensation that she was indeed speaking for someone else (rather than for a subconscious personality, for example, who just called itself Seth).

" 'Now the three of you see your reflections clearly in the mirror, just as you should. Watch, for I'll change Jane's image and replace it with another,' Seth said. And Jane's image did begin to change. Her head dropped lower. At the same time, the shape of the skull changed, the hair grew shorter and fit about it much more closely. The shoulders of the mirror image hunched over, and grew more narrow. And then the head in the mirror tilted, and looked down, while Jane herself sat with her head erect, staring straight ahead into the mirror.

"Jane said later that this shocked her more than anything else. I looked at her first beside me, then in the mirror. There was no doubt as to the difference between the two. I also saw a shadow suffuse the mirror image. At the same time I had the feeling that the face hung forward from the body. The mirror head seemed to grow smaller. I detected a faint glow about it as it hung in space, seemingly between the mirror reflection and the three of us.

"It was also obvious that the mirror image sat several inches lower down than Jane herself sat. And now and then the mysterious head would dip down and then hang forward from the body." End of Rob's notes.

During the séance I hadn't been a bit nervous or frightened. Toward the end, though, I was shocked to see such a difference between my mirror image and myself. I think that I was momentarily afraid that I really looked like that. After all, that's a normal enough reaction—usually when you look into a mirror, it gives a faithful reproduction, and no woman is going to be pleased to see a weird-looking apparition staring back.

When Seth took over, his confidence knocked all other ideas or doubts from my mind. Yet my eyes were open all the while. I could examine the differences between my hands, for example, and see the other set of fingers, and the white glow that ran up to the edge of my rolled-up sweater. I seemed to "click out" when Seth spoke, yet a tremendous sense of energy rushed through me as he did so. Except for the mirror image at the end, nothing bothered me.

But as soon as the séance was over, I was appalled. Instead of being encouraged by Seth's part in the events, we were upset. We all knew what we had seen. Rob had even touched the hand at one time, and Seth had given us many occasions to check effects as they occurred. We couldn't accept the evidence of our senses, nor could we really deny such obvious evidence. Though we were trying the experiment for the book, we thought that séances were kooky, somehow unrespectable. We didn't want Seth involved, and specifically had made a point of *not* asking for him.

My intellectual skepticism was aroused simply because the affair had been so successful. We argued back and forth as to whether or not suggestion could have been responsible, but we knew that this could not explain half of what happened. It could hardly explain the bumpy quality Rob had felt in my hand, or the second set of fingers, though we decided that it *could* perhaps have accounted for the odd mirror image.

Actually, for the first time in our lives we found ourselves experiencing events that we couldn't explain, and doubting the obvious evidence of our senses—an uncomfortable spot for anyone. The affair had such an effect upon us that I wouldn't try that kind of a séance again for three years. (As you will see, however, Seth appeared in apparition form in session #68.) From then on, we always kept lights on for easier checking of any effects that might appear.

Later work has convinced me that psychic phenomena do not simply appear because we want them to, or as the result of suggestion alone. Other, later effects happened in full light, in a few of my ESP classes, for example. The Seth apparition also appeared in full light. I've also known incidents since, when groups of highly suggestible people with little critical sense have gathered in dark rooms expecting all kinds of apparitions—and nothing happened at all.

I think Rob and I were angry at being brought up short, forced to face issues we weren't ready to face. Everything was happening so fast. It hadn't been a month yet since we began with the Ouija board. Our ideas of what was possible were being turned topsy-turvy. We decided to hold one other session to see what Seth had to say about the affair, and again we considered dropping the experiments, book or no book. Yet we could hardly blame Seth, since the séance was our idea to begin with. I had to write up the séance results for one of my early chapters, and I hardly knew how to go about it.

The next night we held what we thought might be our last session. After it, we knew that we were committed, and to us the session really marks the beginning of the Seth Material, the end of the preliminary data.

For the first time Seth really "came through" as a definite other personality, laughing and joking. Rob just couldn't believe that he was speaking to me, in any ordinary terms. But more than this, Seth's long monologue on the nature of reality captivated and intrigued us. We had no idea that it was actually a highly simplified explanation, cleverly geared to our own level of understanding at the time. It made a tremendous impression on us nonetheless.

For nearly three hours I spoke for Seth, striding up and down the room, joking, pausing now and then for Rob to catch up with his notes, and delivering this monologue, using gestures and facial expressions, verbal expressions and inflections, entirely different from my own. I spoke steadily, without hesitation, breaking up serious philosophical material with jovial comments, much like a professor at a small seminar. The session so aroused our intellectual and intuitional curiosity that all thoughts of discontinuing went out the window.

"Consider a network of wires, a maze of interlocking wires endlessly constructed so that looking through them there would seem to be no beginning or end. Your plane could be likened to a small position between four very spindly wires, and my plane could be likened to the small position in the neighboring wires on the other side. Not only are we on different sides of the same wires, but we are at the same time above or below, according to your viewpoint. And if you consider the wires as forming cubes—this is for you, Joseph, with your love of images—then the cubes could also fit one within the other, without disturbing the inhabitants of either cube one iota. And these cubes are themselves within cubes, and I am speaking now only of the small particle of space taken up by your plane and mine.

"Again think in terms of your plane, bounded by its small spindly set of wires, and my plane on the other side. These, as I have said, have boundless solidarity and depth, yet to one side, the other is transparent. You cannot see through, but the two planes move through each other constantly. I hope you see what I have done here. I have initiated the idea of motion, for true transparency is not the ability to see through, but to move through.

"This is what I mean by fifth dimension. Now, remove the structure of the wires and cubes. Things behave as if the wires and cubes existed, but these were only constructions necessary even to those on my plane. . . . We construct images consistent with the senses we happen to have. We merely construct imaginary lines to walk upon.

"So real are the wall constructions of your room that you would freeze in winter without them, yet there is no room and there are no walls. So, in a like manner, the wires that we constructed are real, though there are no wires. The walls of your room are transparent to me, though I am not sure I would perform, dear Joseph and Ruburt, for a party demonstration.

"Nevertheless, those walls *are* transparent. So are the wires, but for practical purposes we must behave as if both were there. . . . Again if you will consider our maze of wires, I will ask you to imagine them filling up everything that is, with your plane and my plane like two small bird's nests in the nestlike fabric of some gigantic tree. . . .

"Consider that these wires are mobile, constantly trembling, and also alive in that they not only carry the stuff of the universe but are themselves projections of it, and you will see how difficult this is to explain. Nor can I blame you for growing tired, when after asking you to imagine this strange structure, I then insist that you tear it apart, for it is no more to be actually seen or touched than is the buzzing of a million invisible bees."

It was in this session that Seth suggested we hold sessions twice a week, saying that a schedule was far better than spasmodic activity. He went on: "At one time or another, all of us on my plane give such lessons, but psychic bonds between teacher and pupils are necessary, which means that we must wait until personalities on your plane have progressed sufficiently for lessons to begin. Lessons then are conducted with those psychically bound to us.

"What you call emotion or feeling is the connective between us, and it is the connective that most clearly represents the life force on any plane, under any circumstances. From it is woven all material of your world and mine."

When the material given above was finished, Seth stayed around, as if to emphasize an informal social period. He invited questions, gestured frequently, paused in front of Rob, looking right at him through my open (but un-Jane-like) eyes.

"There is nothing wrong and perhaps much to be gained," he said, "in trying whatever experiments you want on your own. Call it homework if you like. Perhaps I'll even give you a Gold Star, although if I know you, you will probably insist that the teacher give the proverbial apple to the pupils instead of the other way around. . . ."

Then, with strong humorous accents he spoke about the Ouija board which we still used to open and close sessions. "It is a matter of formality in that it renews contact in a familiar manner, and also, I have always been partial to formality to some extent. The board gives us a breathing spell and is a method of saying good day or good evening, or tipping one's hat. I'm also of the opinion that small ritual tends to emphasize data in the mind, and set it off to advantage, in the same way that good cuisine is set off by fine dishes. . . . At the end of a session it would be most cordial to touch your hands briefly to the board. You're lucky that I don't request you to wear full-dress clothing."

Rob laughed at this, and so did I when he read me the notes. We were fascinated by the monologue on the fifth dimension—which ran much longer, incidentally, than the excerpts given here. Seth's personality impressed Rob to such an extent that he, at least, was convinced that Seth was a completely independent personality. He knows me so well, of course, in almost every mood, that he's in an excellent position to judge the differences and similarities between my personality and Seth's.

After having Rob describe the session, and after reading the notes, my attitude was one of simple astonishment. Rob and I are very informal; our friends are informal. The men don't wear hats and suits, for example, but jeans and shirts or sweaters. I found Seth delightful, whoever or whatever he was. Who else did we know, so "old school" who'd even speak of tipping one's hat, or refer to food as "good cuisine?" Anyway he certainly didn't sound frightening, and the fifth-dimensional monologue was really provocative.

I was already beginning to study my own psychological behavior, though, and the question of Seth's independent reality came more and more into my mind. Since I "become" Seth in some fashion, I'm never able to see myself as Seth in the way that Rob can, or that my students can in a class session, but I do know that he makes a definite impression on others. Who or what was he? I questioned Rob constantly. How did I look? How did he know someone else was speaking? What was there about Seth that so convinced him that Seth was more than a dissociated part of my own subconscious?

Far from looking for Seth in every corner, I guarded my mental integrity with all the determination of my nature. Then I felt silly, because Seth made absolutely no attempt to "invade" my normal working day. Worse, I felt that he was amused but understanding, and felt that my efforts, if basically unnecessary, were still important for my peace of mind.

Still, I was never aware of new developments until they actually occurred spontaneously, and to my own surprise. If we thought that Seth "came through" as himself in the last sessions, we had a lot to learn in the next one, when Seth's own, more powerful voice suddenly emerged.

The first session with Frank Withers had been held on December 2, 1963. In the fourteenth session, January 8, I was ready to speak for Seth, deep masculinelike tones and all. We had traveled some way in little over a month. Beyond doubt those thirty-odd days were filled

41

with the most intense psychological activity, excitement, and speculation that we had ever encountered. It would be at least three years and after my book appeared before we even began to understand what had happened.

CHAPTER
FOUR:

The "Seth Voice"

————◆◆————

All during this time I was working at the local art gallery in the afternoons. Mornings I spent on my ESP book, writing up the results of our experiments. We still hadn't told anyone what we were doing, except our friend, Bill. In fact few of our friends even knew what we were up to until the book was out. Now I wonder why we were so secretive, but at the time it seemed much better to keep the world with all of its questions out. We had enough of our own to consider.

Seth's personality was expressing itself much more freely now that it was released from the board, particularly after the surprising fourteenth session. I don't think Rob will ever forget it. We were still astonished by the fact of the sessions themselves. I was nervous before we started, wondering whether Seth would come through or not. In those days I was always afraid that I'd go into trance, open my mouth, and—nothing! Or worse, gibberish. Besides, I wasn't even aware of *how* I knew when Seth was ready. We began sessions at 9 P.M. Five minutes before nine, I'd get that feeling again, that I was going to leap from a high diving board into a deep pool—and without knowing for sure whether or not I could swim.

The session began as usual, with no hint of the voice changes that would occur. I'd like to mention here that by now we had read several books on extrasensory perception, but still hadn't come across anything about voice communication. We'd read about the Patience Worth case, where a Mrs. Curren produced novels and poetry through the Ouija board and automatic writing, but we were completely unfamiliar with the idea of anyone's speaking for another personality. It had never occurred to either of us that my voice might change in any way.

In this fourteenth session I spoke for Seth for fifty minutes straight, the longest period without a break up to that date. Seth began by advising us to have a more balanced social life—to go out more and mix with people—so as to counter the intense inner activity of psychic experience. Then he launched into his first discussion of the Inner Senses, a subject which was entirely new to us. It was to be elaborated upon in the future.

"Everything on your plane is the materialization of something that exists independently of your plane. Therefore, within your senses there are other senses that perceive inward. Your regular senses perceive an outer world. The senses within the recognizable senses perceive and create an inner world . . . once you exist on a particular plane you must necessarily be attuned to it while blocking out many other perceptions. It is a sort of psychic focus, a concentration of awareness along certain lines. As your ability grows in relation to the environment then you can afford to look around, use the Inner Senses, and enlarge your scope of activity. This is only natural. Survival on a particular plane depends upon your concentration within it. When survival is more or less satisfied through attention, then you can afford to perceive other realities."

Actually this material went on for several pages. As usual, Rob was writing as quickly as he could to keep up with the delivery.

Running into the session's second hour, my voice had sounded progressively more hoarse, and it was the first time in sessions that it had ever shown signs of strain. After the initial discussion of the Inner

44

Senses, Seth said, "I did not intend to make you work so hard this evening, Joseph. If your hand is working as quickly as Ruburt's mouth, you must be exhausted. Would you like to take a break, or end the session? I am always thinking of your convenience, at least when I am not concerned with your education," he added with a smile.

Rob asked for a break, but then he urged me to end the session before my voice gave out. I knew that he was concerned about me, but also tremendously interested in the material Seth had been giving. Besides this, as Seth, I had been extremely active, making funny remarks now and then to break up pages of serious monologue. The sense of another independent personality was stronger than it had ever been, and so I decided to continue. By now it was after 10:30. While we were talking, Rob had wondered aloud about the meaning of time; when we resumed, Seth started discussing this question.

"Time has no meaning without barriers. To put it another way, time has no meaning without the necessity to counteract against other actions. Basically, this is a gem of a description, if I do say so myself. The sad part is that you probably won't be able to understand it yet. It all takes time! As I try to counteract your ignorance, I couldn't resist. I mean it kindly, for you have no idea of the difficulties involved in explaining time to someone who must take time to understand the explanation.

"The study of time will teach you much about the nature of fifth dimension also. Our imaginary wires composed of solidified vitality are fluid, I hope you understand this, even while they are solidified. For solidity is illusion."

Here, as Seth, I pounded on the desk for emphasis, and suddenly began speaking in a stronger voice. At the same time the hoarseness disappeared. Word by word the voice grew deeper, more formal, louder. As Rob looked down to take his notes, he realized that a vocal metamorphosis of some kind was taking place. He wrote as fast as he could, so he could also look up now and then to see what was going on. Now I stood almost in front of him, the un-Jane-like open eyes staring at him as if to make sure he understood what was being said.

"I have also said that this feeling of vitality—and I prefer that

45

term, vitality—is moving and itself a part of the living stuff of the universe. Now as these wires pass seemingly from plane to plane, they actually form the boundaries of each plane and become subject to the particular laws within each. Therefore, they become subject to time within your particular three-dimensional system."

During the last passage the voice became louder and louder, as though it were trying to fill a good-sized hall. I'm reading that session, of course, as I write this chapter, and I've just come across Rob's original notes, scribbled in between this passage and the next. They show his reaction rather clearly:

"Looking at Jane and knowing her natural feminine voice so well, I had to think twice to realize that this other new voice was issuing from her in such volume, and with no strain at all. I don't know whether I was more surprised at the fact that Jane seemed not at all disturbed by this voice, or by the fact that it had such a definite deep and masculine tone."

Rob had little time to make extra notes, though, as the passage continued without pause. "The motion of the apparently solidified vitality gives the illusion of time. The counteraction involved in this case is counteraction within the core of vitality itself, in much the same manner that we spoke of a closed mental enclosure earlier. . . . The action and counteraction is the time trigger. On some other planes motion is simultaneous and time unknown. To me your time can be manipulated; it is one of the several vehicles by which I can enter your awareness. . . .

"Now, as an example of my good intentions, I will end this session. I would continue if I did not have your physical limitations to contend with. I am able to come through very well this evening, and when this happens I like to take advantage of it. After all, do you blame me? . . . In any case I shall say good night. You should know that I too enjoy a moment of social discourse, or I would not keep you so long. I regret the necessity to keep Joseph so occupied [with notes]. Good night, dear friends."

Instantly my voice returned to normal. The hoarseness had long since disappeared. Now it was almost impossible for us to end the session. We were too intrigued. Despite Seth's parting words, I could

46

"feel" him still present, along with a tremendous sense of vitality and goodwill. Rob told me about the heavy masculine voice with its astonishing volume, and all around me I felt this high energy and great humor as if an invisible Seth were sitting there, smiling, ready to start a friendly chat.

As soon as we decided to continue, that deep voice boomed out of me again, and as Seth, I began walking about the room, pausing to speak directly to Rob or to look out the window. I really felt that someone else was settling down inside my body, getting used to moving it about and glowing with satisfaction at the achievement.

"I enjoy speaking with you for a few moments of what you might be pleased to call normal conversation. Friends do not always talk of high and weighty matters. . . . Previously we have been too concerned with other matters for any emotional interchange. And if Ruburt's voice sounds rather dreary in this transitional phase, I myself am in a very playful, you might say, frisky mood. By all means, ask any questions you have in mind."

As Seth I paused, smiling, looking Rob directly in the eye. Rob was newly surprised at the deep voice that had started up again, and it took him a minute to think of something to ask. Besides, he was still laughing at Seth's jovial manner, and the humorous gestures and voice inflections that were so unlike mine.

"Uh, do you have friendships on your plane as we do here?"

"I have friendships, of course. The one thing about your plane that makes it such a tempting field of endeavor for us here is that some of us still have ties of an emotional kind, and we attempt, though often clumsily, to make contact with old friends. As you write letters to friends in strange countries and do not forget them, so we do not forget."

Rob asked several other questions, and the two of them, Rob and Seth, chatted back and forth for three quarters of an hour. About the voice, Seth said: "Ruburt's voice is an experiment. The immediacy of our sessions would be enhanced if more of my personality could come through. I could go on happily, you might say blithely, for hours, but I shall not. I am not some old fogy. Now and then old Frank Withers comes through simply because he was the latest independent materialization and is used to taking things upon himself. I have not assimilated him completely, but you can believe me, I intend to."

Here Rob started laughing again. Seth had spoken jovially but not maliciously about Frank Withers. The tone of his voice and broad smile softened the actual words spoken. Rob made a comment about Seth's attitude and Seth said, "I'm afraid I haven't learned humility yet. On the other hand, you knew me before I knew Frank Withers, and my vanity then was astounding. You were quite vain yourself, and as a woman, you certainly put your present wife to shame as far as vanity is concerned."

He was referring, of course, to some reincarnational data he had given earlier. Eventually we learned that Seth, Rob, and I were part of an ancient entity; this will be discussed in chapters 14 and 15. Seth was also to say later that this past relationship was partially responsible for our communications.

As the give and take between Rob and Seth continued, Rob got used to the voice and really enjoyed himself, there being no doubt in his mind now that Seth was Seth, someone entirely different and independent.

The impression Rob got from the voice, gestures, and manner was that of an energetic, educated gentleman of the "old school," in his sixties perhaps, extraordinarily intelligent but aware of his own foibles—a man with a highly developed yet old-fashioned sense of humor. As Seth I touched a begonia plant (one of my favorites) and said, "I like Jane's plant. Green things are a touchstone of your existence. You notice that earlier I used the term 'plane' rather than 'planet,' because you do not have the whole kettle to yourself. . . .

"I fear that as a man's voice, Jane will sound rather unmelodious. I do not have the voice of an angel by any means, but neither do I sound like an asexual eunuch, which is all I've been able to make her sound like tonight . . . and Ruburt, if you want a cigarette, get one. She's been walking around with a match in her hand for the last ten minutes."

I don't recall any of this, but according to Rob I then got a cigarette and sipped a glass of wine. "If I could have a glass of wine with you and enjoy it, I would. If you want to talk for a few moments

48

without the necessity of taking notes, do so. I'll certainly last as long as Ruburt will, and a lot longer. And if ever your wife's features change some night as we talk, I suggest you do not mention it to her until the end of the session."

Seth went on until past midnight. The remark about the change in my features was included in the notes, of course, but it was otherwise forgotten until a year later when it was brought rather forcibly to mind. When the session was over, my own voice was still fresh and clear, with no trace of the earlier difficulties. I wasn't even tired.

Again, on reading the notes we were fascinated by the material, particularly since Seth told us that he was going to explain these Inner Senses more fully, and teach us how to use them. He was as good as his word, for as you will see shortly, he did give us instructions and we were to have all kinds of new experiences as we followed them. We didn't know that this information was geared to our own level of understanding and quite simple in comparison with the elaborations that would follow.

We didn't realize either that the emergence of the Seth voice completed the psychic structure through which we would receive the Seth Material, and through which Seth's personality would express itself. From this session on, there was always some voice change during sessions, but the deep booming tones were the exception rather than the rule for some time to come. On occasion there is the sense of really tremendous power behind the voice; and my own voice is never strained. Much later, Seth told us that this psychic energy can be translated into sound like this, or it can be used for other purposes. Now when Seth gives clairvoyant material, for example, the voice is seldom loud. The energy is used to gather the data instead. (As you will see later in this book, that energy can also be a springboard into other dimensions.)

When the voice is deep and booming, I feel very small and surrounded by terrific energy. From what we have learned, the voice was a sort of indication of the amount of energy available; it served many purposes, besides helping to express Seth's personality.

Looking back, though, it does seem that with the initial emergence of the Seth voice the structure of the sessions was completed. Even the basic principles of the material had been given in highly simplified form: the blocks upon which the foundations would be laid.

Talk about psychic explosions! Our first Ouija board session had been on December 2, 1963. By the end of January we had twenty sessions and some 230 pages of typewritten material. We knew that the voice change was significant, of course, but we didn't realize that the power behind the voice was the more important issue. We saw that the sessions had a kind of order, but its significance escaped us. Actually, the structure provided continuity and stability, but also was flexible enough to nurture latent developments of which we were then completely unaware. Within it my own training as a medium would take place safely.

At this point, there were several courses we could have taken. We could have told no one what was happening, we could have contacted a spiritualist group or we could have informed the parapsychologists. We definitely decided not to tell any of our friends or relatives, at least for the time being. The spiritualist groups would have been out in any case, because of my views at the time on religion in general. But the ESP books we'd read all advised that anyone having such experiences contact a qualified psychologist or parapsychologist.

As a result of Seth's instructions, both of us began to have some clairvoyant experiences on our own, and we thought we should write to someone who knew more about such matters than we did. Besides, there was that pressing question: Was Seth part of my subconscious? Could the psychologists tell us? So we decided to contact a parapsychologist who would have a knowledge of ESP and psychology.

I guess I'd do the same thing if I had it to do over. But I'm not sure.

The next few chapters will deal with our efforts to be "scientifically responsible," to "test" Seth for ESP. We didn't really come to any overall decision, but I think that I was driven by the need to make all of this intellectually or academically legitimate. It was, of course —but I had a lot to learn.

CHAPTER FIVE:

*A Psychologist's Letter
Gives Me the Jitters—
Seth's Reassurance*

In early February, Rob wrote to Dr. Ian Stevenson, who was connected with the Department of Neurology and Psychology at the University of Virginia. Dr. Stevenson was interested in reincarnation, and we had just read about his work. Rob also sent him copies of a few sessions, including some of the information we had been given about our own past lives. According to this, we lived several existences in the very distant past, including one in Denmark three centuries ago when Rob and I were father and son and Seth a mutual friend. Our last lives were in Boston in the nineteenth century.

I was unhappy with the reincarnational material simply because I still didn't want to accept the idea—it just seemed too far out. I didn't exactly encourage Rob to ask Seth to enlarge on this information or to fill in on the details he'd given. But it was a part of the material—I could hardly deny that.

Dr. Stevenson wrote us a letter much like one I would probably write today to someone else under the same circumstances. He thought that the fluency of the material suggested a subconscious origin, but emphasized that at this stage it was impossible to tell. He also told us that amateur mediumship could produce mental symptoms under certain conditions.

"Oh, great," I said to Rob. "Do I act any nuttier than usual?" Rob solemnly assured me that there had been no change in my behavior. Actually he had been watching for such signs, and so had I. But Dr. Stevenson's well-meaning warning did throw me for somewhat of a loop, even though we had read the same cautions ourselves in some of our psychic books.

In a way, Dr. Stevenson's letter came at an unfortunate time. It had been impossible to keep the sessions absolutely secret. Eventually some of our friends were bound to come around on a Monday or Wednesday evening, and hear the odd voice from outside the door as Phillip did just before we wrote Dr. Stevenson. As a result, Phil began to attend occasional sessions. I'm using the entity name that Seth gave him, since his family doesn't understand his interest in psychic phenomena—a situation we've encountered more than once. Phil lives out of state but travels to Elmira every six weeks or so on business.

Just a few days before we received Dr. Stevenson's letter, we had an unscheduled session with Phil present. We gave him paper and pen to write down any questions he might have, but Phil never got a chance to write anything down. According to him, Seth answered each of his questions in turn as Phil formed them in his mind. Phil wrote and signed a statement to this effect.

This was the first sign of any kind of telepathy or clairvoyance in the sessions. Phil was really astonished, and so was I.

I took Phil at his word, but I also thought that coincidence could have explained the episode. Just the same, my spirits rose. Then a few days later, Dr. Stevenson's letter came and I went into a slump. "See if Seth has anything to say about the letter," Rob said. I agreed, but when I became tense it was difficult to relax enough to have a session. I skipped our next scheduled session as a result, but I'd recovered my equilibrium when the next Monday came.

Seth had quite a bit to say! "A fond and exasperated good evening," he began. "The exasperation comes because your good psychologist almost undermined the confidence I managed to give Ruburt in our session with your friend, Phillip. I tried to build Ruburt's confidence, and some stranger tore it down. His intentions were of the best, but I suppose that I must now feel obligated—and I do—to go into the matter of mental and emotional stability and any dangers to such stability that might be involved here.

"As far as Ruburt is concerned, there is no danger. For one thing I am a sensitive but disciplined and sensible—if somewhat irascible—gentleman. None of the communications from me are in any way conducive to instability. I may make bold to remark that I am more stable than you or Ruburt or the fine psychologist.

"I feel a strong responsibility for you and for any results coming from our communications. If anything, the personal advice I have given you both should add to your mental and emotional balance and result in a stronger relationship with the outside world. . . . I do depend upon Ruburt's willingness to dissociate. There is no doubt that he is unaware at times of his surroundings during sessions. It is a phenomenon in which he gives consent, and he could, at any time, return his conscious attention to his physical environment.

"There is no danger of dissociation grabbing hold of him like some black vague and furry monster, carrying him away to the netherlands of hysteria, schizophrenia, or insanity. I have consistently advised contacts with the world at large, and told you both to use your abilities to meet outside challenges. Withdrawal into dissociation as a hiding place from the world could be dangerous, and many have fallen prey here. With Ruburt this is not the case.

"For one thing, Ruburt's ego is extremely strong. His intuition is the gateway that relaxes an otherwise stubborn and domineering ego." At this, Rob looked up and laughed. "The intuitive qualities, however, are not frivolous and the personality is well integrated." Seth went on to describe dissociation, saying that I was always aware of my surroundings to *some* degree in sessions. "It is true," he said, "that a state of dissociation is necessary. But because you open a door, this does not mean that you cannot close it, nor does it mean that you cannot have two doors open at once, and this is my point. You *can* have two doors open at once, and you *can* listen to two channels at once. In the meantime you must turn down the volume of the first channel while you learn to attune your attention to the second. This process you call dissociation."

When Seth paused, Rob asked, "What do you have to say about Dr. Stevenson's idea that this may all be Jane's subconscious?"

"We have gone into this before," Seth said, "and I have no doubt that we will on endless occasions; and if I succeed in convincing you of my reality as a separate personality, I will have done exceedingly well. It should be apparent that my communications come through Ruburt's subconscious. But as a fish swims through water, but the fish is not the water, I am not Ruburt's subconscious.

"The slight evidence of telepathy I gave you had a purpose. I wanted to show you that telepathy did exist, and I wanted to show Ruburt that more than his own subconscious as he knows it was involved. . . . Now Ruburt assembles me or allows me to assemble myself in a way that will be recognizable to you, but regardless of this, I exist in an independent manner."

Later elaborations on the above statement gave us a pretty fair idea of what inner processes go on so that Seth and I can make contact. This involves the construction of a "psychological bridge" that will be explained later in this book. At this point I'd been speaking as Seth for about forty minutes, and he recommended a rest period, saying: "Sometime between now and twenty-five years of laying your doubts at rest, I would like to go into some other matters that I have been trying to tackle for several sessions. But take your rest, pussies."

I used to envy Rob his viewpoint of the sessions. He could see and hear me as Seth and I couldn't. Now during break I questioned him again. I hated to have to depend on someone else to tell me what was going on, but I had learned one thing: I couldn't be Jane and Seth at once. For Seth to come through I had to stop such mental quibbling—at least temporarily.

After break Seth said, "Again, I am not Ruburt's subconscious, though I speak through it. It is the atmosphere through which I can come to you, as the air is the atmosphere through which a bird flies. . . . A certain reassembly of myself is necessary. This is done partially by me and partially by the combined subconscious efforts of you and Ruburt. Will this satisfy you for now?"

"Sure, Seth," Rob said.

"Please be frank, as I do not like this hanging over our heads," Seth said. Then he went on to give us some information concerning entities and the various personalities that compose them. Rob was particularly curious about the differences between entities and personalities.

"Individual life, or rather the life of any present individual, could be legitimately compared to the dream of an entity. While the individual enjoys his given number of years, these are but a flash to the entity. The entity is concerned with these years in somewhat the same manner with which you are concerned with your dreams. As you give inner purpose and organization to your dreams, and obtain insight and satisfaction from them though they involve only a part of your life, so the entity to some extent directs and gives purpose and organization to his personalities.

"Infinities of diversity and opportunity are given to the personalities by the entity. . . . Your own dreams are fragments, even as in a larger sense you are fragments of your entity." Seth also said that an inner part of each personality was aware of its relationship with its entity—and that this portion did man's breathing for him and controlled those bodily processes that we consider involuntary.

The session lasted until 11:30 P.M. Rob was reassured by Seth's statements about my ability to handle dissociation, and by his responsible attitude. I was, too, but I kept thinking of the remark in Dr. Stevenson's letter. "Of course, Seth said that everything was okay," I said. "What else could we expect him to say?"

For a while I think I spent half the time trying to psychoanalyze Seth and the other half trying to analyze myself. Caution is one thing, but sometimes I went overboard. Even so, Seth said that my strong ego was an asset to our work when I didn't overdo it, since it kept my whole personality on an even keel and allowed me the psychological strength to handle and develop my abilities.

One small but amusing incident came up that illustrates my attitude during those early months. We have a lovely large apartment that has, unfortunately, a tiny closet-sized kitchen. When we moved in to our present apartment, the kitchen held a stove and a small refrigerator that didn't begin to hold all our food. We got a larger one for foods that we didn't use every day, and this second refrigerator I put in our huge bathroom, a great old-fashioned tiled room that's easily five times as large as the kitchen. I knew that this was a crazy place for a refrigerator, but after a while I became used to it.

In early spring Rob came down with several annoying gumboils and one night he asked Seth how he might get rid of them. Seth immediately launched into a rather hilarious discussion of the unsanitary aspects of a refrigerator in the bathroom. He made a few kindly but definite statements to the effect that we should know better, and suggested that the appliance be moved into the kitchen, where it would hold all our refrigerated food. If so, he assured Rob his gumboils would disappear.

"No control personality or whatever is going to tell me how to run the house," I said. "This is one of those suspicious signs that we've read about. The control personality starts throwing its weight around and trying to dominate the medium's normal personality. Remember what Dr. Stevenson said? Besides, there's no room in the kitchen for the big refrigerator."

"Do what you want," Rob said. "I've got gumboils, but so what? I can live with them."

"Well . . ."

"Besides," Rob said, "Seth didn't order *you* to do anything. I asked him a question, and he answered it."

When I'm reacting emotionally and Rob gives me a reasonable reply, it always puts me on the defensive. So I agreed.

The next day we moved the big refrigerator. To save my pride or whatever, I put the little refrigerator in the bathroom and turned it into a towel chest. The big refrigerator is still in the kitchen. I got rid of the small one long ago. Oh, yes—Rob's gumboils cleared up in two days, and never returned.

In other words, I used to watch Seth like a hawk, particularly during the first year or so, but he always behaved intelligently, with dignity and humor. As soon as I began judging him by his actions and his effect on us, I dropped this habit. He won my trust. He has given us excellent, psychologically sound advice, but he never tried to give us orders.

Sometimes we followed his council, to our advantage. Other times we didn't go along, for reasons of our own. In 1964 we went house-hunting, for example. Seth suggested we purchase a particular house. We liked it very much but it was in poor condition. Seth might very well be right, we thought—and we might be happier if we bought the house—but we just weren't willing to take the chance.

About a year and a half ago, Seth suggested that I leave my job at the art gallery and give psychic classes. He even told me how many students I would have within three months' time. I followed his advice, though I didn't really think there would be much response in this area. Seth was correct: I've enjoyed the classes, learned a great deal from them, and enlarged my own abilities as a result, in ways I didn't know were possible.

During the first six months or so of the sessions, our cat, Willie, began behaving in a most unsociable manner. A few times he began to hiss and spit quite madly just before sessions. One night he really startled us. We were getting ready to begin, and Willie was sleeping in the bedroom closet. Suddenly he ran out of the closet, fur on end, bolted through the living room, and hid behind the curtains. Once he nipped at my ankles as I was speaking for Seth, and in trance I dragged him half across the room while he hung on to the bottom of my slacks. Rob had to shut him in the studio.

Finally, Rob asked Seth if he knew what was wrong. The reply was that Willie's very acute senses picked up Seth's presence just before session time. He told us that the cat's behavior would change as Willie became more accustomed to the situation. A month or so later, Willie became himself again. Now he pays no attention to the sessions, and even occasionally jumps into my lap when I'm in trance.

During this time Rob had a recurrence of back trouble, though far less severe than before. Seth devoted several long sessions to an analysis of Rob's condition and explained the reasons for the symptoms. They disappeared without medication, and we think that the knowledge Rob gained through these sessions was responsible. Earlier we had purchased a Kennedy rocker because of Rob's back. He used to sit in it to take session notes and for a while it was the only chair in which he was comfortable. He no longer needed it when he recovered, and I got into the habit of using it. Much later, when I finally consented to sit down during sessions, it would be my favorite "Seth" chair.

We quickly learned that Seth regarded physical symptoms as the outward materialization of inner dis-ease. He emphasized the importance of suggestion and the dangers of self-pity. He did tell us then that when one of us was ill, the other was not to offer excessive consolation and thereby reinforce the idea of sickness. In later sessions he would give some excellent material on maintaining good health. This will be covered in Chapter 13.

I've devoted some time and space to the early Seth sessions so that the reader could become acquainted with part of the material as it was given to us. Some of it seems so rudimentary to us now that it's difficult to recall the amazement we felt at the time. It was the continuing sense of discovery and intellectual curiosity that led us on, and that finally resolved my own doubts.

So many developments occurred in the following months that it is difficult to cover them all. We were both to have our first out-of-body experiences, or "astral projections." Our experiments in what Seth calls "Psychological Time" helped us develop our own psychic abilities. The quality and scope of the Seth Material constantly grew, and we were to make some contacts with others in the field of parapsychology. We were shortly to discover that Seth was indeed clairvoyant, and that my own training as a medium had only begun.

CHAPTER
SIX:

Seth Meets a Psychologist

To say that my editor was surprised by the first eight chapters of my ESP book is putting it mildly. He'd had dealings with me before and knew me well enough to be personally interested. He wrote enthusiastic letters, but he was also worried about the book as it stood. My experiences proved that I'd been a medium all along without knowing it, he said, and this could invalidate the book's premise—that the experiments would work for anyone to some extent, regardless of their psychic background.

"But the experiments *did* release my abilities," I protested to Rob. "That proves the point, doesn't it? I never had any psychic experiences before—"

"Don't tell me, tell the publisher," Rob said. "For the life of me I can't understand why Seth's emergence doesn't make it a far better book than it would be otherwise."

As it turned out, it *was* Seth's part in the book that bothered the publisher. If I'd played down Seth's importance and concentrated on

59

some of the other experiments that were also proving successful, then the book would have a very good chance, the editor told me. The other experiments included daily predictions and dream recall; and our dream recall work already had shown us the validity of precognitive dreams.

Rob and I were both practicing with predictions; they took but a few moments daily. We cleared our minds of objective thoughts and wrote down whatever came into our heads, trying to predict the day's events. The trick was to give the intuitional self freedom and not to intellectualize. Results surprised us, and convinced us that most people have more knowledge of the future than they realize. We discovered, among other things, that we would often foresee different portions of one event.

I'm sure that most of us react ahead of time to some events, and I'll have more to say about this later in the book. Since in all of these experiments Seth was helping us through actual suggestions and explanations as to how we perceive such information, I simply couldn't minimize his importance just to get the ESP book published. To us, Seth and the Seth Material was making everything else possible.

Finally, though the editor was for the book, his publisher turned it down. I was really disappointed at losing the sale. As a result, I played around with the idea of publishing some of Seth's ideas as my own and hiding their origin. This seemed dishonest, though, and I decided against it. Besides, I felt that the very fact of the sessions was psychologically fascinating, and brought up questions that were answered in the material itself. So I sent my eight chapters somewhere else, stopped work on the book for nearly a year, and devoted my working time to short stories which were published in various national magazines.

In the meantime we decided to write someone else in the field. Dr. Karlis Osis of the American Psychic Society would have experience with cases like ours, we thought. So in March 1964 we wrote him a letter. He soon wrote back asking for a few sample sessions and suggesting that Seth clairvoyantly describe his office in New York. I don't know what I expected from Dr. Osis, but I sure as the devil wasn't ready to see what Seth could or could not do. Seth offered to carry out the experiment, but I held back. I don't know if I was more afraid that Seth could or couldn't follow through.

"It's put up or shut up time. That's what it amounts to," I said tearfully to Rob. "If this isn't a lot of bunk, then let's see you or Seth walk through walls!"

"But Seth said he'd do it," Rob said, reasonably enough.

Yet even to Rob I couldn't voice my fears. Suppose Seth couldn't? Wouldn't that mean that everything else was some kind of subconscious fraud? Why had Seth agreed when he knew, whoever he was, that I was scared stiff?

"You're afraid of putting this stuff to the test," Rob said. "But that's all right at this stage of the game. I'd rather you didn't push it."

"I can make mistakes and that's okay," I said, trying to explain. "But suppose Seth makes them, too? Suppose he tries to do what's asked of him and fails?"

"Is he supposed to be omnipotent?" Rob asked, grinning.

"No, of course not," I said. "But it sure would be a great help if he was." Just the same, I went into another slump. I still wasn't at all sure that I believed in the survival of personality after death, and if we didn't survive, then from whom was I getting these messages? My subconscious? While I used that explanation as a handy whipping boy at times, I didn't really believe that either: my subconscious was getting enough expression in my short stories and poetry—and without adopting other personality characteristics. A secondary personality? Perhaps, but Seth didn't fit the picture of any of the case histories we'd read—and neither did I.

While I hesitated trying the experiment, Rob sent Dr. Osis some more of the material. Dr. Osis wrote that he wasn't interested in the material itself, since it didn't fall within his field of empirical psychology. He asked us not to send more unless it contained reports of ESP demonstrations. Even though he expressed interest in "testing" Seth for ESP, and suggested again that we try the clairvoyant experiment, I was put off by the letter. So I sulked: If he didn't express interest in the material, which I thought was terrific, then he could just go find someone else to go looking through his walls!

Remember, this was March of 1964. The sessions had only begun the previous December, and we'd had few instances of ESP in sessions, except for the physical effects that alternately intrigued and frightened me.

I just wasn't ready, apparently, to put Seth or myself under any kind of test. I was afraid that Seth's claim to clairvoyance might be subconscious bluff—his or mine—and I didn't know if I had enough courage to call the bluff or not. And suppose it wasn't bluff? I wasn't ready to face that either! I just hadn't come to terms with my experience yet. I thought of "testing" Seth in a highly rigid, uncompromising manner. Seth had to be right or wrong. The idea of hits and misses in ESP investigations was unknown to me. I had little notion of the inner mechanics involved in mediumship, and most likely my attitude effectively blocked any consistent demonstrations at that time.

I was angry at Dr. Osis for looking for signs or wonders (my interpretation, then, of his letter). Yet I knew that I was going to demand the same sort of thing when I got up enough nerve to put Seth, or myself, on the spot.

In the meantime, changes were occurring in my trance states. For the first year I paced the room constantly, while speaking for Seth. My eyes were open, the pupils dilated and much darker than usual. But in the 116th session, December of 1964, I sat down and closed my eyes for the first time. Rob wisely said nothing until the session was over. Seth told us that this was an experimental procedure and would not continue unless I gave full consent.

It seems ridiculous now that it took me 116 sessions before I'd close my eyes or stop pacing the floor. By the time this first change happened in my trance states, I'd already had my first out-of-body experience, and following Seth's instructions I was having clairvoyant experiences during daily exercise periods. But I felt in control of these, while Seth was in control of sessions, and to me this made a difference. I agreed to the new trance procedure, but it was still some time before it became the rule rather than the exception. The trance was a deeper one, though, and the material launched into more complicated subjects. It was also during this time that Seth started removing my glasses just before he began to speak.

(It would be January 1966 before the next change in my trance behavior. After having sessions for a year with my eyes closed, I suddenly began opening them again, though the trance was even deeper than before. There was quite a noticeable alteration of muscle pattern and facial gestures—an overall personality change. The expression in the eyes was not only un-Jane-like. It definitely belonged to Seth. To all intents and purposes, Seth was comfortably ensconced in my physical body. This is our current procedure also, and apparently it gives Seth a certain freedom of expression. He often looks directly at Rob, for example, or at anyone else to whom he is speaking.)

In 1964, though, when we wrote to Dr. Osis, the trance hadn't achieved this depth, and I was just getting used to the idea of sitting down in sessions. During 1965 the Seth Material constantly accumulated at our twice weekly sessions. Early that year, Frederick Fell gave me a contract for the ESP book, and I had a deadline to meet.

The idea of ESP tests still frightened me, but I felt that they were inevitable and necessary.

In spring 1965, about a year after we wrote Dr. Osis, Rob wrote to Dr. Instream (not his real name), who was connected with a state university in upstate New York. Dr. Instream had been one of the nation's foremost psychologists in his earlier years, and had investigated many mediums in the past. If Seth was a secondary personality he would know it, I thought. Again we enclosed a few sessions with one letter. Dr. Instream wrote back, expressing interest and inviting us to attend the National Hypnosis Symposium to be held in July 1965.

By now we'd experimented with hypnosis in some age-regression and reincarnational work. In these I acted as hypnotist, with Rob as subject. We had never used hypnosis to induce a trance in Seth sessions, however, and we had no experience with hypnosis when the sessions began. Would Dr. Instream want me to go under hypnosis? I wasn't at all sure that I would consent. Now, after reading about the hypnotic testing undergone by Mrs. Eileen Garrett, the famous medium, I know I'd never stand for it myself. (Self-hypnosis is something else—I use it now to give myself general good-health suggestions.)

We were delighted at the prospect of meeting Dr. Instream, but in order to pay for the trip, including fees for symposium attendance, we would have to use our vacation money. Besides this, Rob was now working in the art department of a local greeting card company in the mornings, and painting in the afternoons. So we would have to take vacation time to make the trip.

It was the craziest and most vexing vacation we've ever spent. At the first lecture we attended, the speaker gave a demonstration in hypnosis. Except for ourselves and a few students, the symposium was attended by psychologists, doctors, and dentists. The lecturer was a psychologist who is well known for his work in hypnosis. Lowering his voice, he said that since most of those in the audience used hypnosis professionally, they should know what it felt like to be hypnotized themselves. So he began.

Rob sat on one side of me and Dr. Instream on the other. I decided that I wasn't going to be hypnotized, but I lowered my eyes so as not to be conspicuous. When it became apparent that most of the audience had dutifully gone under—sitting there and reminding me somehow of pigeons with wings neatly folded—I looked up cautiously to see what Dr. Instream was doing. He was looking back. Rob was grinning, watching both of us.

Dr. Instream was delightful. Later, we were in a Howard Johnson's restaurant in Oswego talking with the good doctor when I abruptly felt Seth about. We'd never had a session away from home. Nervously I kept trying to make eye-signs at Rob. Once I kicked his leg, hoping that I didn't kick the doctor's by mistake. Finally I caught Rob's eye. He got the message and shrugged comically.

"Uh, I don't know how to put this," I said, "but if you want to meet Seth you can. He's around."

I had no intentions of having a session in a Howard Johnson's restaurant. Neither did Dr. Instream. He took us to his office and closed the door.

We had a Seth session, the first in which I went in and out of trance so quickly that both Seth and I could take part in a normal conversation.

After greeting Dr. Instream, Seth said: "My field is education, and

64

my particular interest is that these [seemingly paranormal] abilities of human personality be understood and investigated, for they are not unnatural, but inherent. . . . I am indeed aware of the difficulties which shall be encountered.

"I have said this often—I am no misty-eyed ghostly spirit, materializing in the middle of the night. I am simply an intelligent personality no longer bound by your physical laws. . . ." Seth went on to speak about the ESP tests that Dr. Instream had suggested in our earlier conversation. "I have some difficulties with Ruburt's own stubborn attitude at times; but we must also take this into consideration, and so we shall . . . I will seriously endeavor to do what I can do, within our circumstances. My cooperation can be counted upon. It goes without saying that all of this cannot happen overnight, but we shall begin. In a regular session I will discuss what can be done. We can do much. Much we cannot do. But since we understand both the potentialities and limitations, then we can make the most of what we have."

I guess we might have set some kind of a record. First I'd say something, then Dr. Instream, then Seth, then Rob—like a round robin. Seth called Dr. Instream by his first name, and the two of them sounded as if they were old cronies. I was a bit appalled. After all, Dr. Instream was a distinguished elderly gentleman. Rob took all the notes he could, scribbling furiously.

Seth said: "Spontaneity must be allowed for. Then the sort of evidence with which you are concerned can be obtained. If we are overly concerned for effects, then the spontaneity disappears. The ego comes in, and we are lost."

"Exactly," Dr. Instream said. "We must proceed carefully, without pushing . . . I'm out of my depth here, Seth. Spontaneity is important, but—"

"It is our doorway," Seth said. "If any evidence is to come through, it comes through that doorway—"

"Yes," Dr. Instream said. "But our human limitations . . . Our methodology is important to us here, if we are to get others to listen."

"In a regular session we will take this into consideration," Seth said. "We will work within them [the limitations] and see what we can do. It would be of great benefit if you and others understood that these limitations exist only because you accept them."

"Yes."

"Human personality is not innately limited. The waking state, as I have often said, is as much a trance state as any other. Here [in sessions] we merely switch the focus of attention to other channels. Consider all types of awareness as trance states. Consciousness is the direction in which the self looks. . . .

"We have many fields of common interest, you and I. The personality must always be considered in an elemental way as patterns of action. When you attempt to tamper with various levels, you change them. When you crack an egg to discover what is inside, you ruin the egg. There are other ways to go about it. We do not need a hammer to crack the eggshell. . . . I am an egghead, but do not need a hammer to be cracked." Here, Seth was smiling broadly.

"We'll need to get some insight on this," Dr. Instream said. "I'm human. I need to learn. We need proof."

"Your attitude may allow you to get some. But those who have a closed mind will not get any evidence that will satisfy them."

"Some [evidence] that we have is difficult to deny, but we must conduct a methodical investigation of these things," Dr. Instream said.

"This is one of the reaons that we have not tended toward a séance atmosphere . . . and also why I have largely avoided displays—"

"Again, I'm in over my depth. I need time to consider what we can do, what your ideas are."

"There may be a time lag as I build up Ruburt's acceptability in these directions," Seth said, "but I anticipate no difficulties."

Dr. Instream treated Seth with deference, great deference—and I admit that I found this somewhat suspicious at the time. I wasn't sure myself as to who or what Seth was, and the thought crossed my mind more than once that the doctor's attitude was simply a device to gain my confidence—the psychologist's pretense that he believed in the existence of his patient's delusion as unquestioningly as the patient did.

Before we finished with that visit, Dr. Instream told us unofficially that Seth had a "massive intellect" and certainly didn't seem to be a secondary personality. He cheered me considerably by telling me that I appeared to be in excellent emotional and psychological health.

Unfortunately, we also spoke to another psychologist at the symposium, one much closer to my own age. We met during one of the informal get-togethers. When he discovered that we weren't connected with the medical profession in any way, he asked what our interest was in the symposium. So we told him. One thing led to another. A discussion about Seth followed, and Rob showed him some of our notes, later, in our room.

After speaking to us for less than an hour, the psychologist assured me that I was schizoid, using the sessions to dominate Rob. Once, he grabbed the notes from the bureau and approached me like some wrathful god, waving them in my face. "You think it's necessary to take all these records, don't you?" he demanded.

"We need them. Rob takes them," I managed to say.

"A-hah," he shouted—and he *did* shout. "That's one of the main symptoms!"

"But Rob's the one who takes them . . ."

It was no good. Whenever I tried to say something in my own behalf, he'd yell triumphantly. "See? See? You feel the need to defend yourself, don't you?"

This happened between our first and second interviews with Dr. Instream. In the meantime we drove around the deserted college town, and stopped once for a drink in a hot little bar. Never had I been so filled with self-doubts. The psychologist had spoken aloud the most exaggerated of my own inner fears.

"He only talked with us for thirty minutes or so, hon," Rob said.

"But suppose he's right? I wouldn't know it—that's the awful part. Neither of us would know it or want to admit it!"

"But anyone that emotionally damaged would show symptoms in normal daily living."

"But the sessions," I cried. "The sessions that I think offer such a contribution . . . the material I'm so sure offers insights into the nature of reality! Suppose the whole thing is just a symptom of mental disorder instead?"

We drove up past the stately university buildings. How neat and orderly! If only life were that neat, I thought. Rob was still trying to comfort me when we arrived at Dr. Instream's office. Was I really one of those talkative domineering women who used any kind of trick to control their husbands? I looked over at Rob. He stood there, quiet but assured, "cool" versus my "hot"—my idea of a man. Usually I'm talkative. Now I shut up and let Rob do the talking—or tried to let him.

Dr. Instream told us that the psychologist's behavior was an example of the sort of performance that so upset parapsychologists. But more, he told me once again that he'd found no such tendencies on my part. "The man's had no experience in the practice of psychology," he said. "He's only read textbook cases of this or that." Then he told us that while the experience was unfortunate, perhaps it was best that we encountered it early in the game. Academic psychologists were apt to take a dim view of mediumship, he said. I would have to let such comments roll off my back. I should have laughed at the young psychologist. I should have said, "Well, it takes one to know one," or some such.

But the affair bothered me. It was to be some time before I completely trusted myself and my own reactions again. I also felt that I could no longer drag my feet: I had to find out what Seth could or couldn't do.

Dr. Instream explained the parapsychologists' attitude toward the testing of ESP and suggested that Seth try clairvoyantly to perceive objects upon which the doctor would be concentrating. We would do this in each session. At 10 P.M. Mondays and Wednesdays, Dr. Instream would concentrate on an object in his study in the town in which he lived. At the same time Seth was to give his impressions, and each week we would mail the sessions to Dr. Instream. This time I agreed; so did Seth.

Then, on our return home, Rob had another idea. Suppose we tried something along the same lines on our own? So at the same time we initiated our envelope tests, in which Seth was asked to give his impressions of the contents of double sealed envelopes.

I wanted to find out if Seth could do what he said he could do. Dr. Instream wanted scientific evidence for the existence of clairvoyance, and we all hoped we could supply it. We'd set ourselves some goals! The months between August 1965 and October 1966 contained enough triumphs and disappointments to keep my head spinning. In the next chapter I'll deal with that exciting—and perplexing—year.

CHAPTER SEVEN:

Out-of-Body Episodes—
I Pop into a Taxi
While My Body Stays at Home

———————————◆•◆———————————

We started the Instream tests and our own envelope tests in August of 1965. In October my first book was coming out, and Peg Gallagher, a reporter for the Elmira *Star Gazette*, interviewed me. I'd known her slightly in the past, but now she and her husband and Rob and I became good friends. Bill is assistant advertising director of the *Star Gazette*, and he and Peg were soon leaving for a vacation in Puerto Rico. We decided to set up an experiment.

We wouldn't communicate at all through usual means. Instead, we would ask Seth if he could "tune in" on the Gallaghers during their vacation. During their trip we would substitute this experiment for our envelope tests. We knew that Peg and Bill were going to San Juan, but that was all we knew. Besides, neither Rob nor I have ever been to Puerto Rico.

We were in the middle of a Seth session and Seth was giving his impressions of the Gallaghers' trip. As I sat in my favorite rocker speaking as Seth, suddenly I found myself in the back seat of a cab. The next instant the cab took such a sharp turn to the right that I was shoved over into the corner of the seat. For a minute I was really frightened. I wasn't used to being comfortably seated in the living room one minute and in the back seat of a swiftly moving cab the next!

I had just enough time to see the cab driver's neck from the rear—it was thick and stubby. I didn't see his face. While this was going on, I lost all contact with my body in the living room. My subjective sensations were those of someone suddenly thrown off-balance by the sickening swerve of the car's turn. Yet while this was happening, my physical body sat upright in the rocker, speaking without pause as Seth:

"A cab ride. Our cat lover laughs [Seth's nickname for Peg, who dislikes cats]. A three-dollar fare which seems too much. An old, rather than young, cab driver with a stubby neck. A destination that is mainly to the right after one turn."

When Peg and Bill returned, we found out that these impressions were quite legitimate. They had paid a three-dollar cab fare to go to the motel from the airport. Peg was quite angry about this, since the same ride two years earlier had cost less than two dollars. Their cab took a very sharp turn to the right. Peg and Bill remembered this vividly, not only because of the sudden turn, but also because this happened right after the driver had run through a traffic light. The turn had been so sharp that it upset them considerably. But the cab driver was not "old, rather than young." Interestingly enough, Peg said, he did look old from the rear, though, because his neck had a peculiar rough, mottled look. It was also thick and stubby.

I was really delighted when the whole thing checked out. I saw just what I could have been expected to see had I been in the cab physically. Peg and Bill were never aware of my presence.

The incident had several intriguing implications. I was definitely the one who was "out," yet Seth described what I saw. His voice and personality were in control of my physical system, while my consciousness was someplace else—and a good many miles away. I didn't have to tell Seth what happened—he described it immediately.

He didn't mention my sensations when I was thrown into the corner of the cab, though. Was this because he didn't feel them? Or because I was certain to remember these myself? And consider this puzzler: Granted my consciousness traveled from Elmira to San Juan in space, what about time? The session was held on Monday, October 25, 1965, but the incident happened to the Gallaghers *one week earlier,* on Monday, October 17. Yet I lived that experience just as vividly as though it transpired at that moment in Puerto Rico. (Seth also gave other correct impressions of that same trip.)

The next episode didn't involve Seth directly, except that I was following his directions in the use of the Inner Senses. I decided to see what impressions of the Gallagher trip I could get on my own. So one morning that same week I lay down, closed my eyes, and gave myself the suggestion that I would find Peg and Bill.

Suddenly, without transition, I found myself descending through the air to land on a long narrow porch that was surrounded by a low railing. I knew that my body was in bed, but lost all contact with it. Regardless of where it was, I was someplace else entirely. Looking around I saw that I stood on the veranda of an oddly constructed double-story motel.

The building was raised up from the ground in a manner different from the usual. Over the railing, a small body of water was visible, and beyond this there was a much larger body of water, an ocean, I thought. Was this Puerto Rico? I had no idea.

Doors opened off the veranda, which extended the full length of the motel. I wondered if this was where the Gallaghers were staying. Instantly I knew that it was, and that the center door led to their room. Peg and Bill weren't in sight, though. Before beginning the experiment at 11 A.M., I had set the alarm clock for 11:30. Now it rang. My consciousness returned so quickly to my body that my physical head was swimming. I sat up in dismay—couldn't I find out more? Couldn't I see a sign, or get a more definite idea of the location?

I didn't know if it would work or not, but I reset the alarm for thirty minutes later, then I lay back down and told myself I would return to the same place. Brief but definite traveling sensations followed. Mountains and skies swept by. Then I found myself hovering in the air above the same motel.

I was too high to make out details, so I willed myself to move down closer. Without any difficulty I changed position and came down, though still not to the ground. A man was directly beneath me, and slightly ahead of me. He wore a business suit and hat, and carried a briefcase. As I watched, he crossed a blacktop expanse to a sidewalk, and entered a large building on the other side of the motel. I remember thinking it odd that he wore business clothes in what I took to be a resort area. It seemed that only moments had passed, but the alarm rang once again. I snapped back to my body.

Talk about being excited! Immediately I drew a diagram of the motel and surrounding area. I couldn't wait for the Gallaghers to return, so I could check this and the Seth impressions. I asked Peg to draw a diagram of their motel and its nearby neighborhood. Peg's diagram matched mine! My description of the motel was correct, including the center door that led to their room. The motel was on St. Thomas, an island near Puerto Rico. Peg and Bill were there the day of my experiment, and the following day.

Not only that, but the man I saw was one Bill noticed on both mornings, specifically because he wore business clothes. The man was a native—another reason Bill noticed him. I didn't know this, having seen him from the rear. The building he'd entered had been the post office.

I was fascinated; there was so much to learn. In the cab episode in the Seth session, Seth had described everything while I saw it. This time I had to wait until I got back to my body to write down what had happened, and draw my diagram.

As far as I was concerned, I had enough evidence to convince me that both episodes were legitimate. They started me on my own work in out-of-body experiments, in which I'm still trying to find answers to the many questions posed by such phenomena. Later, Seth was to give us instructions. As a matter of fact, as I write this book, Rob and I are just starting a joint series of projection experiments that Seth initiated. These first instances greatly increased my confidence in Seth's abilities and my own.

74

How much more fun this sort of thing was than the Instream tests, which we were also conducting! Even our own envelope series was dry in comparison. We mailed copies of the Gallagher material to Dr. Instream. I was really excited about the whole thing and waited eagerly for his comments. I took it for granted that he wouldn't consider that we had any *scientific* evidence, but we did have the nearly identical sketches, and the impressions were correct. "He may not consider this scientific enough," I said to Rob, "but he has to admit, at the very least, that clairvoyance occurred."

We held seventy-five Instream tests and eighty-three envelope tests between August 1965 and September 1966. Like most people with no background in psychic work, I espected things to be pure and simple. If Seth was what he said he was, then he should be able to look into time and space and closed envelopes as easily as you and I can see the objects in a room. I didn't realize how much depended on the depth of my trance and on my willingness to give him freedom—I had to learn not to "block" information that came through. I didn't realize either that little is known about normal perception, much less extrasensory perception, or that no medium is expected to be 100 percent correct. The impressions had to come through me, and as the old saying goes, to err is human.

Yet Seth managed to use the tests to demonstrate his own clairvoyant ability, further my education, and instruct us on the processes involved. He varied the depth of my trances during tests so I could get the feel of various stages of consciousness, and also showed me how to let him use my own personal associations in order to get certain data. He used the tests to demonstrate ESP; but more, he gave me constant practice in changing my subjective focus, explaining the whole thing as he went along.

Usually no one was present at these sessions but Rob and I—hardly a scientific state of affairs. But with the envelope tests we weren't trying to convince scientists or psychologists of anything. We were trying to see what we could and could not expect of the sessions. We wanted something we could check out for ourselves right away. I wanted to know how we were doing!

Sometimes Rob prepared the envelopes just before a session, and sometimes way ahead of time. He used all kinds of things for test items, some that I had seen, recently or in the past, and some that I had never seen. He might use a letter, for example, that had come the day before, and which I had read, or a bill from several years back, or an item he picked up that I had never seen, or an envelope prepared by a friend—in which case the contents were unknown even to Rob. Pieces of paper Rob picked up in the streets, leaves, beer coasters, chunks of hair, photographs, sketches, bills—all were used at one time or another. Sometimes Rob chose items specifically because they had strong emotional charges connected with them. Other times he purposely used neutral objects. We wanted to see if Seth did better with certain kinds of targets than others.

The items were enclosed in one sealed envelope between two layers of lightproof bristol cardboard, and then the whole thing was placed in another envelope, which was also sealed. I never knew when we would have such a test, and I never saw the envelope before a session. Rob would hand an envelope to me in the middle of a session. I was always in trance, and usually my eyes were closed. (In any case, the test item was enclosed within the two pieces of cardboard and two envelopes, and was quite opaque.) Sometimes I held the envelope to my forehead while delivering impressions. After the session we checked our results. (Specific examples will appear in the next chapter.)

Talk about a seesaw! When Seth did well on the tests, I felt light as a feather for days. When anything didn't check out to my satisfaction, I felt as though I weighed 450 pounds and was gaining a pound an hour. I thought that anything less than a perfect performance cast doubts on Seth's independent nature.

All in all our own tests proved invaluable, not only as a part of my training and as a means of increasing my self-confidence, but also in preparing me for some other out-of-body-experiences that would take place during later Seth sessions. The tests, and Seth's comments, also gave us insights into the nature of inner perception that literally could not have been achieved in any other way.

As Seth varied the trance depths, I became aware of two lines of consciousness, his and my own, and to understand at least to some degree when my own personal associations were an aid and when they were a detriment. In a very deep trance, the inner processes are hidden even from the medium. With most mediums the mechanics are so automatic that little can be learned about the inner psychological actions involved in such work. Seth maintained that our situation would work to our advantage in this respect.

In the data he would often differentiate between his impressions and any of mine that had slipped in, connect mine to their source in personal associations, and tell us whether or not they were legitimate. I am seldom so "blacked out" as to feel as if I were sleeping. Usually I know what is going on, although I may almost instantly forget what has happened. On occasion Seth and I can take turns talking so that I can go in and out of trance in seconds. Sometimes it seems I merge with Seth, feeling his emotions and reactions completely, rather than my own. In this case the Jane-self is far in the background, dozing but dimly conscious. Other times, though less seldom, I am in the foreground and Seth advises me as to what to say.

Our own tests gave me a standard against which to measure my performance and Seth's, providing an immediate check of accuracy and teaching me to sharpen my subjective focus to go from the general to the specific. All of this training was important as far as my reception of the Seth Material itself was concerned. Seth has often spoken about the necessary distortions that must occur in any such communications, and he is most concerned that the material be as little contaminated by distortions as possible. He discusses this thoroughly in later sessions.

I started the autumn of 1965, then, with high hopes, particularly because of the two out-of-body episodes mentioned earlier in this chapter. I waited to hear what Dr. Instream had to say about them. I was sure he'd have to admit that they were encouraging, even if they didn't involve his own experiments with us. We'd already begun his series of tests and were sending the results to him each week. So far we'd heard nothing from him about these, and I also looked forward to see how we were doing here. If they turned out even half as good as the out-of-body data, I thought, we'd still be getting off to a great start.

In the meantime, I'd left my gallery job and was writing full-time. I also began angling with one of the best-paying and most popular magazines in the country. The editor turned down story after story, assuring me each time that I was certain to sell him the next one. I lived by the mail, waiting for an acceptance from this editor, or for a report from Dr. Instream.

Trying to prove the existence of telepathy and clairvoyance to a self-professed "hard-nosed psychologist," sell fiction to one of the best magazines in the country, and conduct our own tests in the Seth sessions was rather a bit to take on in one year—as I discovered.

CHAPTER
EIGHT:

*A Year of Testing—Seth
"Looks Into" Envelopes
and Gives Rob a Few Art Lessons*

For the next eleven months, the Seth sessions dealt mainly with test data of one kind or another. At 9 P.M. as usual, Seth would begin with the theoretical material in which we were increasingly interested. At 10 P.M. he gave impressions for Dr. Instream, and after that Rob gave me an envelope if there was to be such a test that evening. If we did have one of our own tests, then we'd sit up after the session, trying to evaluate the results. By then it was usually past midnight, and we would be exhausted.

Although my confidence had risen with the two out-of-body episodes, I felt that I was putting Seth and myself on the line with each test session. I never knew whether or not we would have an envelope test. Often I was afraid of having a session for fear we'd have an envelope test and the results just would not apply. (This never happened, incidentally, though the impressions given were not always as specific as we would have liked.) Actually I didn't care *what* was in the envelopes—I just wanted to know if Seth could tell us, and I wanted him to be absolutely right each time. My attitude was bound to have an effect. Now I wonder that Seth was able to do anything with me at all in those days, but most of the time he managed to do very well indeed.

Here's an instance where Rob was trying to test for clairvoyance rather than telepathy. Like many others, this test had surprising results. Rob's notes show clearly the procedure he followed in choosing the test item:

> In my studio was a pile of old newspapers. Most of them were of *The New York Times,* both daily and Sunday copies. Shortly before the session I removed a few local papers from the stack. Then backing up to the pile, I pulled out a section without looking at it, and tore off a portion of a page. I folded this behind me until I was sure it would fit between the regular double bristol and into the double envelopes.
>
> Still without looking at the paper I'd chosen as object, I sealed it in the envelopes. Then, with my eyes closed, I picked up the section from which the object had been taken, groped over to a floor-to-ceiling bookcase, and placed it on a high shelf where I would not see it.
>
> This procedure left me knowing only one thing about the object: that it was from some section of *The New York Times,* date unknown. After the experiment was over, Jane opened the envelopes containing the test object; then I went back to the studio, and from the hidden section I picked out the page from which the object had been torn. It turned out to be pages 11–12 of Section One of the *Times* for Sunday, November 6, 1966.

Seth gave thirty-nine impressions. Almost all of them had direct application. Here are several, pertaining to the test object, grouped together for convenience:

"A paper item, rougher rather than smooth background." (The object was a piece of newspaper, coarse newsprint rather than, say, a coated magazine paper stock.)

"A gray view." (Portions of illustrations were visible on both sides of the item, all in gray tones.)

"Liberal giving." (The words *"liberal* discounts" appear on the object.)

"Connection with a telephone or telephone call." (On one side of the item we find "No mail or phone orders," and on the other side, "Mail and phone orders filled," plus a long series of telephone exchange numbers.)

"Something identical to something else . . . two or two of a kind." (The word "twin" appears on the object, referring to the size of a blanket on sale. I had the strong subjective impression, however, that this was a reference to the fact that the envelope object was a *part* of a similar object.)

The above impressions referred to the test object itself. Now here are some about the page from which the object was taken. Seth said, in consecutive order: "A method of disposal . . . Something in the vernacular . . . Gubatorial." (I was after the word "gubernatorial" here, but as usual Rob recorded it the way I pronounced it in trance.)

For a minute this data stumped us when we went over the test results. Then Rob looked at the full newspaper page.

Both of us caught on at once. "Wow," I said. "A method of disposal—that must be sales! But what a crazy way to put it."

"And look at this," Rob said, holding up the item in one hand and the full page in the other.

" 'Election Day Sales,' or 'Values,' is printed in black headlines at the top of both sides of the page. And gubatorial, or gubernatorial, applies because the election's for New York State governor on November 9. I'd also say that the phrase 'Election Day Sales' is certainly in the vernacular."

Refer to the illustrated section for reproductions of the test item and the page from which it was torn. Both sides of the test item contained portions of advertisements that were tied in with election day, yet the words "Election Day" didn't appear on the object itself at all —only on the whole newspaper page that had lain on a high shelf of Rob's studio bookcase.

"But why didn't Seth just say 'sales'?" I asked in exasperation.

"Listen," Rob said, laughing, "we have to go along with the way the data comes through and try to learn from it. You did well . . ."

Now I think that this is an excellent example of the way extrasensory perceptions are sometimes received. Sales *are* a method of disposal, yet verbally the final connection isn't as concise as we would like. There's more than just the idea of conciseness involved, though: such answers are also just different—unexpectedly so, and they make us consider old objects or ideas in new and equally valid ways. I'll have more to say about this sort of thing later in this chapter.

There were quite a few other surprises in this test. Not only did Seth pick up this excellent identifying information, but he gave further impressions concerning the whole page from which the test item had been taken. Besides all the sales, there were four articles on the large section. The envelope item didn't include these, yet Seth gave impressions referring to three of them.

"A mission with unforeseen consequences . . . 1943 . . . Illia, and perhaps an F and R . . . Something happening all over again, as a commemoration . . . A connection with something green, as a meadow . . . a child . . . Januarious."

All of this referred to an article dealing with a Dominican seminary founded in Aldeia Nova, Portugal, in 1943. We believe "Illia" an attempt to get at "Aldeia." The given date was correct, and the article goes on to tell about a young priest, Father Fernandes (F and R—the abbreviation for "Father" is Fr.), who was on a *mission* in this country to get funds to modernize the seminary. He was also described as organizing a pilgrimage to *commemorate* the fiftieth anniversary celebrations at Fatima, which is only ten miles from the seminary. The article states that the seminary includes, among other things, its own farm, vineyards, and vegetable and fruit gardens. We think that the "green, as meadow" impression referred to these. The "Januarious" connection doesn't seem to be related, yet it is highly important because for me personally it had a strong religious connotation: one of my favorite grade-school teachers was a nun, Sister Januarious. The article speaks of the three children who saw the apparition at Fatima, and Seth mentioned a child.

Other impressions dealt with another article headlined "Portugal Shows Dip in Prisoners." This specifically referred to the need to modernize the "big, old antiquated prisons" that were "of very low standard," and made several remarks concerning the crime rate in Portugal. The article also stated that Portugal has the lowest per capita income in Europe. Seth's impressions were fairly obvious here:

"Connection with a monstrosity, as of a monstrous building . . . A disturbance . . . a determination and a disadvantage . . . an inadequate performance."

Seth also gave some other impressions of the page from which the envelope item was taken, besides those dealing with the articles. "A date above . . . Buttons . . . some figures and a distant connection with skull shapes . . . the colors, blue and purple and green . . . and other round shapes."

The date of the paper was at the top of the page, of course. Buttons, many of them, are clearly shown in the photographs of clothing for sale. These same models are also the figures Seth mentions, and as you can see from the photograph of the page, the women's faces give a skull-like impression, with their hair pulled back. The colors mentioned by Seth are listed in the sheet advertisement. Purple, I believe, refers to "Orchid mist."

This test brought several questions to mind at once, though. How had Seth picked up the information about the entire page, when only a small section of it was in the test envelope? Had some kind of projection on my part been involved, back to the studio bookcase? Seth hadn't first given impressions of the envelope object itself, then neatly moved on to deal with the entire page; he had shifted back and forth between the two, as if viewing both at once. And why had he not confined his data just to the envelope object?

We asked Seth about these points in a later session, and got some very interesting answers: "A portion is always connected to the whole of which it is part," he said. "From the torn section, then, to me the whole [page] was present, and from portions of the whole, the whole can be read. With enough freedom on the one hand, and training on the other, Ruburt, speaking for me, could give you the entire copy of *The New York Times* from a torn corner.

"This does not involve projection.

"There were other issues, having to do with Ruburt's own characterics. Now it is true, generally speaking, that material of an emotional nature actually has a stronger vitality and is easier to perceive. Beyond this, however, Ruburt has *no* love for detail" (Seth smiled) "and will always use it as a clue to see where it leads him.

"He would not be content simply to give the details on the snatch of paper. This is a fairly automatic tendency of his mental life. We use it, I hope to advantage, in our sessions in other ways. . . . In the tests, however, we tried to utilize this characteristic, since we could not deny it. Ruburt's abilities are what I have to work with and through—besides, of course, my own. So we used this tendency here to enlarge the picture and bring in further details that gave you rather respectable data . . . and in a way that was fairly natural to Rubert."

About the tests in general, Seth said: "I was teaching him, and I went along with his natural interests and inclinations. The antagonism he had for testing came not from the idea itself, as much as from the idea of focusing upon detail for detail's sake. Only when you had that kind of a test did he become antagonistic. In extrasensory perception—as in so-called normal perception—the natural inclinations of the personality dictate the kind of information that will be sought from any available field of data.

"There are many areas of knowledge in which any given individual is uninterested. He will not bother to use [even] normal perception to obtain it. I give Ruburt access to large fields of focus. I help him change the energy that he uses in perception into other directions, to turn it inward. I make information available to him. Then, according to his basic characteristics, he uses the information."

The test just described stressed clairvoyance. An earlier test was extremely illuminating from a different standpoint, convincing us that the original extrasensory perception is general, like an overall view of a large area. Somewhere a narrowing-down process must occur to give it a more specific focus.

This test was funny, really, because Seth was doing beautifully on his own. Then he threw the ball to me, and I nearly fell flat on my face. The envelope item was a bill of Rob's, dated July 15, 1966. The session was on August 1. I'd been with Rob at the lumberyard when he got the bill. (See the illustrated section).

Rob had purchased two four-by-eight-foot pieces of Masonite and a roller pan. The salesman who waited on us became quite talkative when he learned that Rob was going to use the Masonite for paintings. He told us that a European artist had done a portrait of him while he'd been a soldier in World War II. Somewhat humorously, he described how the artist had drawn his face as though it were symmetrical and without blemish, while actually it was quite asymmetrical with an impaired eye. The salesman also wore glasses.

Here are some of Seth's impressions: "Four square, or four and four square." (We thought this was very good. Rob had the two pieces of Masonite cut in half so they'd fit into our car. This gave him four pieces, each four-foot square.)

"Writing or printing on the lower left hand corner, very small, holding the object horizontally. Something on the back also." (Both of these applied, except that the very small print was on the left side, not only the left corner.)

"1966, looking forward to 1967." (Written on the bill is the date and the year, 1966, and underneath, "Account forwarded.")

"A connection with a photograph or other like object." (This, we believe, refers quite validly to the portrait.)

"An oval shape or eye shape, that is, this kind of an eye, inside of a rectangle or triangle, you see." (According to Rob's notes, I pointed to one of my own closed eyes. The salesman, as mentioned earlier, specifically mentioned his poor eye in connection with his portrait, and his glasses.)

"Connection with transportation and with water." (A rather unique way of referring to a ten-mile car trip to *Well*sburg. The name of the town appears on the bill. So, incidentally, does the word "*car*load" on the back.)

"A word beginning with *m*, and another *M*, this time the initial of a name." (Rob had purchased *M*asonite, by its brand name, but the salesman listed it as "Presdwood" on the bill. A capital *M* appears in the bill's heading: Glenn *M*. Schuyler.)

"A rectangular item with some dark coloring on it, perhaps dark blue." (The bill is rectangular. The back of it is printed in heavy black.)

All in all, Seth gave twenty-four impressions. Each of them did apply, though some were not as specifically connected as others. For example, Seth said: "Connection with black, symbolic of death; and with a tournament, again symbolic, as of a crossing of swords." We believe that this was a reference to World War II, when the salesman who waited on us had his portrait done as a soldier. Another example was this: "Numbers . . . perhaps 01913." The bill did have numbers on it, and in a series that began with 0 (this seemed unusual to us), but not in the order given by Seth. One series begins with 09 (not 019); and the last two digits, 1 and 3, do appear by themselves on the front of the bill.

Up to this point the impressions had come through with no concern on my part. I was in a deep trance. Then Seth said: "The feeling of something hanging over, threatening or overhanging, on the upper half of the object, and dark." As I spoke these words for Seth, a rift seemed to open up—a doubt as to the information's interpretation. I knew that Seth wanted me to narrow this down myself, and that this was part of my training.

I had the feeling of something very heavy hanging over me. Was this to be translated into an object like, say, a heavy roof over my head, or to an emotional feeling that "hung over me"? I didn't know—and at that point I couldn't figure it out. The correct specific connection wasn't made. Seth threw me another: "Something bright and small also, beneath this overhanging or threatening portion." Here again, left to my own devices, I couldn't work my way to the specific data we wanted.

Yet Seth was trying to lead me to the word "roofing." It was in the heading of the bill, on the upper half. See how correct and yet ambiguous that unfinished impression was—"the feeling of something hanging over, threatening or overhanging, on the upper half of the object, and dark."

The second impression that I was supposed to complete ("something bright and small beneath this overhanging or threatening portion") was to lead me to the word "roller pan," which also appeared on the bill beneath the word "roofing." A roller pan *is* small, bright, and shiny, and the one Rob purchased that day had been a shiny aluminum color.

Here Seth's impressions had been quite literal, as if the words on the bill were coming to life and being described as objects instead of as words *describing* objects. Later I was to do much better when Seth left some impressions up to me, but this kind of training was invaluable. Even though I didn't do a very good job, we learned something about the nature of perception, which was Seth's intent. This test made us suspect that all impressions, extrasensory or otherwise, are initially nonverbal and nonvisual, more like pure feeling that is only later interpreted in sense terms.

We tried all sorts of things with the envelopes. In *The New York Times* test, Rob himself didn't know what was on the test object. He didn't always know what the test object *was,* in any case, and sometimes he didn't even know that a test would be held! For example, occasionally friends would come unannounced to a session and bring their own test envelope. This was just handed to me in the middle of the session, without my knowing beforehand whether or not a test would be held. Sometimes Rob would use such an envelope at once; at other times he would save it for a future session.

It didn't seem to make any difference in the results whether Rob knew what the test envelope contained or not. One night Nora Stevens (not her real name) came unannounced. She was the friend of a friend, and had attended two sessions previously. During this period we encouraged people to drop in with test envelopes, though actually few did. (Before and after this we preferred to keep our sessions private.)

We knew that Nora was a secretary in a hospital office that had to do with the purchase of drugs and supplies, but that she had nothing to do with patients, their records, or medical procedures. I didn't know she'd brought an envelope. She slipped it to Rob after the session began.

Seth said: "A connection with a family record, as a page, for example, from a book . . . connected also with a turbulent event or unpleasantness . . . four numbers in a row, and other numbers, the initial *M,* a connection with another city."

After the session we opened the envelope. It contained a patient's record sheet, a page from a pad that Nora had picked out of a wastebasket in another office. At the bottom corner were four numbers in a row, with other numbers on the top by the patient's name, Margaret. Her hometown also began with an *M;* she was from out of town. A hospital stay is certainly unpleasant, often turbulent. Seth also gave other impressions concerning the woman's background, but we couldn't check these out.

Yet sometimes I'd get discouraged even over good results. One test had pleased me no end at first. It was our 37th, held in the 237th session on March 2, 1966. The target item was a print Rob had taken of his own hand a week earlier, when we were reading some books on palmistry. Seth's impressions couldn't have been more concise. I went around the house with a smile on my face just thinking of it for days afterward.

I was doing the dishes when a drawback suddenly occurred to me. Rob was in the living room. I went in. Slowly. "I bet Dr. Instream would throw out the results of that hand-print test because we both worked on palmistry the week before," I said.

"He might," Rob admitted. "But the fact is, we've received plenty of letters that I could have used since then. We also did work in handwriting analysis; I could have used one of those samples. I could have used something older than you are—as I've done before. I could have used *anything*. No matter what we use, Seth still has to describe a particular item. And those impressions weren't general; they could only refer to that specific hand print."

I agreed with him. But after that, Rob often made up several test envelopes at once, shuffled them, and then chose one just before a session.

And what about the Instream tests? First of all, I kept waiting to hear what Dr. Instream thought about my two out-of-body episodes. *And he simply never mentioned them.* To me this was terribly disappointing. The results had checked out, whether or not they could be considered scientific. If these didn't convince him that something was going on, I didn't see what would!

The overall results of our own envelope tests encouraged us to hope that Seth was doing fairly well on the regular Instream data, too. We started these with zeal and energy.

For one year, twice a week, Seth gave his impressions as to Dr. Instream's activities. These included specific references as to names, initials, dates, and places. Some of this data could be easily checked out. Dr. Instream wanted Seth to concentrate on naming a particular object, though, upon which he would be concentrating in the distant town in which he lived. It became obvious that emotional elements were more important; that activities of an emotional nature "came through" more clearly than impressions of a more neutral object. Seth did give material pertaining to objects also, but he was more apt to give specific information on Dr. Instream's daily life.

One of our favorite topics of conversation that year was when will we hear from Dr. Instream? For months on end we would hear nothing. Perhaps, we thought, he wanted to give us no reports until the experiments were finished. If so, why didn't he just tell us? When finally the suspense was too much for me, I would write: were we getting any hits or weren't we? Dr. Instream always assured us of his continuing interest, told us to go on with the tests, and said that he had no evidence yet strong enough to "convince the hard-nosed psychologist." But that was all. He said nothing about the numerous names and dates, the visitors or letters mentioned in the sessions. Was the data all wrong? Partially right? We never found out. *He never told us.*

Knowing that Dr. Instream would be concentrating on each session put me under a strain, perhaps because of my own attitude. But now I felt that I really had to have a session each Monday and Wednesday evening, come hell or high water. And even when we were alone, which we usually were, I felt that the sessions were no longer private— that an invisible Dr. Instream was an audience. We seldom missed a session before the Instream tests. But now my idea of great defiance was to miss a session, to go out and get a beer and let the psychologist go stare at his old vase or ink spot or whatever he'd chosen for that night's test.

I didn't feel this way in the beginning, but I was really furious that he didn't tell us the results of the tests; all those hours seemed to be going down the drain. One night, really angry at not hearing from him, I did go with Rob to a nearby bar—only to rush home at the last minute so as not to miss the session!

With no idea of how we were doing, I couldn't have cared less, finally, *what* Dr. Instream was concentrating on. The tests just became time-consuming, cutting down on the amount of theoretical material we could receive. Once more I wrote the good doctor, suggesting that he not spare my feelings in case the data was just wrong. If so, we were wasting his time and our own. Again he wrote of his continuing interest and suggested we keep on. But he would not say we were doing well, fair, or poorly, and he gave no reports on the many specific details given.

He *was* obsessed with statistical proof for the existence of telepathy and clairvoyance, and hoped that we could produce it. At first it seemed tremendously exciting to me to be a part of such an endeavor. But as we continued to read everything we could get our hands on, excitement turned to bewilderment. As far as we could tell, the existence of telepathy and clairvoyance had been scientifically proven time and time again by Dr. J. B. Rhine at Duke University, and demonstrated by others such as Croisset, a psychic, working with Professor Wilem Tenhaeff at the University of Utrecht in the Netherlands. The work of Harold Sherman and other psychics certainly added circumstantial evidence at the very least. Was Instream throwing out all of these results and countless other evidence gained in parapsychology laboratories throughout the world?

Apparently he was. And our own results were presenting difficulties. Dr. Instream admitted that he didn't know how to evaluate them statistically. A hit had to have so many known odds against it before it could be credited, and it was nearly impossible to set up odds against any particular statement made by Seth.

Seth told Dr. Instream that he would be moving to a Midwestern university by the end of the year, for example. I have no idea if Dr. Instream had any indication of this ahead of time, but he did move when Seth said he would, and to a Midwestern university. We never learned how many correct impressions even of this sort checked out. Enough of them would have added up to something. So would a high enough percentage of hits on specific names and dates and so forth, statistics or no.

We started all the ESP tests just before our friends the Gallaghers took their 1965 vacation. In the meantime, they took another trip, and we decided to try the same kind of experiment with them as we had earlier.

This time Peg and Bill went to Nassau. Again, neither Rob nor I have been there. Again, we exchanged no cards, letters, or communications of any kind. But to my delight, Seth certainly knew where the Gallaghers were staying. In a series of impressions one night (October 17, 1966), he accurately described their hotel:

"A building with a long narrow section; a roof supported by posts. The roof is long and narrow also. With a floor of stone or cement, sand-colored. A veranda outside their door, and a large bucket filled with sand. There are rocks beneath the veranda, and beyond that, the ocean or bay. Right at the shore, down and ahead, is a scooped-out circular indentation where there is a swift current because of the rocks. And at this particular point, by this indentation, there is no beach, though there is a beach to the left and right, rather large ones."

Each point was correct. We went over the material with the Gallaghers on their return. But there was much more. Seth had correctly described a nightclub they'd visited, then went on to mention that there had been a "nuisance there." Bill and Peg wholeheartedly agreed. They'd been annoyed by a loud-mouthed English tourist. So, obviously, had others. The Englishman insisted upon whistling with the band. Seth also said that there were eighteen shrubs out in front of the nightclub, but Bill had to admit that though there were shrubs out front, he hadn't thought of counting them.

Seth seemed to pick up things that had particular emotional meaning for Peg and Bill. For instance, he included among other impressions, "a commemoration of a murder . . . a statue . . ." It developed that the Gallaghers had passed a statue, a memorial to Sir Harry Oakes who had been murdered in a sensational, well-publicized case in 1943. Peg was so curious about this that she even questioned a cab driver on his knowledge of the murder events.

Then, strangely, Seth gave a very specific description of a place Peg and Bill visited, but with one distortion, apparently of wording. "A fountain with steps leading up to it; a circular formation surrounded by flowers, with closely crowded, old, two-story structures to the left of the street and very close to it, in rows." Everything was correct, except that there was a water tower rather than a fountain.

All told, a total of forty correct impressions were given in the three sessions held while Peg and Bill were in Nassau; more, actualiy, since many impressions consisted of several points. But so much work is involved in such an experiment! Memory is fallible, so we always tried to get anyone involved to write up their reports at once for easier and more reliable checking.

In any case, I always think of that "testing year" as beginning with the Gallaghers' trip to Puerto Rico and ending with their Nassau trip. As far as we were concerned, Seth had proven himself. After a year's work we wrote to Dr. Instream, ending the tests and giving our reasons. After a few more envelope tests, we ended those, too.

Actually, I'm not sorry that we took so much time for the tests, but I'm glad we ended them when we did. I'm not temperamentally suited to putting myself under fire twice a week, which is what I was doing with the attitude I had at the time. Emotionally I disliked the tests; intellectually I thought them necessary. Seth didn't seem to mind them at all, but I forced myself to go along because I thought I should. The fact remains that in our sessions the best instances of ESP have occurred spontaneously or in response to someone's need, and not when we were trying to prove anything. I knew I was disappointed not to get some sort of "certificate of legitimacy" from Dr. Instream. On the other hand, we didn't ask for one; we were too burned up not to have reports on the results.

Now we could concentrate on the Seth Material. Freed from the test structure, the sessions were ready to go places. We were in for many surprises. If I'd had more faith in Seth's abilities and my own, I could have saved myself a lot of trouble. Actually, even while we were conducting the ESP tests, other things were happening and not only in sessions.

Very shortly after the sessions began, Rob started to see visions or images. Some were subjective, but others were objectified—three-dimensional, or nearly so. Some were of people, and Rob began to use them as models for his paintings. Now our living room is full of portraits of people we don't "know." Seth has said that some depict ourselves in past lives. One, used in this book, is a portrait of Seth in the form in which he chose to appear to Rob. (Since then, a student and a friend of ours have both seen Seth as he appears in this picture.)

Rob has a strong visual memory. Once he sees such an image, he retains it and can refer back to it at will. My visual memory is poor, in contrast, and so is my eyesight (I have no depth perception). Rob is a professional artist, an excellent draftsman and technician. Yet in sessions, Seth has given Rob excellent advice and information on the techniques and philosophy of art. This strikes us as really funny, since I paint as a hobby, with a stubborn lack of perspective. Rob used to try to teach me perspective, but the lessons just wouldn't take. I've never studied art, and my paintings are rather childish in execution, done with raw color. Yet Seth told Rob how to mix and use certain pigments, and Rob has added the information to his repertoire. Seth says that he has no artistic ability either, but questions artists who have entered his own field of reality.

In one session, Seth gave some pointers that Rob immediately put to use. The picture is one of our favorites, and belongs to Rob's "people series"—portraits of people we've never met. The inspiration for this particular painting came to Rob suddenly a few days after the session in question, and he used the techniques Seth had given in its execution.

Here are a few excerpts from that session: "In a portrait," Seth said, "do the same exercise as given earlier: [that is], imagine the individual as the center of all life, so that when the painting is completed, it automatically suggests the whole universe of which the individual is part. Nothing exists in isolation, and this is the secret that the old masters knew so well.

"In the smallest detail they managed to suggest the reality of the spiritual universe of which that detail was a part and through which the energy of the universe spoke. Use your talents—and they are considerable—to this end. You can do no less. . . .

"Now, oils suggest the earth. Let that medium stand for the physical appearance of permanency in any object, the physical continuity of any given human form in a painting. Let the transparent oil colors represent the constant renewal of energy that always escapes the form.

93

"One of the attractions of your portrait of me is that it automatically suggests an unseen audience to whom I appear to be speaking. Not a formal audience, but unseen listeners who represent humanity at large. The unseen is there. The figure manages to suggest the universe of men and the world that holds them, yet nowhere do these appear.

"Now, this information is from an artist who always used sienas for initial flesh tones, with a suggestion, very lightly, of violets. These were then very cleverly built up with a transparent ocher which he had, and a particular green, muted. The top complexion tone lay on this lightly, as if a wind could blow it away."

After the session Rob told me he was quite certain that I didn't consciously possess such knowledge—that my mind "didn't work that way." Rob had never tried this particular method of building up color tones in portrait work, and it is this technique he used in the painting idea that "came to him" a few days after this session. Later Seth added to this information. We are still accumulating material on art, art philosophy, and painting techniques.

Seth has dropped some hints as to the identity of the artist who is passing on this data to him. According to what he's said so far, the artist was a fourteenth-century Dane or Norwegian, and was known for his domestic scenes and still lifes. We have been told that his name will come in future sessions, along with other information on art.

Seth did say, however, that Rob's picture using the color-building technique is a portrait of the artist in question. (See illustrated section.) He also said that Rob would do other paintings of both the artist and his environment, including possibly the artist's studio.

In the past, Rob's portraits were representations of personalities involved with us personally through association or past life connections—as far as we know. Some of them still have to be identified. Lately, however, the range of the portraits has been extended. Rob did one of a young man recently, for example (see illustrated section). He had no idea who it was. Later one of my students, George, picked out the painting as a portrait of a personality called Bega, who communicates with him through automatic writing. Seth

94

corroborated this, and said that Bega is one of his own students in another level of reality.

Though the sessions continued as usual, we found ourselves having other experiences then, like Rob's visions, that also developed out of the Seth Material in one way or another. And as if to stress our new sense of freedom and further add to my confidence and training, Seth was to send me to California during a session, while he and Rob talked in the living room of our apartment in Elmira, New York. So much more fun than trying to tell the contents of sealed envelopes! This time complete strangers were involved in an experience that would really satisfy my seemingly endless search for proof after proof.

CHAPTER NINE:

A Psychologist and Seth Talk about Existence—Another Out-of-Body

―――●◦●―――

One day while we were still up to our necks in tests, I saw an Associated Press article that really surprised me. Dr. Eugene Barnard, a psychologist then at North Carolina State University, came out publicly with a statement favoring astral projection. He said that he had propected his consciousness out of his body, and that no hallucination was involved. The article also gave details concerning his academic research in the field of parapsychology.

I was really excited to think that a psychologist would do his own experimentation with projection, and I wrote him. We corresponded for a while, and then in November of 1966, Gene and his wife visited us. We got along beautifully. He never made me feel that I had to prove anything, which was pretty tricky of him actually, since he wanted to satisfy himself as to the authenticity of the Seth sessions.

We had a fascinating session one night, lasting several hours. Not until it was over did I realize what he'd been up to—now that's a good psychologist! Gene had questioned Seth in what I guess you could call "professional philosophical jargon," making frequent references to esoteric Eastern theories with which I was totally unfamiliar. Gene has his Ph.D. from the University of Leeds, England, in experimental psychology, and taught at Cambridge. He also had an excellent knowledge of Eastern philosophy and religion. Yet Seth not only took him on, but in some way I still don't understand, he used Gene's own terminology and jargon to beat him at his own game— and with humor and grace.

This session ran fourteen typewritten pages, and is so of one piece that it's difficult to give excerpts, without including a good bit of background information. Here are portions of the last half of the session. Earlier, Seth and Gene had been discussing reality, and Gene had commented that existence was "kind of a lovely colossal joke." Seth answered that "it is no joke. It is a means for the Whole to know Itself."

Now Seth said: "The 'joke' is highly relevant. If you realized thoroughly that your physical world was an illusion, you would not be experiencing sense data."

"Can't I experience an illusion that I create for myself?"

"You can experience the illusion, but when you experience the illusion as an illusion, you no longer *experience* it. You are running ahead of yourself."

"But there's nowhere to go," Gene said.

"You do not *know* it. You think it. You will not be where you are."

"Is there anywhere else to be?"

"No and yes," said Seth.

"Is there anywhere else to be that is not illusion?"

"I say this to you: Yes."

"How would I know the difference? Is there any way to distinguish between reality and illusion other than by a creation of my own mind?"

"You do not know it now. When that point is reached, you will be able, if you prefer, to experience any 'reality . . . illusion' at your will, but the self who experiences these 'reality . . . illusions' will know itself as reality. There is no place for it to go, because it is the only reality, and will create its own environment."

"But that is a discussion of the me here and now."

"In your terms," Seth said.

"In yours, too."

"In your terms," Seth repeated.

"In yours, too."

"Look at the last statement then, carefully."

"We have come full circle. I am one with what reality I create. There is nowhere to go," Gene said.

"You must still be able to experience any one of these illusions, knowing they are illusory, with full knowledge of their nature, and still know that the basic reality is yourself. There is no place to go because you are the place—and all places—in those terms. But the 'joke' is relevant. The most important thing I have said this evening is that the joke is relevant. You must be free enough to explore the nature and experience of each living thing within your own system, knowing that it is yourself, and then leave your system. These must be direct experiences."

"But I can't leave the system because I am in all systems simultaneously."

"I am speaking in your physical terms . . . but even in those terms, you are still dealing with other systems."

"I have no choice."

"I am using terms of continuity now simply for explanation. First there must be a period, and then it has passed, when you are completely immersed in a given system as if no other existed; value fulfillment as a rule being achieved in this manner. This does not mean that you are not dwelling in other systems simultaneously. The illusion must be probed to its depth."

"Of which it has none," Gene put in.

"You create the depth."

"Right, and in so doing the probing has been done. There is nothing to probe."

"The probing is necessary. Some games are necessary and always relevant."

"Isn't the object to play the game . . . not to create or probe?"

"You are yourself the game, in those terms."

"In all other terms also."

"You are creating your own limitations," said Seth.

"Is there really more than one viewpoint?"

"Yes. You are not granting the diversity that exists."

"I would be willing to grant a multiplicity of illusory forms of that same thing . . . namely, you and I. All one . . ."

"There can be no self-betrayal," said Seth.

"Right, nor any betrayal of others."

"But the idea of self-betrayal can lead to distortions."

"But these distortions are part of the game that Shiva plays."

"I would prefer to call it a loving endeavor."

"Of course," Gene said. "Think of the classical statue of Shiva standing on the crushed baby—a loving participation in the illusion of tragedy. Even in the illusion of self-delusion."

"You are trying to cut out many steps for yourself."

"But there aren't any steps, are there?"

"For you, now, there are steps."

"Aren't they illusory?"

"They are indeed," said Seth.

"If they are artificial barriers which I create in my own path, surely I can remove them."

"Theoretically it is so indeed. Practically it would behoove you to watch your footing."

"Yes. That was the comment to Siddhartha."

"These are tender children we lay to rest. We must mourn them though they be [words lost]. . . . We must feel for them though they be cow dung," Seth replied.

"We must love them for they are ourselves."

"You cannot do less," said Seth. "You can hardly do more."

"To do that is to have opened an eye and to see that there is but one short step to take."

"You are playing a game," Seth admonished.

"Of course. So are you. We say that Shiva is playing a game, and who is Shiva besides yourself?"

"You are indeed playing a game with yourself, but it is not relevant, and it may be irrelevant. But you had better play it reverently."

"With reverence for whom?"

"With reverence toward the self."

"Okay. We're not talking at cross purposes."

"There is a holy irreverence and a flighty irreverence. You are playing a game. They are both one. But you had better be certain that you know this thoroughly."

Dr. Barnard was kind enough to write a letter to the publishers of this present book, giving his opinions and mentioning that session (Number 303). (More than this, he let me use his real name, rather than hiding behind a pseudonym.) In his letter he said: In the session "I chose topics of conversation which were clearly of tolerable interest to Seth and considerable interest to me, and which by that time I had every reason to believe were largely foreign territory to Jane. Also . . . I chose to pursue these topics at a level of sophistication which I felt, at least, made it exceedingly improbable that Jane could fool me on; substituting her own knowledge and mental footwork for those of Seth, even if she were doing it unconsciously. . . .

"The best summary description I can give you of that evening is that it was for me a delightful conversation with a personality or intelligence or what have you, whose wit, intellect, and reservoir of knowledge far exceeded my own. . . . In any sense in which a psychologist of the Western scientific tradition would understand the phrase, I do not believe that Jane Roberts and Seth are the same person, or the same personality, or different facets of the same personality. . . ."

Besides the session, Rob and I and the Barnards had a great time discussing out-of-body experiences.

Shortly after their visit, my book, *How to Develop Your ESP Power,* finally appeared in the bookstores. I began to get some mail, though I was hardly deluged. One of these early letters was responsible for my next out-of-body trip during a Seth session.

On May 3, 1967, Peg and Bill Gallagher dropped in for our regular Monday night session, and as we sat around chatting, I told them about a letter I'd just received that amused me—and sort of outraged me at the same time.

"It was registered, and I had to sign for it," I said. "How about that? It's from two brothers out in California someplace, and they want to know what Seth can tell them about themselves."

"Are you going to answer it?" asked Peg.

"I'll drop them a short note, thanking them for their interest or something. Seth can do what he wants. I doubt he'll do anything."

But, as often happens when I try to second-guess Seth, I was really wrong. Our session, the 339th, started shortly afterward, and almost immediately I left my body, though I had little sensation of doing so. I just found myself hovering in midair, looking down on a particular neighborhood that was obviously someplace in Southern California. Back in the living room, Seth was describing what I was seeing, but I was only distantly aware of his voice. To me it sounded far less distinct than a very poor long-distance telephone call.

I had no idea how to tell Rob that I was out of my body, as Seth was carrying on as usual. My body, I knew, would be animated, as Seth talked. Once I laughed to myself and thought: "I'll have to send him a telegram." In the meantime I floated in the air, quite high, looking down on the location Seth was describing. I was able to move about, changing my position to get a better view. But I had no connection at all with the body that sat in the living room. Seth was saying:

"Now there is a small yard with lemons for the brothers; a pink stucco house, two bedrooms to the rear, not a new house. They used the Ouija board in the kitchen. They are near the right corner of the block, but not at the corner. They are not far from water. There is high grass for a while, and some wooden posts and wires."

In here, because of the specific material, Rob began to wonder if projection was involved. "Are you at the location now?" he asked.

"To some degree. There are sand dunes of a sort. There, I've changed my position. Now I am facing the house. The directions have changed somewhat due to my position. A garagelike structure to my right now, and behind it other structures leading to the water. Beyond, a dune area and a beach. The tide is in."

Now in here, I was changing *my* position in the air. As far as I can figure out, I was the one at the location, not Seth.

"What time of day is it?" Rob asked. (It was after 9 P.M. in Elmira.)

"Early evening. There are fairly thin wooden posts, not round, rectangular at the top, you see, perhaps hip-level." Seth gestured to Rob, to show the shape and size of the posts. At the same time, I floated above them, puzzled because I couldn't see what they were being used for; I was also mystified by their rectangular tops.

"Then a bay effect to the left. The land is like this, you see, not straight. The land here curves and juts out again." Here again Seth gestured broadly to indicate the shape of the seacoast. He also said that the family had a strong foreign connection, though the name was not particularly foreign, and made some other remarks about the family's history and members.

Rob sent a copy of the session to the two brothers. They sent back a tape in which they evaluated the information. Later they signed a statement which is in our files. Seth's information about their house was right in every particular, including the data on the area, and the shape of the seacoast there.

The brothers lived in Chula Vista, a place I'd never visited. They lived in a pink stucco house with two bedrooms to the rear. The corner was two houses to the right. The house itself was half a mile from San Diego Bay. Numerous sand dunes were nearby and wooden posts, exactly as described, were scattered along the dunes.

The family had come from Australia and hoped to return. Several other impressions, not mentioned here, were also right, others wrong: For example, Seth said that the mother was dead. Actually she was quite alive, though the family had cut her off emotionally and she did not always live at home.

Again, this experience suggested all kinds of questions concerning Seth's and my relationship in an out-of-body episode. Presumably he stays in my body, while I go out of it, but this is a simplification, I'm sure. We're still accumulating information on such questions, both through sessions and through work on our own.

As always, when things like this check out, I smile all over. I've never been one to accept other people's word about the nature of things, even though at times I have accepted more than I should have. I've always wanted to find out for myself. No one could have been more critical about his own experiences than I have—while still maintaining enough freedom to experiment. So after this episode, I began to relax. I'd been out of my body again, and again things had checked out. How did Seth help me do this? How could he record my perceptions when my consciousness was across the continent? I was more intellectually intrigued than I can say. One thing I knew: He was pretty tricky—sending me "out" without my prior conscious knowledge of what he was planning. I do much better that way, because I don't feel that I'm being tested, and I don't have time to fret about results. (*He's* a good psychologist, too!)

This experience and my new confidence obviously made other later developments possible. Other strangers wrote, some urgently wanting help of one kind or another. While Seth insists that help comes from within, he did offer excellent advice to a few, along with correct clairvoyant impressions of their environments—probably to let me know we had the right person more than anything else.

Our Monday and Wednesday sessions, where Seth develops the theoretical material, are still private, although a guest may drop in occasionally. Seth sometimes does hold a session for my ESP students on class night, and in class he deals with the practical application of the material.

Actually the only person who has attended our private sessions with any regularity is Phillip. Seth has given him information concerning his business dealings, correctly predicting the behavior of certain stocks among other things; and Phil is keeping record of Seth's percentage of "hits." The time ranges for some of the predictions cover several years, but Seth has been correct about a large number of items that Phil has been able to check. Seth doesn't make a habit of giving advice in sessions, though: he insists that people make their own decisions.

We really never know what is going to happen in a session, and one night Seth really surprised us. That night Phil turned up, unannounced as always. He told us he'd received a raise. With a comic shrug he left the amount up in the air. When the session started, Seth promptly named the amount to the dollar, smiling broadly. Then Phil asked Seth if he knew anything about a voice that he'd heard in a local bar.

"The voice was male, was it not?" Seth asked.

"Yes," Phil said.

"And you did not recognize it? Then I shall not tell you. I shall not indeed."

"Was it your voice? It happened so quickly, I didn't have time to think," Phil said, grinning. As Seth, I nodded humorously.

During our first break, Phil explained: A month earlier he'd been speaking to a young woman in a local bar, when he heard a clear, loud, male voice say, "No, no," very emphatically. It seemed to come from within Phil's head. Nothing like this had ever happened to him before, and he was so startled that he muttered a quick excuse to the woman and left the bar.

Seth admitted that he was the one who spoke to Phil. After our break he said, "The woman is grasping in a way that is disastrous to those with whom she comes in contact." He added that the woman "would have used you as a buffer between herself and another male, and as a bargaining point, exaggerating your slightest interest. An unpleasant situation would have resulted. Because you listened to me, the probable future was changed." Then he gave considerable background information, saying that the woman had a child and was involved with another man. "The male involved with her has something to do with mechanics." He also said that she was a Catholic, and that her problem concerned a legal paper.

After this, Seth proceeded to tell Phil where she lived, though he didn't give a specific address. "She lives in . . . the third or fourth house in the middle of a dead-end street, in the northeastern section of town, but west of the establishment in which you met her. . . ."

All of this was highly interesting to Phil, who had no idea where the woman lived, and knew nothing about her except her name and probable age. Since he was to be in town the next day, Phil went back to the bar and started asking questions. He found out the woman's address from the bartender and drove down the street to discover that Seth knew what he was talking about. She lived in the third house before the end of a dead-end street, in the northeastern section of town, but west of the bar. She was Catholic and had a child and a male friend who was a car salesman rather than a mechanic.

Phil hasn't gone back to that bar since!

105

Rob and I didn't know what to make of the affair. It certainly seemed to give some kind of evidence for Seth's independent nature, unless Phil hallucinated the voice and Seth took advantage of the fact and claimed it as his own. If so (and I doubt it), then Seth certainly had information about the woman and the affair that Phil didn't have.

Obviously, according to Seth, we can change the future. As he told Phil: "At no time are events predestined. With every moment you change, and every action changes every other action. I am able to look from a different perspective, but still see only probabilities. On that particular evening I saw a probability that was not attractive. You and I changed it."

In another episode, a friend claimed to have seen Seth, and under peculiar curcumstances. One night as I lay in bed I had a spontaneous out-of-body experience in which I seemed to be in a crowded room speaking urgently to Bill Macdonnel (our artist friend). I shook his shoulder none too gently and instantly snapped back to my body. I hadn't been in bed ten minutes yet and I got up immediately, wrote down what happened, and told Rob.

Exactly a week later Bill called us, sounding very nervous. He told me that something very strange had happened, and since he was still upset about it, he thought he'd discuss it with me. Instantly I remembered my own experience, and told Bill to wait while Rob got my notes, so I could check them as Bill talked. Bill told me that exactly a week before he had been awakened suddenly. Seth stood by his bed, fully three-dimensional, looking just like Rob's painting of him. He shook Bill's shoulder and disappeared. Bill told his mother at breakfast the next morning, and wrote a report out for us.

The incident upset his mother, who made some joking comment to the effect that she wished Seth and I would stay at home. Only I don't think she was joking. It was Bill's uneasiness that kept him from calling earlier, and I didn't want to call and prompt him.

First of all, I thought I had been in a crowded room in my out-of-body experience, but Bill was obviously in his room, alone. Another thing, he saw Seth smoking a cigarette; I smoke. Did Bill hallucinate Seth's three-dimensional image? If so, he did this at the same time that I felt I was with him. And he felt Seth shake his shoulder while in my experience I shook it.

Several people have told me that Seth communicated with them through automatic writing, but Seth denies any such contacts, saying that his communications will be limited to his work with me, in order that the integrity of the Seth Material be preserved. According to his statements, however, he has "looked in on" friends occasionally.

One day I met Mrs. Brian, a former student who dropped out of class due to illness, who told me she had read a newspaper article about this present book that appeared in the local paper. It contained a few excerpts of the Seth Material, and a reproduction of Rob's painting of Seth. Mrs. Brian had a terrific headache while reading the article; suddenly she thought she felt Seth's presence. An inner voice, presumably Seth's, told her that she had been feeling sorry for herself, that she must stop brooding over her health at once, get up, and go out for a walk. If so, she would improve at once.

Considerably startled, she did as she was told. In that instant the headache vanished. By the next day she felt better than she had in six months. She began to take walks again and felt rejuvenated. When she told me the story, I just nodded and smiled. Quite frankly, I didn't know what else to do.

We asked Seth about the incident. In this case, he said, Mrs. Brian had used him as a symbol of her inner self, or supraconsciousness, to deliver help and healing influences as well as advice. The experience helped the woman to use her own abilities, and the idea of Seth enabled her to activate her own healing forces. Seth told me not to concern myself. Apparently he is delighted to inspire others in such a fashion and serve as a focal point for their own creative energies.

He absolutely refuses to let people use him as a crutch—this goes for me, too—and maintains that the Seth Material itself provides a means by which people can understand themselves better, reevaluate their reality, and change it. Despite the sessions held now and then to help particular persons, and despite their incidents of extrasensory perception, the sessions remain focused primarily on the material. It is here we feel that the real significance of the sessions rests.

We are far more interested in the Seth Material than in demonstrations of ESP, and we always were. We think it offers excellent explanations as to how ESP or any perception works, and to us this is far more important. We also accept Seth's statements as meaningful, significant explanations of the nature of reality and mankind's position within it. His theories as to the multidimensional personality are not only intellectually provocative but emotionally challenging. They offer each individual the opportunity to enlarge his own sense of identity and purpose.

Demonstrations of ESP in sessions have always had a purpose: either to help increase my confidence or train my abilities, to illustrate a point made in the material, or to offer information to someone in need. It's easy for me to forget my earlier feelings that Seth should prove himself; easy for me to forget that I, too, insisted on my "wonders," and on several occasions even denied the evidence of my own senses out of the mistaken belief that I was somehow being more scientific that way. I will say that I always highly respected the Seth Material, and recognized the scope and daring of some of the concepts it contains.

Since we had read little psychic literature when the sessions began, everything was new to us. It wasn't until much later that we discovered that some of Seth's concepts had appeared in esoteric manuscripts dating back thousands of years. As our own knowledge increased, however, we found that in some critical areas Seth's ideas departed from those generally accepted in much spiritualist and metaphysical literature.

For one thing, Seth does not agree on the existence of one historical Christ, though he grants the legitimacy of the Christ spirit—as you will see later in this book. While he sees reincarnation as a fact, he places it in an entirely different time context, and reconciles the theory with the idea of "simultaneous" time. Perhaps more important, he describes reincarnation as only a small part of our entire development. Other equally important existences occur in other nonphysical dimensions.

All of this is interwound with the idea that personality is composed of action. Seth's description of the three creative dilemmas upon which identity rests is thought-provoking and original. His ideas on God are a natural and fascinating extension of these theories.

To our knowledge at least, the inverted time theory and the system of probabilities are entirely original with the Seth Material. Seth's idea of the nature of pain is also quite divorced, I believe, from current metaphysical thought. He views suffering as simply an attribute of consciousness and an indication of vitality, considered alarming only by those areas of identity that still fear death as an end.

But from now on I'll let Seth speak for himself. I've chosen excerpts dealing with the subjects at hand. In some cases, Seth gave demonstrations to make his point. In the chapter on health, for example, I've included excerpts from some readings for specific people. I've followed the same procedure with the data on reincarnation. To explain his theories on the nature of physical reality, I'm using excerpts from a session in which he really demonstrated that he knew what he was talking about—if an apparition in the living room can pass as a legitimate approximation.

I'd like to close this chapter with excerpts from Session 329 recorded in March 1967 for a teacher-friend's high-school group. Though Seth is speaking to teen-agers here, the message is meaningful to each of us.

"You create your reality according to your beliefs and expectations, therefore it behooves you to examine them carefully. If you do not like your world, then examine your own expectations. Every thought in one way or another is constructed by you in physical terms.

"Your world is formed in faithful replica of your own thoughts. . . . Certain telepathic conditions exist that we call root assumptions, of which each individual is subconsciously aware. Using these, you form a physical environment cohesive enough so that there is general agreement as to objects and their placement and dimension. It is all hallucinatory in one respect, and yet it is your reality, and you must manipulate within it. The world in which your parents live existed first in thought. It existed once in the stuff of dreams, and they spawned their universe from this, and from this they made their world.

"If you sell yourselves short, you will say, 'I am a physical organism and I live within the boundaries cast upon me by space and time. I am at the mercy of my environment.' If you do not sell yourselves short, you will say, 'I am an individual. I form my physical environment. I change and make my world. I am free of space and time. I am a part of all that is. *There is no place within me that creativity does not exist.*' "

CHAPTER TEN:

The Nature of Physical Reality

What do you think this physical universe is? You may not have thought of the question consciously, but each of us has an opinion and we guide our daily actions by it whether we realize it or not. By physical universe I mean everything with which we come into contact in any way at all—stars, chairs, events, rocks, flowers—our entire physical experience. What you really believe about these things causes much of your behavior. You'll feel safe or panic-stricken, happy or sorrowful, secure or insecure, according to your private view of reality.

Some people think that we are stuck in physical reality like flies in flypaper or victims in quicksand, so that each motion we make only worsens our predicament and hastens our extinction. Others see the universe as a sort of theater into which we are thrust at birth and from which we depart forever at death. In the backs of their minds people with either attitude will see a built-in threat in each new day; even joy will be suspect because it, too, must end in the body's eventual death.

I used to feel this way. When I fell in love with Rob, my joy served to double the underlying sense of tragedy I felt, as if death mocked me all the more by making life twice as precious. I saw each day bringing me closer to a total extinction that I could hardly imagine, but which I resented with growing vehemence.

Many people, of course, feel that death is a new beginning, but most of us still think that we are formed and bound by our physical bodies and environment. Many who believe in an afterlife think that current events are thrust upon us indiscriminately. Still others believe that good or bad events are sent to us as rewards or punishments. But most people take it for granted that we are pretty much at the mercy of events over which we have little control.

I'm dealing with this subject, the nature of physical matter, first, because it is basic to any understanding of Seth's theories. Seth says that we form the physical universe as unselfconsciously as we breathe. We aren't to think of it as a prison from which we will one day escape, or as an execution chamber from which all escape is impossible. Instead *we form matter* in order to operate in three-dimensional reality, develop our abilities and help others. Physical matter is like plastic that we use and mold to our own desire, not like concrete into which our consciousness has been poured. Without realizing it we project our ideas outward to form physical reality. Our bodies are the materialization of what we think we are. We are all creators, then, and this world is our joint creation.

These are Seth's ideas as simply as I can put them. We are not at the mercy of events. We form the events to which we then react. Look at it personally: You are not at the mercy of your childhood environment or background, unless you believe you are. You merely cooperated with your parents in forming it.

This simple statement alone liberated Rob and me from all kinds of preconceptions that had inhibited our daily lives.

Seth says that not only do we form our own reality now, but we will continue to do so after physical death, so it is of the utmost importance that we understand the connection between thought and reality.

Seth explains exactly how we translate thoughts into physical

112

reality. To our knowledge, this explanation is original with the Seth Material. To say the least, the supposition that we actually create matter gives rise to all kinds of questions, and Rob and I have considered many of them at one time or another. Was Seth saying that we created tables and chairs as well as events? And when we were ill, were we creating our own disease? If we create reality to begin with, then can we change it for the better?

Seth answers these questions and many we hadn't even considered. I thought that the whole subject was fascinating when he began, but I didn't expect a demonstration in the middle of our living room, which is exactly what happened in the 68th session (July 6, 1964). Seth was describing the intimate connection between expectation and perception—what we see and observe—to Bill Macdonnel, when the incident took place. It was a session none of us would ever forget. Before I give you the high points of that episode, however, here are a few excerpts from immediately previous material:

"Because I say that you create physical matter by use of the inner vitality of the universe, in the same way that you form a pattern with your breath on a glass pane, I do not mean that you are the creators of the universe. I am saying that you are the creators of the physical world as you know it.

"Chemicals themselves will not give rise to consciousness or life. Your scientists will have to face the fact that consciousness comes first and evolves its own form. . . . All the cells in the body have a separate consciousness. There is a conscious cooperation between the cells in all the organs, and between the organs themselves. . . .

"Molecules and atoms and even smaller particles have a condensed consciousness. They form into cells and form an individual cellular consciousness. This combination results in a consciousness that is capable of much more experience and fulfillment than would be possible for the isolated atom or molecule alone. This goes on ad infinitum . . . to form the physical body mechanism. Even the lowest particle retains its individuality and its abilities [through this cooperation] are multiplied a millionfold.

"Matter is a medium for the manipulation and transformation of psychic energy into aspects that can then be used as building blocks.

113

. . . Matter is only cohesive enough to give the appearance or relative permanence to the senses that perceive it.

"Matter is continually created, but no particular object is in itself continuous. There is not, for example, one physical object that deteriorates with age. There are instead continuous creations of psychic energy into a physical pattern that appears to hold a more or less rigid appearance.

"No particular object 'exists long enough' as an indivisible, rigid, or identical thing to change with age. The energy behind it weakens. The physical pattern therefore blurs. After a certain point each re-creation becomes less perfect from your standpoint. After many such re-creations that have been unperceived by you, then you notice a difference and assume that a change . . . has occurred. The actual material that seems to make up the object has completely disappeared many times, and the pattern has been completely filled again with new matter. . . .

"Physical matter makes consciousness effective within three-dimensional reality. As individualized energy approaches your particular field, it expresses itself to the best of its ability within it. As energy approaches, it creates matter, first of all in an almost plastic fashion. But the creation is continuous like a beam or endless series of beams, at first weak as they are far off, then stronger, then weak again as they pass away.

"Matter of itself, however, is no more continuous, no more given to growth or age than is, say, the color yellow."

Session 68 was held on a very warm night. All the windows were open. We were drinking iced coffee, and as the session started, my glass sat on the wooden table. At that time I still paced the room as I spoke for Seth, my eyes open with the pupils dark and dilated. As usual, Seth addressed us by our entity names, referring to me as Ruburt, and Rob as Joseph. Bill Macdonnel he called Mark. (As I mentioned before, these names refer to the whole personalities of which our present selves are only a part.)

Shortly after the session began, I picked up the abandoned glass and held it out to show to Rob and Bill. At the same time Seth's voice began to grow deeper and stronger, with the masculine tones starting

114

to creep in. Then Seth began to use the glass as a point around which to build his discussion.

"None of you sees the glass that the others see. . . . Each of the three of you creates your own glass, in your own personal perspective. Therefore you have three different physical glasses here, but each one exists in an entirely different space continuum."

Here Seth's voice really boomed out. Bill was sitting in the rocker in the middle of the room. He moved the chair closer to see better. Rob was taking verbatim notes as usual, and looking up to watch whenever possible.

"Now, Mark, you cannot see Joseph's glass, nor can he see yours," Seth said. "This can be proven mathematically, and scientists are already working with the problem, though they do not understand the principles behind it. Now there is an infinitesimal point where Mark's perspective and Ruburt's overlap. Again, theoretically, if you could perceive that point, you could actually each see the other two physical glasses.

"Physical objects cannot exist unless they exist in a definite perspective and space continuum. But each individual creates his own space continuum . . . I want to tie this in with the differences you seem to see in one particular object. Each individual actually creates an entirely different object, which his own physical senses then perceive. Since we have here this evening such an elegant and welcome guest," Seth smiled, "Let us then perceive him in terms of a slight discussion of matter, in which he will be our guinea pig."

At the time, no one thought anything in particular about Seth's last sentence. For one thing, Rob was so busy taking notes that he didn't really pay much attention to what was being said, beyond making sure he took Seth's words down accurately. As far as I remember, I wasn't even aware of speaking them.

Here I'm going to quote the additional notes, which Rob wrote immediately after the session:

Jane's delivery was unbroken as she paced about the room at a rather fast rate. Her voice was strong and deep, much deeper than usual, yet she spoke without apparent effort.

From my writing table at the right of the entrance to our

bathroom, I could easily look at Bill as he sat in our Kennedy rocker, facing the bathroom entrance itself. . . . As Jane continued her delivery, I noticed that Bill was staring quite consistently into the open bath doorway, yet I didn't pay any particular attention to this. I just took it for granted that Seth's remark about using Bill as a guinea pig meant that he was to be a topic of conversation.

In the meantime the session continued.

"You, Joseph, perceive Mark sitting in the chair," Seth continued. "He sits in his own chair which he has constructed in his own space continuum and personal perspective.

"You and Ruburt perceive Mark, and yet neither of you sees *Mark's* Mark. As he sits in his chair, he is constantly creating his own physical image, using his own psychic energy, and using particular atoms and molecules for the construction of his body. So far we have here, then, one Mark, constructed by himself, and before the evening is out you will be amazed at how many Marks we end up with.

"I suggest your break. And mark my words, Mark: You are more than you know. Incidentally, I would like particular attention paid to this session, as the material will be of great value."

As soon as break arrived, Bill announced that he had seen an image in the bathroom doorway. This is what he had been staring at the whole time. He asked for a sheet of paper and immediately set to work on a sketch of what he had seen. He is an artist and schoolteacher.

For one who felt poorly at the start of the session, Jane now said she felt fine. Seth had "knocked her out quickly," she said. Our cat, Willie, now became active. He began to stalk through the apartment, crying out. He behaved in quite a scary fashion, looking all about him, though there were no bugs about, or unusual sounds to upset him.

As soon as Bill told us he had seen an image, Jane and I both looked into the doorway, of course. But we could see nothing; for that matter, Bill said, the image had vanished during break. Now Jane began dictating again in the same strong and very deep voice. Bill continued working on his sketch, saying that he was not satisfied with it and would try another.

116

The session resumed.

"I will have something to say about the apparition shortly. First of all I would like you to notice that Ruburt's voice is somewhat lower, and then with your permission, I will continue.

"While Mark creates his own physical image, you do not see it. At this time, there are three entirely different Marks in this room."

Here Jane, as Seth, pointed at Bill as he sat in the rocker, working on his second sketch. Then she pointed at me. In the meantime Bill kept staring into the open doorway. As before, I could see nothing from my position at the table. The open door completely blocked my vision. I did not want to risk moving around, since I had to continue taking notes to make certain that our record was complete.

"There is the Mark which Mark has created, an actual physical construction. There is another, created by you, Joseph. There are two more physical Marks, one created by Ruburt, and one by your cat. If another person entered the room, there would be still another physical Mark.

"In this room, then, there are four physical Ruburts, four physical Josephs, and four physical cats. There are indeed four rooms."

From my studio at the back of the apartment came Willie's cry. He was still stalking about.

"Your friend Mark, to digress, is an excellent witness in one way because he is sensitive to constructions that appear within the physical realm from other planes. His span of attention is short. I did indeed stand momentarily in the doorway, though if I do say so . . ."

Here Jane paused beside Bill and picked up the first pen drawing he had made of his sighting of the apparition.

". . . I am a much more cheerful-looking fellow than here portrayed. You missed a certain cast along the cheekbones. And if you watch the image closer now, I may be able to make it clearer."

Jane handed the sketch back to Bill, who continued to stare into the doorway.

"This is the first time that I have attempted to approach in this manner during a session. I am pleased that I have been perceived, and I have been watching you from my own vantage point. The image in the doorway is indeed my own, though there is bound to be a distortion in Mark's perception of me. It is through the Inner Senses that he perceives me, and this data he then attempts to transform into information that can be physically perceived."

Now Jane stood in back of Bill, looking over his shoulder as he sketched.

"There is a smugness about the lips, very good, that I am rather pleased with. The construction is being created by myself. Just to appear within your plane, any construction, whether perceived by you or not, must be composed of atoms or molecules.

"The motion and speed varies from regular constructions. I am in this particular instance speaking through Ruburt while I have also stood by in the construction and watched him speak. At a later date I may be able to speak from my own construction."

Jane took the second sketch from Bill's hand and paced about the room, talking as she examined it. I caught a glimpse of the drawing as she waved it briefly in my direction. All the while Bill continued to stare into the doorway.

"It is true that in some ways I am no beauty in your terms, yet you must attest that I am not altogether ugly. I will let you take your break. And I wish to thank Mark. When I said that he would join me in a demonstration, I meant that he would join me in a demonstration."

Seth-Jane ended the monologue with a laugh at Bill. Now I asked Bill exactly what he had seen. He said that the dark open bathroom doorway turned a foggy white. He then saw the form of Seth's apparition stand out against this lighter background. The form was mainly a silhouette, Bill said, without strong detail, and yet during the first monologue he got a good look at the face. The effect was rather like that of a photographic negative. Bill added that the face of the apparition was about six feet above floor level. A copy of his sketch is included in the notes [see illustrated section].

Rob's hands were tired from taking notes; we took a break. I was somewhat bewildered. Bill swore up and down that he had seen the apparition for nearly an hour. It was not as solid as an ordinary body, but it was far from transparent. Seth had made numerous comments about it. Yet I had seen nothing. Rob hadn't been able to leave his

118

chair, so he had seen nothing. The lights had all been lit, but I just couldn't accept the idea of an apparition.

"Bill, you didn't see a thing, I bet." I said. "You just want us to agree that we saw something, and then you'll break up laughing and tell us you made it up—"

"That's a great thing to say," Bill said angrily. I was sorry as soon as I'd made the remark.

"Your imagination?" I asked weakly.

"I've got as good an imagination as anybody, but I don't normally go around seeing stuff like this—"

"Hon, why don't you just take Bill's word for it?" Rob said.

"Oh, all right." Suddenly I felt silly. I sort of danced around to the doorway, laughed, and said, "Okay, Bill, now exactly where did you see your man in the doorway?" I clowned about, moving around in the open doorway. "Here? Or was it here?"

Suddenly I saw Bill's and Rob's expressions change. They'd been standing in the middle of the room, laughing at me. Now Rob whitened. Bill's mouth dropped down. "What's wrong?" I said.

"Just don't move," Rob said very quietly.

I had a tingling sensation, but I saw nothing. I knew something odd was going on from Rob's and Bill's reactions, so I just stood still as I was told. And I stopped laughing.

Again I'll quote Rob's notes:

Bill and I noticed at the same time that Jane's animated features were changing. As she spoke to us, her jaw became more square in outline against her long black hair. Her nose enlarged. Her mouth acquired heavier, thicker, and wider lips as they moved with her speech, and her neck thickened. Neither Bill or I noted any change in her eyes or forehead.

At our request, Jane remained standing where she was. There was no doubt about what we saw. The effect lasted for perhaps a minute or two. The room was well lighted. The change in Jane's features seemed to take place on a plane an inch or so in front of Jane's actual physical features. The new set of features might have been suspended on a clear screen of some kind. As I watched them

I saw or sensed behind them—or through them—Jane's real features as I knew them.

After this Rob asked me to move a few inches forward. I did, and the effect diminished and then disappeared.

We resumed the session, with all kinds of questions in our minds. Bill told us that he still sensed the first apparition, sometimes quite strongly. He had made two sketches, and was still making corrections. Since the session began at nine and lasted until midnight, I won't attempt to include it all. The deep masculine voice was to last for the entire session, becoming more and more Seth-like as the evening continued.

When the session resumed, as Seth I picked up Bill's second sketch and said, "This picture represents an outward transformation as Mark attempted to construct an accurate replica of material that he sensed with the Inner Senses, and as such it is a reconstruction of what I am.

"It represents the appearance that these abilities of mine take on when closely connected with the physical plane. This does not necessarily mean that in all planes I have the same image. It is the first such representation of me, and I am quite fond of it.

"I would not be surprised if you wondered about the part that suggestion might play in such a demonstration. . . . Generally speaking, however, no physical object can be constructed, and no action can occur, without what you are pleased to call suggestion. No action and no material object can be perceived without inner consent and willingness. Behind every action and every construction there is indeed suggestion.

"Suggestion is no more and no less than an inner willingness and consent to allow a particular action to occur; and this consent is the trigger which sets off the subconscious mechanisms that allow you to construct inner data into physical reality.

"There is no more truth and no more falsehood in saying that my appearance in the doorway was caused by suggestion than to say that this room and everything in it is caused by suggestion. . . . You will understand that it is erroneous to think in terms of one physical universe. You now exist in four different ones at this moment. . . ."

Seth explained that the apparition's appearance was distorted by

Bill's own ideas, though. The high forehead represented Bill's interpretation of great intelligence, for example. Bill interpreted the available data in his own way: this was the Seth that Bill saw, regardless of Seth's own appearance.

Seth then continued, in a rather amusing fashion, giving "advance information" to Bill concerning a vacation trip he was going to take the following week. He described people and events that checked out perfectly on Bill's return.

At this time Rob and I were thinking of buying the house mentioned earlier. That very day we had gone to look it over again, and were surprised to find the back door wide open. Now Seth told us that we had opened the door ourselves, using psychic energy to do so, and that this was just one instance of mind influencing matter.

I didn't know what to think. When he was finished with the discussion, Seth began joking with Rob and Bill and showed such high spirits and vitality that Rob had trouble taking notes—he was laughing so hard.

The session simply astonished me. We had so many questions to ask, we didn't know where to begin. Exactly *how* do we form events from mental energy? How do we form objects? How do we agree on what we see?

Here are some later excerpts explaining how we project our ideas into events and objects. I'd better mention at this point that Seth says that telepathy operates constantly, providing inner communications to back up all sense data.

From Session 302, November 21, 1966:
"The objective world is the end result of inner action. You can indeed manipulate the objective world from within, for this is the means and definition of true manipulation. . . .

"Thoughts and images are formed into physical reality and become physical fact. They are propelled chemically. A thought *is* energy. It begins to produce itself physically at the moment of its conception.

"Mental enzymes are connected with the pineal gland. As you know them, body chemicals are physical, but they are the propellants of this thought-energy, containing all the codified data necessary for translating any thought or image into physical actuality. They cause the body to reproduce the inner image. They are sparks, so to speak, initiating the transformation.

"Chemicals are released through the skin and pore systems, in an invisible but definite pseudophysical formation. The intensity of a thought or image largely determines the immediacy of its physical materialization. There is no object about you that you have not created. There is nothing about your own physical image that you have not made.

"The initial thought or image exists within the mental enclosure [as explained in earlier sessions]. It is not yet physical. Then it is sparked into physical materialization by the mental enzymes.

"This is the general procedure. All such images or thoughts are not completely materialized in your terms, however. The intensity may be too weak. The chemical reaction sparks certain electrical charges, some within the layers of the skin. There are radiations then through the skin to the exterior world, containing highly codified instructions and information.

"The physical environment is as much a part of you, then, as your body. Your control over it is quite effective, for you create it as you create your fingertip. . . . Objects are composed of the same pseudo-material that radiates outward from your own physical image, only the higher intensity mass is different. When it is built up enough, you recognize it as an object. At low intensity mass it is not apparent to you.

"Every nerve and fiber within the body has an inner purpose that is not seen, and that serves to connect the inner self with physical reality, that allows the inner self to create physical reality. In one respect, the body and physical objects go flying out in all directions from the inner core of the whole self."

This material was given while we were still having the Instream tests. Later, when we had dispensed with these, Seth had more time to answer our questions. Rob wanted to know what other parts of the body were responsible for this creation of material—if any. Here is part of the answer we received:

"Nerve impulses travel outward from the body, invisibly along

122

these nerve pathways in much the same manner that they travel within the body. The pathways are carriers of telepathic thoughts, impulses, and desires that travel outward from any given self, altering seemingly objective events."

This next is quite important, I think:

"In a very real manner, events or objects are actually focal points where highly charged psychic impulses are transformed into something that can be physically perceived: a breakthrough into matter. When such highly charged impulses intersect or coincide, matter is formed. The reality behind such an explosion into matter is independent of the matter itself. An identical or nearly identical pattern may reemerge 'at any time' again and again, if the proper coordinates exist for activation."

Throughout the centuries many people have recognized that mind and matter were related, but the Seth Material specifically gives the ways and means by which mind is translated into the reality that we know. Exactly what force is beneath the smallest units of matter, for example? How does the breakthrough into matter occur? In order to do justice to these questions, I deal with them separately in the Appendix.

And what is the point of all this? Seth says:

"In your system of reality you are learning what mental energy is, and how to use it. You do this by constantly transforming your thoughts and emotions into physical form. You are supposed to get a clear picture of your inner development by perceiving the exterior environment. What seems to be a perception, an objective concrete event independent from you, is instead the materialization of your own inner emotions, energy, and mental environment."

But as you will see, we form our physical reality not only now and after death, but through at least several lifetimes, as we learn to translate energy and idea into experience. We not only form our environment now, but ahead of time we choose our parents and circumstances. Perhaps after reading the next two chapters you'll see why I finally accepted the idea of reincarnation after having been "dead set" against it.

CHAPTER
ELEVEN:

Reincarnation

———◆◆◆———

Have you lived before, and will you live again? According to Seth all of us have been reincarnated, and when we are finished living our series of earthly lives, we will continue to exist in other systems of reality. In each life we experience conditions that we have chosen beforehand, circumstances and challenges tailored to fit our own needs and develop our own abilities.

Think about it: Some of us are born brilliant and some mad, some with bodies swift and elegant, others missing vital organs or whole limbs. Some of us are born so blessed with riches that we live in a world hardly imaginable to the majority of men, and others grow old and die in dark pockets of poverty, equally incomprehensible. Why? Only reincarnation weaves these seemingly disparate conditions into a framework that makes sense. According to Seth these situations are not thrust upon us, but chosen.

Why would anyone choose a life of illness or poverty? And what about children who die young, or servicemen killed in war? All of these questions came into our minds when Seth began speaking about reincarnation. As I mentioned earlier, when the sessions started I didn't believe that we survived death once, much less many times. If we lived before, I thought, and if we can't remember, then what good does it do? "Besides," I said to Rob, "Seth says that we live in the 'Spacious Present,' and that there really isn't any past, present, and future. So how can we live one life 'before' another?"

Some of the answers cropped up in readings given for others, where Seth was dealing with specific cases. I do not give readings or sessions for the public (nor do I charge fees or accept contributions), so the reincarnational readings were those we had for students, friends, or for those who had asked for assistance in a particularly tragic problem. For that matter, Seth doesn't give such readings unless they have bearing on the matter at hand.

Why do some children die young—particularly gifted children with devoted parents? I don't believe that there can be any single answer or blanket explanation, but we have had two readings involving such children, and I can give you the explanations offered in these specific instances.

The first episode involved a couple I will call Jim and Ann Linden. Ann, a complete stranger, called me on the phone one morning. Since she dialed me directly, there was no indication that this was a long-distance call, and I thought she was calling from town, particularly since she mentioned having relatives in Elmira. She told me that her son, Peter, had died a few months ago at the age of three. She and her husband were distraught, she said, and a friend of theirs, Ray Van Over, a parapsychologist in New York, had suggested she call me.

"I've only met Ray once," I said. "He must have told you that I don't give readings but concentrate on our private work and the Seth sessions."

"Yes, he did," Ann said. "But he thought that you might make an exception. He said you did sometimes, in cases like these." She paused.

I waited a long moment, considering. "Well, this is a regular session night. If you want to come—"

126

"We'll be there," she said quickly. "My husband is in New York for the day, but he'll be back by late afternoon."

"Well, maybe he'll be too tired."

She insisted that a shower and quick supper would fix him up like new. We agreed that she and Jim would be at our apartment around eight.

I told Rob, and while he said that it was up to me, he wasn't too happy. "Remember what happened last time you tried to contact someone's deceased relative?" he said. "Anyway, let Seth handle it."

I nodded, remembering only too well the incident to which Rob referred. It had been in the back of my mind all the time I talked to Ann Linden over the phone.

"You wouldn't want anything like that to happen again, would you?" Rob asked.

"Uh huh," I said, and the details of that last episode rushed into consciousness once more. It had been a bright sunny Saturday afternoon several months earlier. I was in jeans, housecleaning, when a student called. She had a particularly knotty problem and she wanted me to try to contact her deceased mother-in-law. The student had been to only a few classes, and her mother-in-law lived and died in Florida. I didn't know her family at all.

I told her to come over, and Rob came out from his studio to take notes. During the proceedings I felt that *I* was the deceased woman, reliving an argument she once had with her husband. As the woman, I banged my fist up and down so hard on our table that Rob was afraid I'd break my hand. The argument was a violent one. The other personality took over rather completely, and Rob was actually concerned for my physical safety. I was able to "pull out" without any strained muscles or bruised bones—she was obviously used to a much larger and stronger body than mine—but since then Rob and I have been cautious.

I started to smile, though, thinking of it: According to Rob the can of Dutch Cleanser had really jumped when my fist came down on the table the first time, and the cleaning supplies next to my elbow had gone flying. It had hardly been an occult setting at that, with the sun shining full through the bay windows. My student was convinced that her mother-in-law had expressed herself through me, because I used her gestures and her language—including some pet phrases that were pretty purple.

Rob was watching my face. "You didn't think it was so funny then, though, did you?"

I had to admit that I hadn't. Yet most of the names and dates I had given that day had checked out, and one point in particular—unknown to my student—was later corroborated by a relative.

"Seth just wasn't around," I said. "If he had been, he probably would have given me the information, and I wouldn't have had to go through all that."

"Or you just wanted to try it on your own," Rob said.

I grinned, a bit guiltily. I'd wondered about that episode. Had I decided to try my own wings to see what evidence for survival I could get on my own?

If it was subconscious role-taking on my part, then it was a darned good job, and if telepathy was involved, then it was a darned good job too, because my student had to check some of the facts with others. But I didn't like it, and I didn't want anything like it to happen again. I'm pretty choosy as to whom I let in my house, and living or dead, people like that weren't going to find a welcome mat here.

"Still, I don't want to go overboard in my reactions," I said. "The Lindens only want to know about their little boy. Besides, I'll let Seth handle it. It's a session night, after all."

I knew Rob was right, though: Some self-protection is necessary on my part. Besides the mother-in-law episode, there had been a few other upsetting ones involving emotional situations I'd "picked up" from living people. In any case, when I can get such excellent material from Seth, it seems that my primary responsibility lies in that direction. All of these feelings were in the back of my mind that night, when Jim and Ann came.

And another surprise was in store. About 6 P.M. Ann called saying that she was in Binghamton, N.Y., a city more than an hour's drive away. She had had no idea that Elmira was so far from Brooklyn!

"*Brooklyn?*" I nearly dropped the phone. "I thought you meant that your husband was in New York for the day, but that you lived here—"

"Oh no," Ann said, "but Jim got home early in the afternoon, and we thought it only took a few hours to get to Elmira."

"Oh, wow," I said, and Rob put down the evening paper. "You mean you're driving here for just one session? New York is full of excellent mediums."

"But you were highly recommended. We'll be late, which is why I called. I hate to ask you, but could you wait until we get there?"

I said "Yes" in a sort of daze, and hung up. Rob was afraid that I'd feel under pressure, knowing that they were driving such a long way and back the same night for a session. I'd explained to Ann that I could give her no guarantee of any kind as to what would happen. Purposely I put the matter out of my mind and watched television during the early evening. Then to top it off, at about eight Phil dropped in, explaining that he was in town for the night and would like to attend a session!

Jim and Ann arrived about 10 P.M. Rob and I liked them at once. They were in their late twenties, intelligent, and, like us, informal. Over wine they told us about their son. "He was exceptionally bright," Jim said. "He was fantastic, and I'm not just saying that because he was our child. From the start he was way above average, quick in his reactions, so much so that we were almost frightened in a way. And then, overnight, he died of aplastic anemia. No one even knows what causes it."

What can you say in a situation like that? I wanted to help. I felt their terrific need, but I also realized that it was well-nigh impossible to *prove* life after death. Suppose I contacted the boy, or thought I had? How would this help? Instead of making them face the facts of his separation, couldn't such an incident simply make things worse? And my own doubts rose: if subconscious playacting were involved . . .

Rob must have read my thoughts. "Relax, hon," he said. I told the Lindens my attitude, and Ann smiled. "Ray said you were one of the most objective mediums he knew."

129

"Too objective, I'm afraid. Sometimes it holds me back from using my abilities fully."

That's the last thing I remember saying as myself. The next moment Seth's deep booming voice came rushing through me: "The boy was briefly with you for his own reasons. He was to enlighten you, and so he did. You have known him in past lives. At one time, he was his present father's uncle.

"He did not mean to stay within physical reality. He only came to show you what was possible, and to bring you both to an understanding of inner reality. He chose his illness. It was not thrust upon him. He did not manufacture sufficient blood, for he did not want to be physical beyond the time he had allotted.

"He wanted to give you an impetus, and his effect was far stronger than had he lived, and he knew this. He had a horror of living to young malehood for he did not want to meet a young woman, become attracted, and continue with another physical life.

"He was a light to you, and the light is not extinguished. It will lead you into knowledge that you would not have known otherwise, for you would not have sought it so vigorously. He is well aware of this, and wanted you to begin the pilgrimage; but the pilgrimage is within yourselves."

Now Seth was staring out through my open eyes. My gestures were his. He looked Jim right in the face as he talked. Ann and Rob both took notes. Phil just sat, listening.

"He was involved in scientific endeavors both in Atlantis and Egypt, but he had no desire to continue those pursuits now. He had gone quite beyond them. You [Jim] were also involved with him in two past lives in the same relationship, and as priests you both were interested in the inner workings of the universe."

Seth went on to say that Jim had fallen by the wayside in some respects, forgetting what he had learned in the past. "He [Peter] could not force you to remember, but he could give you a nudge and a push, and in this existence he did so.

"It is not time for you to run willy-nilly, looking for truth in any treetop. The truth is inside yourself. Your son is not a three-year-old any longer. He is an entity older than you, and he has tried to point

130

out the way to you. . . . He was not a child taken before his promise was achieved, but a personality who left you when his own reincarnations were finished. He will not return, but go on now to another reality in which his abilities can be used to more advantage."

According to Seth, Peter's own reincarnations had really been completed before he was born this time. He'd returned to die young so that Jim and Ann would be forced to ask the questions they were now asking.

At one point Seth smiled broadly and said, "Now, I have lived and died many times, and you can sense my vitality. And I tell you that the boy's vitality exists in as vital terms. It would have been almost a penance for him to have stayed longer. You helped him 'save his soul' at one time [in a past life] and he was returning the favor. At one time he was tempted to use his abilities to gain power, and to use the priesthood for gain. On that occasion you stopped him."

Seth went on to give an analysis of Jim's present personality as it was connected with events from past lives, and to give him some advice about the future. Jim told us earlier that he had been a disc jockey. Now Seth said, "No one can tell you what road to follow. You have the answers within you. Beware of those who give you ready answers. I am speaking in terms of probabilities, for the future is plastic."

He suggested that Jim stay out of the acting field, because in his case it led to a confusion as to the nature of his own identity. Seth advised him to stay with communications, saying that if he continued in radio there would be another radio job, and then an emergence into another line of work.

Seth gave more information concerning the past lives of all involved, then added, "I am giving you what I believe is the most important information, whether you can check it out or not. . . . Your inner selves digest what I have said, and this is more important than ten pages of notes and dates that you cannot check, since these lives were so long ago."

He said more about the symbolism of Peter's illness, spoke about Jim's past relationships with Ann, and said that Jim had mathematical abilities he was not using. "They result from your two priestly existences where you were both highly involved with calculations having to do with movement of the planets."

He ended in this manner: "It is natural that you come to others for help in your situation, and in my way I hope I have helped you. There is a difference between being told things and knowing them, however. And knowing comes from within. When you know, you do not need to be told, and you can have that kind of knowing. I will be glad to help you find it, but no one can find it for you."

During a break we sat nibbling at crackers and sipping wine. Suddenly impressions came into my own mind. Many of these checked out at once, on the spot. I told Ann, for instance, that her brother used several names and wore a toupee, and this was correct, along with many other statements. At the same time I kept getting impressions about the boy's symptoms.

When this sort of thing happens, I just relax and say whatever comes to mind. "There was an episode with toenails and shoes too small," I said. "This put pressure on the right big toe which affected an artery up the right leg. A bruise that damages function always occurs in such a case, though the bruise may be small."

There was more, much of it verified on the spot. Though they hadn't anything to do with reincarnation, these impressions did have a lot to do with demonstrating to Jim and Ann that we do have the ability to receive knowledge other than through the physical senses. The events that I "picked up" were often emotionally significant to the Lindens, though trivial in other respects.

These impressions also included some statements concerning the origin of the disease that killed Peter. Its cause is unknown, and there is no reason to go into my explanation here. But the characteristic symptoms of the disease I gave also described Peter's condition accurately. The Lindens had not discussed these with us—perhaps they found the subject too painful. Since this information was correct, there is no reason to suppose that the impressions concerning the disease's causes were wrong, though they are unknown. By the same token, there is no reason to suppose the reincarnational material was any less correct, though we can't check it because of the long time periods involved. (Some reincarnational data is much more recent and can be checked to some extent if the people involved have the time and want to make the effort. So far we have run across very few priests, and no one else who lived in Atlantis.)

Seth devoted the very last part of the session to Phil, and it was well past one in the morning before we were finished. Jim and Ann went away convinced that their son's life and death had a meaning, that there was sense and purpose in their lives, and that even this seeming tragedy operated for a greater good.

I felt pretty humble when the whole thing was over. Jim and Ann were almost transformed, and before the session, I had been so dubious that I hesitated. (The thing is, when I consciously think in such a limited fashion, my intuitive inner self rises up and shows me that much more is involved than the ego. Actually I think that these abilities flow through us as the wind flows through the branches.) Ann wrote me a letter shortly after, telling me that she and Jim no longer felt the tremendous sorrow that had burdened them earlier.

More and more I have seen how reincarnation makes sense out of such apparently senseless tragedies, and provides an inner structure to situations that would otherwise seem chaotic and unjust. I was so pleased to be able to help Ann and Jim; and that session and others like it have helped me also by showing me the value of ideas that originally I could not accept. The same thing applies to Seth: I am literally amazed at his capacity to help others, at his psychological understanding, at all the abilities he draws upon and focuses in our sessions.

Another similar case, involving the death of a child, concerned a woman who attended a few of my classes. Her fifteen-year-old adopted son had drowned a few months earlier. Seth said in a session that the boy had been a sailor in several past lives and still regarded death by water as preferable to dying on land. The boy had been related to his foster mother in another life, and also returned to help her gain needed inner development. He died early so that his death would make her question, and search for answers. She had been running from medium to medium, trying to contact the boy. In no uncertain terms, Seth told her to stop this practice and to work for inner development instead.

According to Seth, we choose our illnesses and the circumstances of our birth and death. This applies to every illness, whether it is a broken leg suffered from an accident, or an ulcer. This doesn't mean that we *consciously* make a choice in the way we're used to; we don't sit down and say, "Well, I think I'll get a broken leg this afternoon at three in front of Rand's drugstore." Some part of us is upset and chooses an illness or accident as a way of expressing this inner situation. This will be explained in the chapter on health, along with Seth's instructions on the maintenance of good health and vitality.

But what about serious diseases—and where does reincarnation fit into the picture? To begin with, Seth does not use the word "punishment." We are not "punished" in one life for the "transgressions" of a past one. Nor do we choose illness per se as a given life situation, even though we may utilize such an illness as a part of a larger plan, as a method of teaching ourselves some important truth or as a means of developing certain abilities.

Here is how this process works in a specific instance. Again, a phone call was involved, this time from a man I'll call Jon who called me from another part of the country, right after my first book was published two years ago. Jon and his wife were both in their early twenties. I'll call his wife Sally. After coming down with multiple sclerosis, Sally had been given about a year to live, and Jon wanted to ask Seth if anything could be done for her.

Again I felt this strong desire to help, and again I was filled with doubts. Suppose—just suppose—Seth held a session and suggested treatments or medicine that made Sally worse? I was Jane Roberts, not Edgar Cayce. And how could some stranger have such faith in Seth and my abilities when I was so often filled with doubts myself?

"I'm sure Seth could help," Jon said. "I knew it as soon as I read your book. Even if Sally can't be cured, perhaps he could explain things so that her illness would make some kind of sense. Why Sally? She's never hurt anyone in her life."

I really felt besieged, mostly because I wanted to help so badly. Then again I managed to remember that the inner *I* was so much stronger than the Jane-I, and that Seth knew much more than either of us. So I agreed.

134

Over a period of two years we've had several sessions for Jon and Sally. In that first session, though, Seth gave some excellent advice that is helpful to anyone whenever illness strikes. Before he went into the reincarnational background, which was important in this case, he emphasized the importance played by suggestion and telepathy in the sickroom. Because this has such great general application, I'll include portions of that passage here:

"The mental attitude of everyone involved should be altered to one that is more hopeful. The woman is picking up and reacting to the negative thoughts of those who believe her recovery is impossible.

"The disease cannot be reversed physically. A physical improvement will be the result of a spiritual change. All those surrounding her must refrain from attitudes of hopelessness and negative suggestions, whether implied or spoken. . . . This in itself will enable her to improve to some degree.

"The husband should follow this exercise three times a day: He should imagine the energy and vitality of the universe filling his wife's form with health. This should not be a wishful-thinking sort of thing, but a definite effort to understand that her form is composed of this energy, and in this way he can help her use it to advantage. If possible, he should touch her during this exercise, and it should be done morning, evening, and night.

"Do not manufacture hollow false assurances, but honestly and persistently remind yourself that the physical matter of your wife's image is filled with and formed by universal energy. A block has been preventing her from using this energy with normal effectiveness. You can partially make up for this by your own attitude and the exercises I have given you. This itself will give her a breathing spell, when the disease will cease its progression. If my instructions are followed completely, then some improvement should take place shortly.

"If the instructions concerning a beneficial change in her mental environment are not taken, then no other advice or medicine will be of help. . . ."

Seth also said that he would outline a program designed to change Sally's own expectations, and also suggested treatment by an accredited hypnotist who could instill positive suggestions to rouse her will to live.

He recommended that Sally's limbs be rubbed with peanut oil, and that iron be added to her diet. He emphasized that she would be happier in another room and said: "I believe you have a fairly small sunny parlor. This room has beneficial connotations for her. Let her be moved there." In passing he spoke of several episodes in Sally's present life, some that Jon corroborated in his next letter, and one in particular that he did not know about until Seth mentioned it. Seth said, for example, that she had worked in a five-and-dime store with a girl friend, and that a visit from this friend would be helpful. Jon didn't know that Sally had worked in such a place, but her mother remembered.

Notice that Seth did not mention other topics until he gave the above advice—and that it was for the husband and those caring for the patient rather than for the patient herself. At the end of the first session, Seth said, "There are past life connections operating. Right now it is not as important for you to know these as it is to take the steps I am outlining."

Between the two sessions, Jon wrote telling us that some improvements had been noted, and that he was following Seth's instructions. He also told us that he did have a room like the one Seth mentioned, and that Sally had been moved into it.

The second session for Jon was entirely devoted to reincarnational influences, and it is an excellent example of the way these can affect health patterns. The session also contains some general advice and answers some specific questions applying to the relationship between past lives and present health.

Seth began by saying that Karma does not involve punishment. "Karma presents the opportunity for development. It enables the individual to enlarge understanding through experience, to fill in gaps of ignorance, to do what should be done. Free will is always involved."

The story of Sally's past life is fascinating. Note that this was not the life *immediately* past, but an earlier one in which problems were "shelved" until this existence:

"The woman was a male, Italian, in a hill village. He lost his wife

136

and was left with a highly neurotic crippled daughter for whom he cared for many years. As a man, Sally was called Nicolo Vanguardi [Rob's phonetic interpretation] and the daughter was named Rosalina. He resented the girl, and while he cared for her, he did not do so kindly.

"He wanted to remarry, but no one would have him because of the daughter. When she could, she defied him. She was a handsome-looking young woman, crippled but not deformed. When she was in her thirties, she was more youthful appearing than many women much younger who had to work in the fields. They had a small farm, and itinerant help. A widowed man with no children came from a nearby village to help out on the farm. He fell in love with her, and despite her condition, took her to his home village.

"The father [Sally in the past life] was thoroughly embittered. The daughter had left too late; he was too old; no one would have him, and now he had no one even to talk to. He hated his daughter the more and railed that she had forsaken him in his old age, after he had cared for her."

Seth went on to say that in her next life, Sally was reborn as a woman of some artistic merit in a very successful existence, also in Italy. She was the mother of two sons. "Here the personality was born only fifty miles away, and as the wife of a wealthy landowner, she often drove through the very land where the small house [of her former life] still stood with its farm. This in a town badly bombed in the Second World War."

After that life, however, Sally's personality decided to take on the unfinished problems of development. "This time the personality is being cared for rather than caring for—being physically dependent. The personality in the earlier existence would not and could not try to understand the circumstances and position of the crippled daughter. Not for a moment then could the personality bear to contemplate the inner reality in personal terms.

"This time Sally plays that part, and is completely immersed in it. Jon was the man with whom the daughter left in the past life. Now Sally loves him, and has learned to see the good points of his personality.

"Through the change of roles, Sally now gains insight on past failures, and also helps her present husband to become more contemplative and to seek answers to questions that he would not have asked otherwise. She is adding to his development and also working out serious flaws that existed in her own personality."

He went on to say that the name of the original Italian town was something like Ventura, was located in southeastern Italy, and that a tragic train wreck occurred in the area just after the 1930's.

"While such situations as Sally's illness are chosen by the personality, the individual is always left to work out its own solution. Complete recovery, illness, or early death are not preordained on the part of the entity [or whole self]. The general situation is set up in response to deep inner involvements.

"The problem is a challenge set up by the entity for one of its own personalities, but the outcome is up to the personality involved. This was the last major stumbling block for this personality. . . . One does not choose illness per se for a lifetime situation. In this case, in order for the personality to see its own past activities clearly, it felt that it must develop a position of complete dependency."

Seth went on to say that even in such apparently tragic conditions, the personality is not abandoned. "The inner self, as distinguished from the more accessible subconscious, is aware of the situation and finds release through frequent inner communications where successes are remembered and reexperienced. The dream state becomes an extremely vivid time, for such experiences assure the personality of its larger nature. It knows it is more than the self that it has for a time chosen to be."

But Sally was in such terrible condition, going blind, unable to speak or move voluntarily. Why, Jon wrote, couldn't she have chosen something less damaging? Why couldn't she have been just sickly for three lives, say, instead of being struck down with such a killing disease in this one?

Seth answered, "This is characteristic of that entity, an impatience and yet a daring, because the situation represented such a challenge. All the weak points are intensified, hence the gravity of the physical situation. The entity preferred this, rather than a series of smaller difficulties. In this, Jon subconsciously acquiesced, to learn patience

138

and forbearing—to take what he considered his medicine all in one dose, so to speak."

Seth emphasized that in the life immediately past, Sally had taken a rest from problems, had enjoyed excellent circumstances and fulfilled her creative abilities.

"Such a situation allows the personality to telescope experience needed into one life situation, to delve deeply and face at once problems that could otherwise take several lifetimes. Only a bold and courageous personality would attempt this."

Now, over two years later, Sally is still alive but in poor condition. Seth said that she had solved the challenges she had set for herself, but in so doing had damaged her physical body to such an extent that she had decided to discard it. As of this writing she is in coma. Jon wanted to know what was happening to her in this state. "Is she really conscious someplace else? Or just dreaming? And what happens after death?" In a recent session Seth answered these questions. Many of the answers apply to death in general, so I'll include some excerpts from this session in the next chapter, and also go into Seth's ideas on reincarnation more thoroughly.

CHAPTER TWELVE:

More on Reincarnation— After Death and Between Lives

———— ⚬•⚬ ————

It was just last week that Jon called again. Sally was in the hospital, after a bad attack during which her heart had stopped for a short time. Jon was torn between praying for her recovery and for her release by death, and he asked if we'd have a session on the matter.

Seth had often told us that when we're finished with our lives here, we're actually anxious to leave this existence. When the body is worn out, we really want to get rid of it. The instinct for survival is served quite well, because the inner self knows that it lives beyond death. Still, I hated to say this to Jon over the phone. In theory it sounded fine, but naturally I knew he wanted Sally to live. I knew that he hoped for some miracle—at least a partial recovery, a reprieve.

I did promise to hold a Seth session for him, and later I was glad I did. Not only was the session a help to Jon, but it contains some excellent information on what can go on while a person is supposedly unconscious, in coma, and what we experience just before and after death.

Again, at the time of the session Sally was in deep coma. She hadn't been able to speak for over a year. First Seth gave a page or so of impressions, names, initials, events, and so forth, that he said he "derived from a certain portion of the girl's consciousness—disjointed memories, thoughts, and ideas.

"Her whole reality is far greater, and she is endeavoring to put these memories in place, as you would put furniture into a new house. Time as you think of it has little meaning for her. You could compare the two different time experiences in this way:

"In your dimension it is as if remembered events were like pieces of furniture, all arranged in one room, in a given order. Living in that room, you can find your way between the various pieces easily.

"You then move out into a larger and different kind of room, and here the furniture may be arranged in any fashion, arranged and rearranged to your heart's content. You may form different combinations from it and use it for different purposes. So Sally is rearranging the furniture of her mind. And as you might visit a new residence and move some of your belongings there before you officially make it your own, so she has been examining the new environment. She is in the process of transferring herself to the new location.

"There have been guides to help her. She will hardly notice that she has entirely moved in, for she will feel so at home. In her case, she has been forming memory pictures of her childhood, of days before her physical illness, and entering into them. She is learning that events that seem to be in the past can be re-created.

"This does not mean she thinks that she is a child. She is enjoying the freedom of reexperiencing events. This is a sort of spiritual therapy in her case, so that she loses the identification with illness and does not carry it with her.

"Shortly, training periods will begin. It will be her turn now to help others and be their source of strength. She has already begun a new life, therefore [Seth does not mean another physical life here, of course], though presently her experience is being monitored to some degree by guides.

"She sees herself supported in a religious sense by conventional figures from the Bible. These personalities will explain the nature of

142

reality to her in vocabulary that will make sense to her. Again, she has solved the problems that she set, and brought forth in her husband compassion and understanding, qualities that greatly help in his own development.

"I have appeared to her as a very gentle John of the Disciples, and spoken with her. This is not trickery, but a method of helping that she can accept. It is not unusual for those trying to help to assume such comforting forms and images."

(Later we thought that this last statement had extremely provocative implications for cases in which visions of religious figures are reported. We hope Seth will discuss this more thoroughly in the future.)

During our break, Rob mentioned several questions that he thought Jon would like answered, or that might come to his mind as he read the session. One had to do with the kind of body Sally had at her disposal. Seth said, "Now the new body is, of course, not a new one at all, but simply a body not physical in your terms, one that you use in astral projections, one that gives the vitality and strength to the physical body that you know.

"Your flesh is embedded in it now. When you leave the physical body, the other body is quite real to you and seems as physical, although it has many more freedoms. . . . Sally is delighted with this body, comparing it with the [sick] physical one. She is trying to cut off all identification with her physical body, whether it is alive or dead in your terms.

"Jon must tell her that she is free to leave, and that he joyfully gives her her freedom, so that even after death she does not feel she must stay close to him. She knows they will be reunited . . . and realizes he is not as aware of this as she is."

A few days after this session we were visited by a retired minister and his wife. Rev. Lowe, as I'll call him, publishes a national newsletter which discusses the psychic elements of Christianity. We had been corresponding for a few years, but had not met. I told him about Jon's session, and he was very interested in what Seth had to say about Sally's experience while in coma.

Rev. Lowe and his wife came on a class night, and so of course I invited them to attend. I try to keep classes as informal as possible. Everyone is on a first-name basis, and each of us wears whatever clothing is most comfortable and natural. Men in business suits mix with people in hippie outfits, and we always have wine for those who like it. I admit I wondered what Rev. Lowe would think, and hoped he didn't expect something like a prayer meeting. In our own way we do use prayer—but in a highly creative, unstructured, unconventional manner. Sometimes we play rock 'n' roll music, for instance, while I read a poem—and this I would consider prayer.

I had no idea whether or not Seth would come through that night. In the beginning, I'd jokingly introduced the minister as a rock drummer, to put both him and the class at ease. Someone commented that the presence of a minister must have quieted everyone down, since no one was saying much.

Suddenly Seth came through, saying: "And I thought you were on your good behavior because I was here! I will have to learn to be a reverend rock drummer, and I will keep the beat with you." After this he spoke to various class members, and then invited Rev. Lowe to ask whatever questions came to his mind.

"When we leave the physical body, where do we go?" the minister asked. Everyone else sat about, sipping wine and listening.

"You go where you want to go," Seth said. "Now, when your ordinary, waking, conscious mind is lulled in the sleep state, you travel in other dimensions. You are already having experiences in these other dimensions then. You are preparing your own way. When you die you go into those ways that you have prepared. There are various periods of training that vary according to the individual.

"You must understand the nature of reality before you can manipulate within it well. In physical reality you are learning that your thoughts have reality, and that you create the reality that you know. When you leave this dimension, then you concentrate upon the knowledge you have gained. If you still do not realize that you create your own reality, then you return, and again you learn to manipulate, and again and again you see the results of your own inner reality as you meet it objectified. You teach yourself the lesson until you have learned it; then you begin to learn how to handle the consciousness that is yours, intelligently and well. Then you can form images for the benefit of others, and lead and guide them. Then you constantly enlarge the scope of your understanding."

"What determines the time between reincarnations?" the minister asked.

"You. If you are very tired, then you rest. If you are wise, you take time to digest your knowledge and plan your next life, even as a writer plans his next book. If you have too many ties with this reality or if you are too impatient, or if you have not learned sufficiently, then you may return too quickly. It is always up to the individual. There is no predestination. The answers are within yourself then, as the answers are within you now."

Rev. Lowe asked other questions but no more relating to the subject at hand. He and Seth seemed to get along very well. Later, in a break, I received several impressions of a past life of Mrs. Lowe's. While a general discussion was going on, I "saw" her near a riding academy in fourteenth-century France; and then I saw her and Rev. Lowe as twins in Greece, when he was an orator and she a soldier. There were other details, but the interesting thing was that Mrs. Lowe told me afterward that she was really crazy about horses, and that Greece and France were the only countries in which she had any great interest.

Seth rarely gives reincarnational data unless it is directly tied in with the overall development of an individual's present life, and he refuses to give past life histories, for example, to those he thinks will not apply the lessons involved. Strangely enough, he did give such information once in a class to three college girls who clearly did not believe in reincarnation to begin with. They had just begun classes, and while they were curious about ESP, they had little patience with the theory of reincarnation—before the session, that is.

The girls were all intelligent, bright, alert—and wary. They weren't about to be taken in by any mumbo jumbo. At the same time they were intensely interested in Seth's ideas that consciousness can be expanded safely and without drugs, using his methods. One girl, Lydia, was the most vocal of the group in her arguments against reincarnation.

"You will reincarnate whether or not you believe that you will," Seth began, smiling. "It is much easier if your theories fit reality, but if they do not, then you do not change the nature of reincarnation one iota." He went on to give Lydia a rather detailed description of a past life around the area of Bangor, Maine, in 1832, when she was a male. This was Lydia's first Seth session and she sat wiggling nervously in her chair as Seth gave names, dates, and particular episodes of this past life.

When he was finished, she said, "Well, I don't know what to say, but I'll tell you this. The crazy thing is that I spent my childhood in Bangor, Maine, and when we moved to New York State I wouldn't give New York as my home. I always felt that I belonged in Maine. And Seth said that—" She broke off, and read her notes. Then she said excitedly, "Seth said that a Miranda Charbeau from the French side of my family in that past life married into the Franklin Bacon family of Boston. Again, it's crazy, it really is, because my family this time *is* connected with the Roger Bacon family from Boston."

There was no time for more discussion though, because Seth now began to speak to Jean, the most psychically gifted of the group:

"She lived in Mesopotamia before it was known by that name. Here we find abilities shown, ignored, and misused through a succession of lives; a rather classic example of the 'progress' followed by many psychically endowed, but in poor control of their personalities and abilities.

"China and Egypt. Lives in various religious capacities, but without the necessary sense of responsibility; unfortunately taking advantage of the fortunes made available to the ruling classes through the ages. For this reason, the abilities have not come to fruition. Only in this present existence is there finally some understanding, and sense of responsibility. In the past the psychic abilities were úsed for the wrong purposes; therefore, they did not fully develop and the personality was at a standstill.

"There was death by fire on two occassions." Following this statement Seth gave details from an Irish life of Jean's in 1524. Then he went on to give the following data, which we found most interesting. I'll give it exactly as we received it, though it was somewhat confusing in the beginning, since Seth just jumped into it.

146

"A small town twenty-five meters from Charterous—the nearest approximation here, Charterous or Charteris [Chartres?]. The last name then was Manupelt. Or Man Aupault. A. Curia. Some connection here with the first historical personality we have run across: a very distant connection to Joan of Arc, on the mystic's father's side, twice removed. And that name, approximately as given, in some records . . . in an old cathedral. The family name, the town, and the name of the cathedral are the same."

When Seth was done, for a minute, Jean wouldn't say a thing. Then she really blushed and told us that she'd always been terrified of fire, and that her nickname in high school had been Joan of Arc or The Witch.

But Seth wasn't through. He gave reincarnational material for another student, Connie, and mentioned in particular a life in Denmark when she had died as a small boy of diphtheria. And that really did it! Connie surprised everyone, particularly the other college girls, by saying that since she was a small child she'd been frightened of getting diphtheria, and that she could never understand why.

"Like, who worries about diphtheria these days?" she said.

"If you were afraid of getting, say, cancer, I could see it," Lydia answered.

"That's what I mean," Connie said. "I just could never make sense of it before. No one in my family ever died of diphtheria."

So along with the reincarnational histories Seth had given each girl a point of information, highly significant, and unknown to anyone in the room except for the person for whom it was intended. And this bit of information tied in beautifully with some small unexplainable attitudes that had previously puzzled them. Suddenly they were quite interested in reincarnation, and as usual, their minds were trigger-fast. Now they wanted to know everything at once.

"Seth said earlier that all time existed at once," said Jean. "Then how come he talks about reincarnational lives or a series of lives one before the other? The two don't seem to go together."

Almost immediately, Seth came through and answered her question.

"Your idea of time is false. Time as you experience it is an illusion caused by your own physical senses. They force you to perceive action

147

in certain terms, but this is not the nature of action. The physical senses can only perceive reality a little bit at a time, and so it seems to you that one moment exists and is gone forever, and the next moment comes and like the one before also disappears.

"But everything in the universe exists at one time, simultaneously. The first words ever spoken still ring through the universe, and in your terms, the last words ever spoken have already been said, for there is no beginning. It is only your perception that is limited.

"There is no past, present, and future. These only appear to those who exist within three-dimensional reality. Since I am no longer in it, I can perceive what you do not. There is also a part of you that is not imprisoned within physical reality, and that part of you knows that there is only an Eternal Now. The part of you who knows this is the whole self.

"When I tell you that you lived, for example, in 1836, I say this because it makes sense to you now. You live all of your reincarnations at once, but you find this difficult to understand within the context of three-dimensional reality.

"Pretend that you have several dreams, and you know that you are dreaming. Within each dream, one hundred earthly years may pass, but to you, the dreamer, no time has passed, for you are free of the dimension in which time exists. The time you seem to spend within the dream—or within each life—is only an illusion, and to the inner self no time has passed because there is no time."

Actually Seth has used several analogies to explain reincarnational experiences. On page 3,600 of our own sessions I find this: "The various reincarnational selves can be *superficially* regarded as portions of a crossword puzzle, for they are all portions of the whole, and yet they can exist separately."

In the 256th session he said, "Because you are obsessed with the idea of past, present, and future, you are forced to think of reincarnations as strung out one before the other. Indeed we speak of past lives because you are used to the time sequence concept. What you have instead is something like the developments narrated in *The Three Faces of Eve*. You have dominant egos, all a part of an inner identity, dominant in various existences. But the separate existences exist simultaneously. Only the egos involved make the time distinction. 145 B.C., A.D. 145, a thousand years in your past, and a thousand years in your future—all exist now."

In fact, Seth gave three or four sessions in which he compared cases of "split" personalities to our reincarnation selves. He ended up by saying, "It is interesting that the personalities [in *Three Faces of Eve*] did alternate, and all were in existence at once, so to speak, even though only one was dominant at any given time. In the same way, so-called past personalities are present in you now but not dominant."

As far as we know, this reconciliation of reincarnation and simultaneous time is original with Seth. Most other theories of reincarnation take the time sequence for granted. But what about cause and effect, then? When Seth introduced this idea, this is one of the first questions Rob and I thought of. Seth's attitude toward cause and effect will become clear enough in his later explanations of the true nature of "time," but when Rob first asked the question, Seth answered:

"Since all events occur at once in actuality, there is little to be gained by saying that a past event causes a present one. Past experience does *not* cause present experience. You are forming past, present, and future—simultaneously. Since events appear to you in sequence, this is difficult to explain.

"When it is said that certain characteristics from a past life influence or cause present patterns of behavior, such statements—and I have made some of them—are highly simplified to make certain points clear.

"The whole self is aware of *all* of the experiences of *all* of its egos, and since one identity forms them, there are bound to be similarities between them and shared characteristics. The material I have given you on reincarnation is quite valid, particularly for working purposes, but it is a simplified version of what actually occurs."

So while Seth often explains present life problems as the result of past life difficulties, he makes it clear to those that can understand that the lives really exist simultaneously, just as three personalities can exist in one body at one time. But all problems are not the result of such "past life" influences. In one case, a friend's hang-ups in the

149

present originated right in this life, though her boyfriend's were left over from the past.

Doris was having all kinds of problems. For one thing, she kept falling head over heels in love with men who didn't want marriage under any circumstances. In these relationships she was the aggressor. The men in each case were men who did not date, were overly attached to their parents, or who for some reason or other did not have ordinary relationships with women. Doris was smart enough to see this, but each time she was certain that there was something about the new man that made him more eligible—or at least more liable to accept her advances. In the meantime she was dreadfully lonely, for she would refuse dates with "ordinary" men, since they seemed so inferior compared to the new idol.

Finally after the breakup of one such episode, she asked for a Seth session. She knows both of us well, so I was quite astonished at her behavior before the session. She was so uptight that I found it difficult to go into trance. She just sat there, really white-faced, unsmiling, looking quite terrified.

Seth began by saying gently, "Your feelings toward me are connected with other attitudes deeply ingrained within you. You have been afraid of your father since infancy. Now you think of me as an old but wise, extremely powerful male adult, as you thought of your father when you were a child. This attitude overshadows your relationship with the males with whom you come into contact.

"You see the male in terms inspired in you in this childhood. You felt that your father had godlike qualities and attempt to project these onto the men you meet. Therefore they disappoint you, but this also serves your needs. Because while you see the male as godlike, you also see him as one who gives out punishment, and as unreasoning and cruel. So you are afraid to 'come under a man's thumb' or domination. Because you were a male in past lives, you resent this all the more.

"Therefore you consistently choose men in whom you see feminine characteristics, hoping that these more gentle qualities will protect you against the other feared masculine traits that you have exaggerated."

150

From what Rob said later, Doris sat there red-faced and somewhat embarrassed. Our tape recorder was on. Seth went on citing examples from Doris' early life of which Rob and I knew nothing. The entire session took up nine pages of single-typed copy, in which Seth analyzed Doris' attitudes and traits, illustrating them with specific episodes formerly known only to her, and ending up with some excellent advice.

He told her that she was projecting this image upon each male she met, and then reacting to *it* instead of to the individual. He gave her some mental exercises calculated to help her dissolve this false image. Here Doris began to cry a little. Seth smiled and said, "Now, now, do not sniffle. I am not your father giving you an arithmetic lesson. I put myself out to help you, and for this I get tears. I usually do not have that effect on people."

In answer, Doris managed a grin.

"You can ask questions," Rob said.

"Well, then why doesn't Frank [not his real name] date and have ordinary relationships with women? He's manly enough" she said. Then, almost with a touch of defiance she added, *"He's* not effeminate." And in this case, the main problem lay in "past life" troubles:

"He was a woman. His present parents were his brothers in the American Revolutionary period in the same geographical area as now. His brothers were involved as spies. Your Frank, as their sister, disclosed their hiding place in a cellar beneath an old inn. She was captured when she went out for supplies, gave away the location, and could not warn the brothers. She felt she had abandoned and betrayed them."

Seth went on to say that in this life, Frank chose to return as the son of the two brothers who themselves are now man and wife. "Now he rationalizes his desire not to leave home. The brothers never held him responsible . . . they knew the girl had been terrified and spoken out of fear with no intent to betray them. There is no punishment involved. He has chosen in this life to be of service to them and to help others. His secrecy [he was very tight-lipped] is the result of these past experiences. Once he feels he spoke too much and betrayed too much. Now he is secretive about matters he considers important."

Seth emphasized that for his own reasons, Frank did not want a marriage relationship, and ended by telling Doris that she had chosen him for this reason—that she never saw the man as he was, but only the image she had projected upon him. He gave Frank's name in a past life as Achman incidentally, and much later Doris learned that his present family has an Achman branch.

Much more psychological advice was given. The whole session was of great help to Doris—who hasn't been frightened of Seth since, by the way! But it is an oversimplificaton to say that *all* present problems are *the result of* past life difficulties. We are not "stuck" with our problems, whether they come from this life or another. We don't have to drag them along with us. They can be solved, and while reincarnational influences certainly operate, they don't operate in a vacuum. The following chapter on health will contain some of Seth's methods for maintaining mental, psychic, and physical vitality —and perspective.

Some people are better able to utilize past life experience, I think, while others insulate themselves rather closely in each life, closing themselves off as much as possible from such influences. Some peoples' lives seem to make no sense, for instance, unless you know their "previous" ones. Our fifty- or sixty- or seventy-year life-spans are like self-contained novels, well plotted and executed.

There is no doubt, though, that a knowledge of reincarnational influences sheds invaluable light on the nature of personality and helps us to see our present selves with some perspective. The following excerpts from a reincarnational reading show the continuity and interrelationships that can be involved in the tapestry of the self we now call ours.

An editor I'll call Matt came to visit us from New York. We had corresponded but never met before. He had read a manuscript of mine and knew about Seth. We liked each other at once, but it was primarily a business meeting. And then, I felt that Matt would want me to "prove my abilities" somehow or other, and I didn't want to feel under pressure.

Some people, I've discovered, have the strangest ideas about mediums or psychics. When I first found this out, I used to knock myself out proving how normal I was. People usually found this very disappointing, and I found it very inhibiting. Now, most of this has just worn off. I'm as normal or abnormal as anyone else.

Actually, it was kind of funny: Matt knocked himself out to show me that I didn't really have to prove a thing! So for a while our conversation was rather bright and frantic.

Seth had previously given us some information about Matt, his publishing company, and his associates. And the next evening, when we were all more comfortable with each other, Seth came through and held an excellent session.

Matt has since become a good friend, incidentally, but at that point we didn't know him from Adam. The psychological insights shown were really astonishing—and I don't believe that the most accomplished psychologist could have pinpointed this young man's character, abilities, and liabilities as well as Seth did.

My eyes were open during much of the session—my physical eyes, that is, because at such times they are definitely mirrors of a different personality. "There has been a sense of a void to be filled," Seth began. "A fear of identity escaping and running outward. My cup runneth over, and there will be none of me left—you see? On the other hand it has always been natural for the personality to turn outward in an easy manner and with exuberance.

"So we find two lives devoted to the nurture of others. But in both cases the personality was filled with an inner dread, to some extent resenting those he helped. If he were out helping others, then who would mind the store? He was afraid his stock would be gone.

"In two other lives, there was instead the development of inner abilities to the exclusion of others, a closing down of windows and barring of doors. He would not look out, and no one dared look in. He would make horrible funny faces at the window of his soul to frighten others away. Yet through all of this, the inner abilities did grow. He 'added to his stock.'

"Now he has begun to synthesize these inner and outer conditions. He realizes that the inner self need not be so heavily guarded, that his identity will not escape from him like a dog who leaves the leash. . . . Now, you see that I am a friendly chap, indeed, like an old dog with a *long* leash—"

At this, Rob and Matt both burst out laughing. Then Seth went

153

into some information, connecting some of the young man's present interests with past activities. He mentioned several past lives, but emphasized one as being particularly significant. "You were a member of a monastic group who classified and collected various kinds of seeds. The group worked on manuscripts officially, but our friend here and several others were bootleg seed finders, believing against currently held theories that questions concerning nature could be answered by examining nature.

"They investigated the ideas, folklore, and officially held knowledge concerning botany and seed reproduction, and began behind the monastery their forbidden garden. They were trying to discover the secret of heredity within plant life.

"This was near Bordeaux. The order had to do with St. John. There was a crest, belonging either to the order or to our friend's family: a four-tonged fork with a serpent above the upper portion of the handle in the foreground, and in the background either a castle or monastery.

"The monks were routed out . . . [of] the order . . . in the 1400's. The name of the monk in the order seems to have been Aerofranz Marie [Rob's phonetic interpretation]."

"How did I die then?" Matt asked.

"Three villagers were hunting on monastery ground. You yelled out to tell them that they trespassed, and tripped on a rock. You were knocked unconscious, and the townspeople ran. You came to at night, and wandered through the fields on the far side of the monastery, and came to a body of water. You knelt and began to pray and lost your balance. You grabbed hold of an overhanging branch, but it gave way, and you drowned."

At this point, as Seth talked I seemed to be looking down on the scene he described. I watched the monk from some point behind and above, as he wandered away from the monastery and through the fields. Seth went on to say that the monk's experiments contributed to achievements made later in the same field by another monk.

He also gave some excellent advice that I'm sure many other people could use: "Do not use your intellect like a shiny banner to wave from your windows. You are using it like a gaudy plaything that

154

belongs to you. You wind it up like a fine toy, but you are careful of the directions in which you let it run. Your intellect is a fine one, but you have allowed yourself to be fascinated by its sparkling quality, and not used it thoroughly as a tool."

I'm only giving excerpts from personal readings, picking out passages that deal with reincarnation. Usually the readings themselves include far more—health suggestions as well as character analysis and advice on other matters. And so far, each such session has been highly significant to the person concerned.

Matt, for instance, was astonished by the character analysis which he said pegged him to a T. More, the crest mentioned by Seth was highly similiar, he told us, to his own private doodle that he sketched while on the phone or in odd moments. Another interesting point: a few years earlier the editor had written two plays—one featuring a monk who lived on the seacoast near Bordeaux, and the other also set in France in the thirteenth century. These facts, of course, were unknown to us.

We did know that the editor was interested in botany, however, and Seth tied in this avocation with the past experimental work done with seeds.

I've tried, through excerpts from readings, to show Seth's ideas on reincarnation as they are personally applied But there are several important questions we haven't considered as yet. For example, how many lives do we live? Is there a limit to them? Quite simply, we live as many physical existences as we feel we must in order to develop our abilities and prepare ourselves to enter other dimensions of reality. This will be discussed thoroughly in the chapter dealing with the nature of personality.

Within this framework of development, however, there is a minimum requirement. Seth says: "As a rule, each entity is born so that three roles are experienced—that of mother, father, and child. Two lives would be sufficient to give you the three roles, but in some cases the personality does not function to adulthood. The most important issue, however, is the fullest use of potential."

Seth also told us that some personalities do not develop well in the physical environment, but fulfill themselves in other realities. In other words, the "last" reincarnation is not the end. There are other dimensions of existence in which we have an even greater part to play in the maintenance of life and consciousness. These dimensions, and our part in them, will be explained along with the God concept, probabilities, and time. But central to Seth's discussions of reincarnation are the following excerpts from session 233 that place reincarnation in perspective, individually and historically.

"In the materialization of personality through various reincarnations, only the ego and the layers of personal subconscious adopt new characteristics. The other layers of the self retain their past experiences, identity, and knowledge.

"In fact, the ego receives much of its [relative] stability because of this subconscious retention. Were it not for past experiences in other lives on the part of deeper layers of the self, the ego would find it almost impossible to relate to other individuals, and the cohesiveness of society would not exist.

"Learning to some extent is passed on through the genes, biochemically, but this is a physical materialization of inner knowledge achieved and retained from past lives. . . . The human being does not . . . erupt into existence at birth and laboriously then begin its first attempt to gain experience. If this were the case, you would still be back in the Stone Age.

"There are waves of energy, and waves of reincarnational patterns, for there *have* been many Stone Ages on your planet, where new identities did begin their 'first' experience with physical existence, and changed the face of the earth as they progressed. . . .

"They changed it in their own ways, not in your ways, but this will be discussed at a much later date. Yet all of this occurs, basically, within the blinking of an eyelid, all with purpose and meaning, and based upon achievement and responsibility. Each part of the self, while independent to some considerable degree, is nevertheless responsible to every other portion of the self; and each whole self [entity] is responsible to all others, while it is largely independent as to activity and decision.

"For as many layers of the self compose the whole self [entity], so many entities form a gestalt of which you know relatively little and of which I am not as yet prepared to tell you." (This last remark was to lead, much later, into whole blocks of sessions dealing with the God concept.)

We are still having sessions that deal with reincarnation, and when questions come up, we ask them. This helps to add to our material on the subject, of course, but yet in the entire fabric of the sessions, reincarnation plays a comparatively minor part, as only one aspect of our reality.

Whether or not you understand or accept your reincarnational background, it is highly important to live a sane, balanced life in *this* life. We form our day-to-day reality. We formed our past lives, and we form this one. And by solving problems now, we can make things vastly easier for our "past" *and* "future" selves.

CHAPTER
THIRTEEN

Health

How can you stay healthy? How can you get rid of any illnesses you might have? Exactly what is the connection between your state of mind and your health? Seth's ideas on this subject have been of great value to Rob and me, and to everyone who has come in contact with them. We have put his concepts to work in our own lives, and sometimes both of us wonder how we managed daily life before we understood the close relationship between thoughts, emotions, and health.

A few weeks ago we heard that a former neighbor had just died. Joanie had lived in our apartment house for a year or so, once right across the hall from us. She was thin, red-haired, with a wild temper. I think she was one of the wittiest people I've known, and she was a great mimic. But she often used her wit like a sword. It was cruel humor, even when she turned it against herself, as she often did.

She was in her early thirties, with a good job, but she looked down on all of the other employees. Her marriage had ended in divorce before she moved here, and while she was always talking about getting married again, she had a great distrust of men. I think she really hated them. She didn't think much better of women, yet at times she could be very warmhearted. She took a liking to Rob and myself, and often we would sit, she and I at this same table where I'm writing this book, and chat.

She always began with one of her fantastically funny sarcastic tales about someone she knew. She had an uncanny ability to sense peoples' weak points and make fun of them. For all of that, when she was not sick she had a fine vitality, and a keen, native shrewdness. We played a sort of game: I liked her, but I wasn't going to be besieged by a barrage of negative thoughts and pessimism for an hour, no matter how wittily presented—and she knew it. The worse part was that she really was funny and it was hard as the devil not to laugh at her, even when I knew I shouldn't. And she knew this, too. So she would try to see how far she could go before I would call her on it and begin a "mini-lecture," pointing out that her attitude toward other people was largely responsible for her difficulties.

And her difficulties were illnesses—of such variety and vigor that I think it was impossible even for her to recount what had afflicted her in any one year. Some were serious, and she had several operations. She picked up every infection in vogue, and many that weren't. She went from doctor to doctor and always with quite definite and often appalling physical symptions. Her diet was greatly restricted, and her illnesses began to become more and more severe.

Emotionally, she went from exaggerated heights to exaggerated lows. Her age bothered her; she was certain that "life would be over by the time you reach forty"—and for her it was, by several years. Yet we were all astonished to hear of her death. Even though we realized that she was literally making herself sick, we had no idea that she was "sick to death."

Remember what I said earlier, that we form physical reality as a replica of our inner ideas. This is a major premise of the Seth Material. Joan literally disliked everyone with few exceptions. She was convinced, furthermore, that she was unliked and unlikable. She felt persecuted, sure that people were talking or gossiping about her when her back was turned—because this was precisely what *she* did. Daily life contained all kinds of threats for her, and she kept her nervous system in a constant state of stress. Her body defenses were lowered. She was tired of the constant battle, never realizing that much of the war was one-sided and unwarranted. She projected her ideas of reality outward, and they literally led her to destruction.

Yet she had been warned. Two years before her death she asked to attend a regular Seth session. Seth was quite serious and not as jovial as usual, and at the time I thought that he was being rather hard on her. Now I see that he was trying to impress her with the necessity of changing her attitudes and reactions. He stated his ideas on health as clearly and directly as possible, dealing with their practical application. I can almost see Joan sitting there, legs crossed, before the session. If she had been able to follow his advice, I am convinced she would be alive and well today. I am also sure that readers who understand and follow Seth's ideas on health will find their own greatly improved.

"You must watch the pictures that you paint with your imagination," he said, "for you allow your imagination too full a reign. If you read our early material, you will see that your environment and the conditions of your life at any given time are the direct result of your own inner expectations. You form physical materializations of these realities within your own mind.

"If you imagine dire circumstances, ill health, or desperate loneliness, these will be automatically materialized, for these thoughts themselves bring about the conditions that will give them reality in physical terms. If you would have good health, then you must imagine this as vividly as in fear you imagine the opposite.

"You create your own difficulties. This is true for each individual. The inner psychological state is projected outward, gaining physical reality—and this regardless of the nature of the psychological state. . . . The rules apply to everyone. You can use them for your own benefit and change your own conditions once you realize what they are.

"You cannot escape your own attitudes, for they will form the nature of what you see. Quite literally you see what you want to see; and you see your own thoughts and emotional attitudes materialized in physical form. If changes are to occur, they must be mental and psychic changes. These will be reflected in your environment. Negative, distrustful, fearful, or degrading attitudes toward anyone work against the self."

Joan sat tapping her foot nervously. There were no wisecracks. At the time, she was dating a man who drank too much. "His drinking makes me irritable and angry," she said. *"He's* my problem. He's the one who makes me feel nervous."

Rob laughed; she sounded so put upon, so determined to place the blame elsewhere.

"You must understand something else," Seth said. "Telepathy operates constantly. If you continually expect an individual to behave in a particular manner, then you are constantly sending him telepathic suggestions that he will do so. Each individual reacts to suggestion. According to the specific conditions existing at the time, such an individual will to some extent or another act according to the mass suggestions he receives.

"These mass suggestions include not only those given to him by others, both verbally and telepathically, but also those he has given to himself, both in the waking and dream states. If an individual is in a state of despondency, this is because he has already become prey to negative suggestions of his own and others. Now if you see him and think that he looks miserable"—Seth looked at Joan sharply—"or that he is an incurable drunk, then these suggestions are picked up by him subconsciously, though you have not spoken a word. And in his already weakened condition they will be accepted and acted upon.

"If, on the other hand, under the same circumstances, you stop yourself and say gently to yourself, 'He will begin to feel better now, or his drinking is temporary, and there is indeed hope here,' then you have given him aid, for the suggestions will at least represent some small telepathic ammunition to help fight off the war of despondency.

"There are obviously ways in which you mold your own conditions, protect yourself from your own negative suggestions and those of others. You must learn to erase a negative thought or picture by replacing it with its opposite.

"If you think, 'I have a headache,' and if you do not replace this suggestion by a positive one, then you are automatically suggesting that the body set up those conditions that will result in the continuation of the malady. I will give you a commercial that is better than your Excedrin, you see, the short headache. I will tell you how to have none at all." This was the only touch of humor in the whole session. In a session devoted to a particular person, Seth usually goes out of his way to make a few jovial comments to set the person at his or her ease.

We had a short break, and Joan continued to complain of her friend's drinking habits, how they only added to her own nervousness. She was certain that if she didn't have this to contend with, her health would return. Quite vehemently, she set about blaming her friend for almost all of her problems. When Seth resumed, he was even more serious than before.

"Now, you are not speaking of basic issues," he said. "You are flying paper dragons to be punctured, but these are not the real dragons. You must learn to listen to the voice of the inner self. It is hardly to be feared. You have allowed the ego to become a counterfeit self, and you take its word because you will not hear the muffled voice that is within it.

"You have been examining others, rather than yourself. What you see in others is the materialization—the projection of what you *think* you are—not necessarily, however, of what you are. For example, if others seem deceitful to you, it is because you deceive yourself, and then project this outward upon others.

"These are examples, now. If an individual sees only evil and desolation in the physical world, it is because he is obsessed with evil and desolation and projects them outward, and closes his eyes to all else. If you want to know what you think of yourself, then ask yourself what you think of others, and you will find your answer.

"Another example: A very industrious individual thinks the majority of men are lazy and good for nothing. No one would ever think of calling him lazy or good for nothing, yet this may be precisely his own subconscious picture of himself, against which he drives himself constantly. And all of this without his realizing his basic concept of himself, and without recognizing that he projects his feared weaknesses outward unto others.

"True self-knowledge is indispensable for health or vitality. The recognition of the truth about the self simply means that you must first discover what you think about yourself, subconsciously. If it is a good image, build upon it. If it is a poor one, recognize it as only the opinion you have held of yourself and not as an absolute state."

With all her other troubles, Joan was frequently bothered by severe headaches. Before closing, Seth gave her advice which can be used by anyone:

"You should tell yourself frequently, 'I will only react to constructive suggestions,' for this gives you some protection against your own negative thoughts and those of others. A negative thought if not erased will almost certainly result in a negative condition: a momentary despondency, a headache, according to the intensity of the thought.

"Now, if you find yourself with a headache, say immediately, 'That is in the past. Now in this new moment, this new present, I am already beginning to feel better.' Then immediately turn your attention away from the physical condition. Concentrate upon something pleasant, or begin another task.

"In this way you are no longer suggesting that the body reproduce the headache conditions. The exercise may be repeated."

It does not do to *repress* negative thoughts, such as fears, angers, or resentments. In other sessions Seth makes it clear that these should be recognized and faced and *then* replaced.

Repression has been one of my own habits, particularly after I learned how destructive negative thoughts can be. At first I went overboard, or tried to. I'd catch myself thinking a resentful thought about a particular person or situation and I'd almost recoil, "Wow, that's a terrible thing to think," I'd say to myself.

"If I direct an aggressive thought toward someone, then it can hurt them." I said to Rob. "If I bury it, it can hurt me and emerge as

164

physical symptoms of some kind. So will you please ask Seth in our next session what he suggests?" In this one session Seth explained the difference between repression and the correct approach.

"Ruburt should remember to recognize resentment when he feels it, and then to realize that resentment can be dismissed. The initial recognition must be made, however. Then have him imagine plucking out the resentment by the roots and replacing it with a positive feeling. But he must imagine the plucking-out process.

"This is the difference between repression and positive action. In repression the resentment is shoved beneath and ignored. With our method it is recognized, imaginatively plucked out as being undesirable, and replaced by the thought of peace and constructive energy." (Seth has frequently cautioned me against repressing aggressions out of fear of them. Rob says that it is quite funny—to him!—when Seth, speaking through me, takes me to task in this way. His suggestions have always been excellent, however.)

Later he made a very good point: "If desire for health leads instead to an emphasis upon symptoms to be overcome, you would be better off to avoid all thoughts of health or illness and concentrate in other directions, such as work. Such an emphasis can lead to a focus upon obstacles that stand in the way, and this reinforces the negative condition."

Seth always says that life is abundant, vigorous, and strong. Each of us has our own defenses against negative suggestions, and we should trust in our own immunity. People react to negative suggestions only when their own frame of mind is negative. Then we close ourselves off from the constructive energies we need.

Again, Seth is not suggesting we *repress* emotion. Spontaneity, above all, is the rule. If we were truly spontaneous, Seth says, we wouldn't need to worry about positive suggestions because our health would be normally maintained.

One of my students, a businessman, always gets worried when Seth speaks about spontaneity. He equates it with lack of discipline. Seth calls this man "the Dean," with affectionate humor, because he's one of my best students, and the others listen to his psychic adventures with a good deal of interest. But he's very much a community man also, and the word "spontaneity" can be like a red scarf to a bull, at least as far as he is concerned! And I have to admit that many of us have the feeling that our inner emotions are too hot to handle.

We were talking about this in class one night, when suddenly Seth came through. "Emotions flow through you like storm clouds or blue skies, and you should be open to them and react to them," Seth said. "You are not your emotions. They flow through you. You feel them. And then they disappear. When you attempt to hold them back, you build them up like mountains. I have told our Dean that spontaneity knows its own discipline. Your nervous system knows how to react. It reacts spontaneously when you allow it to. It is only when you try to deny your emotions that they become dangerous."

We had a new student that evening, and someone made the remark that Seth could be quite stern. Now he said, jokingly, "I have been drastically maligned this evening, and so I come to show our new friend here that I am a jolly fellow. That, at least, was my initial intention. Now it has changed. For I must tell you again that the inner self, acting spontaneously, automatically shows the discipline that you do not as yet understand."

Now Seth, through my eyes, stared around the room. Someone picked my glasses up and put them on the coffee table. (As I mentioned before, when Seth comes through, he always takes my glasses off, and often flings them rather grandly upon the rug.) The lights were on, as always. He faced the group and said emphatically, "You are not your body. You are not your emotions. You have emotions. You *have* thoughts as you have eggs for breakfast, but you are not the eggs, and you are not your emotions. You are as independent of your thoughts and emotions as you are of the bacon and eggs. You *use* the bacon and eggs in your physical composition, and you use your thoughts and emotions in your mental composition. Surely you do not identify with a piece of bacon? Then do not identify with your thoughts and emotions. When you set up barriers and doors, then you enclose emotions within you . . . as if you stored up tons of bacon in your refrigerator and then wondered why there was room for nothing else."

166

He said to "the Dean," "Why is it so difficult for you to learn what freedom is?"

"Freedom in the total sense seems like irresponsibility, almost."

"That is indeed your interpretation," Seth said, "and this is because you set demands. Now I ask you, how far do you think a flower would get if in the morning it turned its face toward the sky and said, 'I demand the sun. And now I need rain. So I demand it. And I demand bees to come and take my pollen. I demand, therefore, that the sun shall shine for a certain number of hours, and that the rain shall pour for a certain number of hours . . . and that the bees come—bees A, B, C, D, and E, for I shall accept no other bees to come. I demand that discipline operate, and that the soil shall follow my command. But I do not allow the soil any spontaneity of its own. And I do not allow the sun any spontaneity of its own. And I do not agree that the sun knows what it is doing. I demand that all these things follow my ideas of discipline'?

"And who, I ask you, would listen? For in the miraculous spontaneity of the sun, there is discipline that utterly escapes you, and a knowledge beyond any that we know. And in the spontaneous playing of the bees from flower to flower, there is a discipline beyond any that you know, and laws that follow their own knowledge, and joy that is beyond command. For true discipline, you see, is found only in spontaneity. Spontaneity knows its own order."

Again, Seth stared at "the Dean," but now he spoke to the others in the group. "In the spontaneous working of your nervous system, what do we find? We see here the head of 'the Dean' that rests upon his shoulders, and the intellect that demands discipline. And yet all of this rests upon the spontaneous workings of the inner self, and the nervous system of which the intellect knows little. And without that spontaneous discipline, there would be no ego to sit upon the shoulders and demand discipline. . . . Now that I have proven how jovial I am, you may all take a break."

Everyone laughed. After our rest period, Seth resumed, to answer some other questions, but he ended the last discussion with a smile for "the Dean": "Now, the seasons come each year as they have come

167

for centuries upon your planet, and they come with a magnificent spontaneity and with a creativity that bursts upon the world. And yet they come within a highly ritualized and disciplined manner. For spring does not come in December. And there is a merging of spontaneity and discipline truly marvelous to behold. And you do not fear the coming of the seasons.

"Each of you in your way contribute. For you can consider the body of the earth and all that you know . . . the trees, the seasons, and the skies, to some extent as your own contribution . . . the combination of spontaneity and discipline that gives fruit to the earth."

All of nature operates spontaneously. Our bodies will be healthy automatically if we do not project false ideas upon them.

But, of course, it is not as simple as all this. In speaking directly to people in class sessions, Seth tries to explain matters as clearly as possible and in a way that they can understand. In our own sessions he goes much more deeply into such subjects. In the following excerpts from a private session, he explains the biological and psychic elements of pain and consciousness and also states that illness itself is sometimes a purposeful activity.

As you read this, think back to various illnesses you have had, and see how this applies. Here Seth discusses illness in its relationship not only to the surface personality but to our deepest biological frameworks. Seth had previously spoken about Sally's (Jon's wife's) need to disassociate herself from her "sick" identity. Now he elaborated:

"All illness is momentarily accepted by the personality as a part of the self, and here lies its danger. It is not just symbolically accepted, and I am not speaking in symbolic terms. An impeding action such as an illness is quite literally accepted by the personality structure, and once this occurs, a conflict develops. The self does not want to give up a portion of itself, even while that portion may be painful or disadvantageous. There are many reasons behind this.

"For one thing, while pain is unpleasant, it is also a method of familiarizing the self against the edges of quickened consciousness. Any heightened sensation, pleasant or not, has a stimulating effect upon consciousness to some degree. Even when the stimulus may be humiliatingly unpleasant, certain portions of the psychological structure accept it indiscriminately because it is a sensation, and a vivid one."

Now Seth comes to this point, very important in his theories: "This acquiescence to even painful stimuli is a basic part of the nature of consciousness. Action does not differentiate between pleasant, painful, or joyful stimuli. These distinctions come much later, and on another level [here Seth is considering personality as composed of energy or action].

"Action accepts all stimuli in an affirmative manner. It is only when it becomes compartmented, so to speak, in the highly differentiated consciousness that such refinements occur. I am not saying that unpleasant stimuli will not be felt as unpleasant and reacted against in less self-conscious organisms. I am saying that they will rejoice even in their automatic reaction, because any stimuli and reaction represents sensation, and sensation is a method by which consciousness knows itself.

"The complicated human personality with its physical structure has evolved, along with some other structures, a highly differentiated 'I' consciousness [the ego, in other words], whose very nature is such that it attempts to preserve the apparent boundaries of identity. To do so it chooses between actions. But beneath this sophisticated gestalt are the simpler foundations of its being, and indeed the very acceptance of all stimuli without which identity would be impossible.

"Without this acquiescence to even painful stimuli, the structure would never maintain itself, for the atoms and molecules within it constantly accept such stimuli, and joyfully suffer even their own destruction. Being aware of their identity within all action, and not having the complicated 'I' structure, there is no reason for them to fear destruction. They are aware of themselves as a part of action.

"Now all of this is basic knowledge if you would understand why the personality accepts even an impeding action such as illness despite the ego's resistence to pain."

Seth goes on to say that illness can be a "healthy" reaction, though it always involves personality problems: "It must be understood by the personality that the illness is a hardship on the part of the whole structure, and . . . not basic to the original personality.

169

"The whole focus of the personality can shift from constructive areas to a concentration of main energies in the area of the impeding action, or illness. In such a case, the illness actually represents a new unifying system. Now, if the old unifying system of the personality is broken down, the illness serving as a makeshift temporary emergency measure may hold the integrity of the personality intact until a new, constructive unifying principle replaces the original.

"Unifying principles are groups of actions about which the personality forms itself at any given time. These usually change in a relatively smooth fashion when action is allowed to flow unimpeded. [See how this ties in with Seth's advice to the students on the value of spontaneity and the difficulties of repression.] These impediments [illnesses] may sometimes then preserve the integrity of the whole psychological system and point out the existence of inner psychic problems. Illness is a portion of the action of which personality is composed and therefore it is purposeful, and cannot be considered as an alien force that invades personality from without. . . .

"Illness could not be called an impeding action unless it persisted long after its purpose was served. Even then you could make no judgment without knowing all the facts . . . for the illness could still serve by giving the personality a sense of security, being kept on hand as an ever-present emergency device in case the new unifying system should fail.

"In other words, an action cannot be judged as impeding without a thorough knowledge of the actions that result in the makeup of any given personality. This is extremely important. To overlook this point is to risk the adoption of a more severe illness.

"When action is allowed to flow freely, then neurotic rejections will not occur. And it is neurotic rejection that causes *unnecessary* illness.

"All illness is almost always the result of another action that cannot be followed through. When the lines to the original action are released and the channels opened, the illness will vanish. However, the thwarted action may be one with disastrous consequences which the illness may prevent. The personality has its own logic."

Over and over again Seth tells us that physical symptoms are communications from the inner self, indications that we are making mental errors of one kind or another. He compares the body in one session to a sculpture "never really completed, the inner self trying out various techniques on its test piece. The results are not always of the best, but the sculptor is independent of his product and knows there will be others."

He also has some fascinating comments on the relationship of various kinds of symptoms to the inner problems involved. "Do not forget that you are a part of the inner self. It is not using you. You are the portion of it that experiences physical reality. Now, physical illnesses that are not critical but observable—that do not involve, say, loss of a limb or organ—*generally* represent problems that are in the process of being solved, problems that are 'out in the open.'

"Such illnesses are the end product of a process of discovery. Inner problems are literally brought out where they can be faced, recognized, and conquered, using the symptoms as measuring points of progress. A trial-and-error system is involved, but the inner processes are reflected rather quickly by the physical condition."

As Seth makes clear in other sessions, the symptoms in such cases are themselves part of the healing process. What we are supposed to do, then, is change our mental attitude, search ourselves for the inner problem represented by the symptoms, and measure our progress as the symptoms subside.

"In cases where the symptom itself is interior, as in ulcers, this is a sign that the personality is not yet willing to face the problem, and the symptom itself is shielded from physical sight—quite rightly, symbolically speaking. The relative observability of a symptom is, therefore, a clue to the personality's attitude toward its problem.

"Many problems are never materialized. They remain as blank spots, uncultivated and unproductive areas within the psyche, areas in which there are no problems because no experience is permitted. . . . There is then a mental, psychic, or emotional lack of sight and a complete blockage. Such a denial of experience is far more detrimental than a specific problem, for there is an inability on the part of the personality to express itself at all in that area."

Rob's father has developed hardening of the arteries and is in a nursing home. He doesn't recognize any of us. When we visit him, we're surrounded by elderly people, more or less in the same condition. Accordingly, we were concerned about the problems of advanced age.

According to Seth, each case of senility is different, but generally speaking, the personality transfers the vital parts of consciousness into the next area of existence, and is often fully aware there, and functioning. Gradually the personality's mental focus leaves this life and begins to operate entirely on another level. The physical disease—the hardening of the arteries—is caused by the personality's gradual refusal to accept new physical stimuli, thus avoiding physical experience (either purposefully or through error). People who are terrified of physical death might take this path, since when physical death occurs, consciousness is already acquainted with its new environment and the organism's death is relatively meaningless. In any case, the individual's inner decision causes the physical symptoms, not the other way around.

You can even continue some symptoms after death. For example, Miss C, who lived in our apartment house, finally died of hardening of the arteries. One night I found myself out of my own body in a strange house—strange because while it was extremely old-fashioned, somehow it looked brand-new. Miss C was just going out the door as I arrived. She was very distracted. Suddenly I "knew" that the house was an hallucination she had created, a replica of her childhood home, and I knew that she did not realize she was dead.

At the same moment I realized that my job was to explain the facts to her. I caught up with her, gently led her back into the house, and said, "Miss C, you don't have to worry anymore about dying. It's already happened. Your mind can be perfectly clear now. It's all right." She seemed to understand, and as I finished speaking with her, another person came to take my place.

I'd read about such instances, but I have to admit that I thought they were highly imaginative accounts until I found myself guiding Miss C. The point is that she was so frightened of death, she didn't realize it was all over. Since her physical body was quite dead, she

172

was in her astral body; yet she was acting confused, and her mind was still unclear, as if she still had hardening of the arteries.

According to Seth, during our reincarnational existences we are to realize that we project our thoughts and emotions outward to form reality. When you realize, for example, that ill health is the projection of distorted ideas outward onto the body, then you work to clear up the inner problems. This realization can cure even illnesses that are related to past lives. Since Seth says these existences are actually lived spontaneously, then these "parallel" selves exist in us now, and we can reach them through therapy.

Remember our friend who kept falling in love with men she couldn't have? Finally she grew more and more morose, and attempted suicide several times. One night in her absence we had a session for her, and Seth's advice here has important general implications.

"You have not accepted life on life's terms," he said. "You are demanding that it behave in certain ways and take courses that you have consciously decided upon. You are refusing to accept life gladly, as its own reason and cause within you.

"The idea that you *must* find a man that will love you is a cover to hide this deeper refusal to accept life on life's terms. . . . You are saying, 'Unless existence meets my terms, I will not exist,' and no one has the right to so set themselves against their own innate vitality.

"Once you wholeheartedly accept life on life's terms, then you may indeed get what you are after, but not while you insist upon it as a condition for continued existence. . . . Your own purpose will make life a daily joy when you let your conditions go. You forget what you do have—health and vitality. You forget your intellect and intuitions. You forget what blessings are yours.

"You cannot pervert them by trying to force them to serve purposes that you have set up as a condition of existence. You must live in the faith that your purpose *is,* and will be fulfilled, is being fulfilled. You must live in the faith that you have such a purpose and meaning, or you would not be here.

"The uniqueness that is your own personality is to be cherished.

173

The particular purposes of your present personality can only be met in the present circumstances in the way that is best overall. The challenges can be met at another time and in another life, this is true. But the particular people that you can help now, and the particular good that you can do now, can never be done in precisely the same way. . . .

"Men and women have joyfully honored the evening and the dawn and listened to the heart pulse within them with a blessing and a joy, who have not had one hundredth of your blessings or one-third the reason to look forward to another day, and they have fulfilled themselves and brought joy to others. They accepted life on its terms, and in so accepting they were filled with a grace . . . that comes from giving life all that you have."

But exactly what is good health? In a recent class session, our "Dean" asked Seth.

"You should desire good health because it is a natural state of your being. You should trust in the innate intelligence of your own being. Health is its natural state. Through your physical image the energy of the universe expresses itself. You, as an individual, as individualized consciousness, are a part of this, and you cannot express yourself fully, nor fulfill your purpose as an identity if you are not in good health. For the effects of the body are felt in the mind, and the mind's effects are felt in the body."

"The Dean" wrinkled his brow. "You mean that if I'm in good health, I'm spiritually in good shape?"

"If you are in poor physical shape, this does not mean that you are an evil person. Let us clear that up. It means that you have a block in that particular area in which you are unable to utilize energy constructively. . . . Theoretically, if you are using energy the way you should, you would be in excellent health and filled with abundance. Various kinds of lacks can show up in many ways, however.

"I do not want you to have the attitude that health or status, for example, is automatically an indication of spiritual wealth. . . . Some of you do well in certain areas and are blocked in others. The ideal is to use all of your abilities, and in doing this you will help others and the race of which you are part automatically."

Seth suggests that self-hypnosis and light trance states be used as ways to uncover inner problems that are causing us difficulty. He also suggests that we simply ask the inner self to make the answer available on a conscious basis. If the inner problems are not discovered, we will simply exchange one set of symptoms for another. Various sessions include specific steps to be taken in these areas and others. Dreams are very important, both in uncovering problems and in providing solutions to them. In fact, I'll begin the next chapter with Seth's suggestions on the use of dreams as therapy. The instructions are simple and can be used by anyone.

CHAPTER FOURTEEN:

Dreams—A Pseudo-Demon— Therapeutic Dreaming

One night I had a frightening dream that seemed very real. I found myself in our bedroom, out of my body, and suddenly I realized that someone or something was directly above me. The next minute I was pushed down to the foot of the bed, off into the air, and then down to the dark corner of the bedroom floor. Above me was what I can only describe as a big black thing like a bloated, blurred human form, but larger and very solid.

It sounds ridiculous, but I knew that this thing was "out to get me." I knew that I was out of my body, and I was overwhelmed with astonishment, as well as very frightened. Although I'd read of people being attacked by demons or the like while they were "projecting," I just didn't believe in demons. So what was it? I didn't have time to wonder, because it bit me several times on the hand. It was amazingly oppressive, and kept up its efforts to drag me farther away from my body into the bedroom closet.

In dismay, I heard Rob snoring. In any case, I wasn't in my physical body, and he probably wouldn't know anything was wrong anyhow. And where was Seth? Where were all those "guides" who were supposed to come running to your aid when you got in predicaments like this? All these thoughts went scurrying through my mind as I tried to fight this thing off. I was very conscious of the creature's weight, which was really amazing, and its intent—which was to maul me up as much as possible, if not to kill me outright.

"Don't panic," I told myself, trying desperately to retain some semblance of calm. But the thing pressed down and was about to bite me again. This time I thought, "To hell with not panicking," and I started to yell my head off. I knew it wasn't my physical head, but I hoped that my shout would either frighten the creature away or attract some kind of help.

The thing pulled back for an instant, much like a huge startled animal, and I slipped from beneath it and shot fast as a rocket for my body, with it after me. In other words, I beat a fast cowardly retreat. I hit my body so quickly that my physical head was spinning, but no matter. My body never felt so welcome.

For a minute I was afraid to open my physical eyes. "Boy, if it's still here, I've had it," I thought. But it was gone. At least it was in another level of existence. I thought of waking Rob to tell him, but decided not to interrupt his sleep.

Now that I was safe I was more than a little ashamed of myself for being such a coward, but I wasn't so complacent that I felt like going right back to sleep, either! So I got up, drank a glass of milk, and thought of all the things I should have done—like saying grandly: "Get thou behind me, Satan," or some such. The least I could have done, I thought, was bite back.

The next night we had our regular Wednesday night Seth session. Before I tell you what Seth had to say about this incident, a little backtracking is in order. I'd been depressed for several days before the incident, brooding (though I should know better) on the negative attitudes that sometimes seem to surround us. Worse, I recognized many of them in myself: resentments, fears, and anger.

Now Seth said: "Our friend [meaning me] attempted to choose a different battlefield last night. He decided to think of all negative feelings as enemies, and to give them form in another plane of reality where he could do battle with them. This was not an astral plane, but a lower one.

"The energy behind his 'black thing' was the energy of hidden fears, but such a thing could be formed by anyone, since there are fears in any man. Ruburt tried to isolate them, give them form, and fight them all at once. The thing was actually a rather clumsy lower-dimensional animal, a provoked dumb dog of other dimensions who then attacked him, symbolically enough, by biting. Any 'thing' so created entirely of fears would be frightened and particularly angry at its creator. It could do nothing but attack to protect whatever reality it had, for it knew Ruburt created it only to slay it, if possible.

"It *did* have reality, therefore. Ruburt leapt back to safety and normal consciousness. The thing then dissipated [as far as Ruburt was concerned]. For when Ruburt 'ran home' he automatically withdrew the energy [of his attention] from it. . . . Ruburt tried to separate from himself all those elements he considers negative, and fight them at once, almost as if in so doing he could remove evil from the universe.

"He tried to destroy the 'animal of evil,' and it bit him back. Now, evil does not exist in those terms, and even illness or fear are not necessarily enemies, as much as aids to understanding and means to a greater end. . . ."

Seth went on to say: "The evil that Ruburt imagined he was projecting outward does not exist, but because he believed it did, he formed the materialization from his fears. It was the shape of his recent depression. In larger terms, there is no evil, only your own lack of perception, but I know this is difficult for you to accept.

"But this fact is Ruburt's safeguard in his out-of-body travels—as long as he remembers it. The words 'May peace be with you' will get him through any difficulty in other layers of reality—for as he formed that image, others also form images and he could encounter them. To wish them peace will give them some comfort, for they do have a kind of reality. To fear them is to put yourself into their realm of reality, and then you are forced to fight on their terms. There is no need for this."

In a sort of backhanded compliment, Seth asked Rob to tell me that my abilities were improving—it *was* a well-made thought-form. Now, I don't propose for a moment that any of my readers attempt such a foolhardy venture. But I do suggest that perhaps some of them have already done so without knowing it, waking only with the memory of a particularly bad nightmare.

This episode was an out-of-body experience from the dream state, though, and it will serve to make one point: dream reality is as valid and real as waking reality. Dreams definitely affect daily life. They can improve our health or help deepen a mood of depression. There are ways to use dreams purposefully, however, to improve our existence, even though I admit that the last instance was not a very good example.

It has been known throughout the ages that dreams can give us clues to all kinds of behavior. Psychoanalysts use dreams to delve into subconscious motivations, but few people know how to utilize dreams creatively: to improve health, gain inspiration, restore vitality, solve problems, and enrich family relationships.

Seth offers some evocative suggestions as to how dreams can be used as direct therapy, and some of his concepts could be of great aid in self-help programs and in psychotherapy.

He starts off by saying: "The personality is composed of energy gestalts. As the personality is changed by any experience, it is changed by its dreams; and as an individual is molded by his physical environment to some extent, so is he molded by the dreams which he himself creates. . . . The self is limitless. When your perceptions fail, it seems to you that boundaries appear. For example, it seems to you that dreams cease when you are no longer aware of them. This is not so.

"On one level the personality attempts to solve problems through dream constructions . . . and often gives freedom to actions that cannot be adequately expressed within the confines of waking life. If the attempt fails, then the problem or action [as we've seen before] may materialize as an illness.

"Consider, for example, a situation in which a personality needs to express dependency, but feels such expression inappropriate. If he is able to form a dream in which he plays a dependent part, then the problem may be solved within the dream state. In many instances, this is precisely what happens. The individual may never recall such a dream, but the experience would be valid and the dependency expressed.

"Much work has been done to interpret dreams, but little to control the direction of activity within them. Upon proper suggestion, this can be an excellent method of therapy. Negative dreams tend to reinforce the negative aspects of the personality, helping to form vicious circles of unfortunate complications. Dream actions *can* be turned toward fulfilling constructive expectations, which can themselves effect a change for the better.

"Many illnesses could largely be avoided through such dream therapy. Rather harmlessly, aggressive tendencies could be given freedom within the dream state. Suggestions would be given that the individual involved would experience, say, aggressiveness, within a dream. It would also be suggested to him that he learn to understand his aggressions by watching himself while he was dreaming [watching the dream as he would a play]. If I may indulge in a fantasy, theoretically you could imagine a massive experiment in dream therapy where wars were fought by sleeping, not waking, nations."

When I first read this session I thought this was a great way to get rid of your repressions—dream them away! If you're really furious at someone and don't dare retaliate, then you can give yourself the suggestion before sleep that in a dream, you'll really get even. But it isn't that easy.

Seth says quite firmly: "There are other considerations that must be understood. . . . When aggressiveness is the problem, for example, the preliminary dream suggestion should include a statement that the aggression will not be directed against a particular person. In all cases, it is the intangible element [aggressiveness, here] that is the problem, and not the person against whom the individual may want to vent it.

"We do not want an individual to suggest that he dream of harming another. There are several reasons for this, including telepathic realities that you do not yet understand, and guilt patterns which would be unavoidable. We are not talking about substituting dream action for physical action. We are discussing particular problems that need treatment."

Over and over Seth says that a dream or imaginative experience is as real as any waking event. If you have a period of depression, you are apt to have depressing dreams during the same period. But Seth suggests the following exercise as a dream therapy: before sleep, suggest to yourself that you will have a pleasant or joyful dream that will completely restore your good spirits and vitality. Unless the depression is very deep-seated, it will be broken or greatly weakened when you awaken.

I've used this method often, with excellent results. Sometimes I've remembered the dreams, sometimes not, but I've always awakened refreshed and renewed, and the effects last. The dreams I've recalled during such instances have been inspirational: strong enough not only to conquer a period of the blues but to restore me to exceptionally good spirits.

While all of this is of practical interest, Rob and I are even more intrigued by Seth's explanation of dream reality. Since I've had many out-of-body experiences from the dream state, I was rather concerned about the reality of the environments in which I found myself. Seth began his discussions on the nature of dream reality very soon after the sessions began, and they still continue. Until I learned from Seth to "monitor" my own dreams, and awaken my critical faculties, I was simply astounded by some of his statements.

Consider this early passage from session 92, which I now accept as basic: "Each dream begins with psychic energy which the individual transforms not into physical matter, but into a reality every bit as functional and real. He forms the idea into a dream object or event with amazing discrimination, so that the dream object itself gains existence and exists in numerous dimensions. . . .

"Although the dreamer creates his dreams for his own purposes, selecting only those symbols which have meaning to him, he projects them outward in a value fulfillment and psychic expansion. The expansion occurs as the dream is acted out. A contraction occurs as the dreamer is finished with the dream events, but energy cannot be taken back."

Jane Roberts *(Rich Conz)*

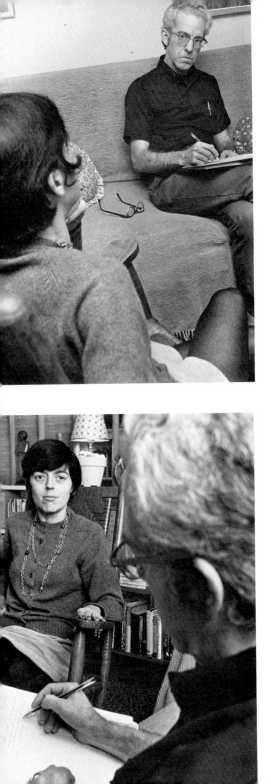

Seth sessions are held in full ligh[t] in the Butts' living room. Jane'[s] husband, Rob, using his own short[-] hand system, takes down Seth'[s] words verbatim. Above, as Jane goe[s] into trance, she—as Seth—re[-] moves her glasses and has throw[n] them onto the couch. (*Rich Con*[...])

Here and on the following pages, Jane's trance expressions and gestures change dramatically to those of Seth. *(Rich Conz)*

"Again, I am not Ruburt's subconscious, though I speak through it. It is the atmosphere through which I can come to you, as the air is the atmosphere through which a bird flies."

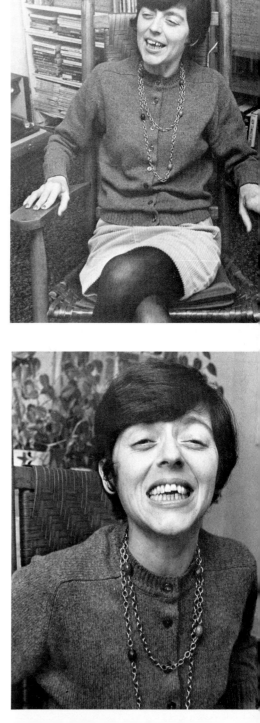

"The human being does not erupt into existence at birth and laboriously then begin its first attempt to gain experience. If this were the case, you would still be back in the Stone Age."

"Jung enlarged on some of his concepts shortly before he died. He has changed a good many of them since then."

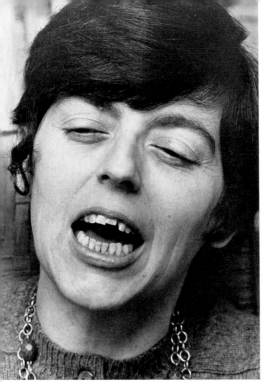

"There is never any justification fo
violence, for hatred, for murder
Those who indulge in violence fc
whatever reason are themselve
changed, and the purity of the
purpose adulterated."

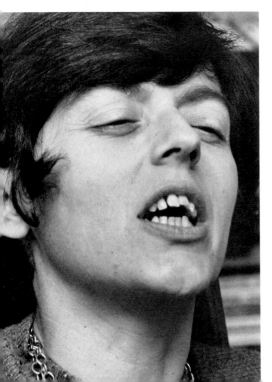

"*You will reincarnate whether or not you believe that you will. It is much easier if your theories fit reality, but if they do not, you will not change the nature of reincarnation one iota.*"

"*Karma presents the opportunity for development. It enables the individual to enlarge understanding through experience, to fill in gaps of ignorance, to do what should be done. Free will is always involved.*"

"When I tell you that you lived, for example, in 1836, I say this because it makes sense to you now. You live all of your reincarnations at once, but you find this difficult to understand."

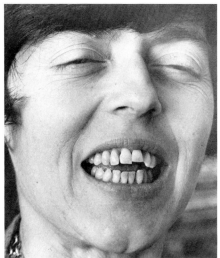

"Because I say that you create physical matter by use of the inner senses, I do not mean that you are the creators of the universe. I am saying that you are the creators of the physical world as you know it."

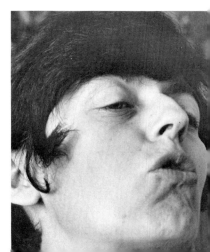

"Now, I have made my friend Ruburt sit fairly quietly for some time, so out of the goodness of my heart I will now end our session; though I may indeed drop in a word now and then."

For the envelope test in Session 300 (which is described in Chapter Eight), the target item was a scrap of paper torn from *The New York Times* of November 7, 1966. Note the words "Election Day" and the models on the major portion of the page, which Seth alluded to in giving his impressions of the fragment. (*Rich Conz*)

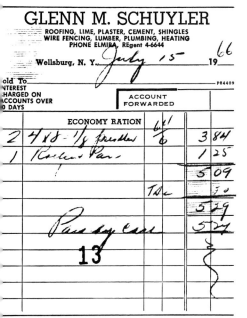

For Session 276, the test envelope contained this bill. Note the line "overhanging" the name "Glenn M. Schuyler." For details, see Chapter Eight. *(Rich Conz)*

THANK YOU

We appreciate your patronage, and if there is anything about this bill, or the goods that is not correct, please report the same to us and we will gladly make it right. This is our way of doing business and we want to have you continue as one of our customers.

GLENN M. SCHUYLER

150 CARLOAD STORAGE AT YOUR
SERVICE, AND MODERN MACHINERY
TO MANUFACTURE AND MIX
FEEDS TO YOUR ORDER

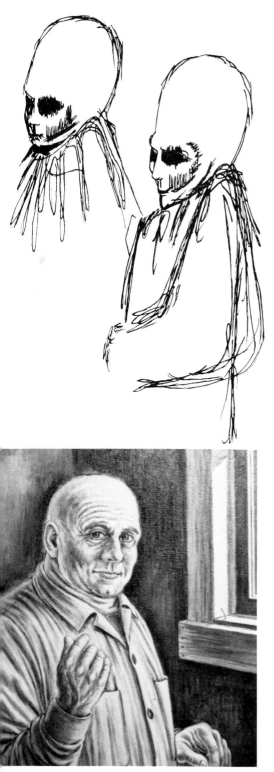

The Seth "apparition" as seen and sketched by William Cameron Macdonnel. The original drawings were done in blue ballpoint on separate sheets of paper, and here have been superimposed and traced in black to facilitate reproduction. The first drawing is in the upper left; note the obvious improvement in the later sketch.

Robert Butts' portrait of Seth. Two of Jane's students have also visualized Seth in this form. (Robert Butts)

Another of Rob's "vision" portraits, this one is of Bega, a personality who communicates through one of Jane's students via automatic writing. *(Robert Butts)*

In this painting, according to Seth, Rob depicts himself in a previous incarnation, when he was a woman and mother of five. *(Robert Butts)*

Rob's painting of the fourteenth-century artist from whom Seth gleans advice on painting techniques. *(Robert Butts)*

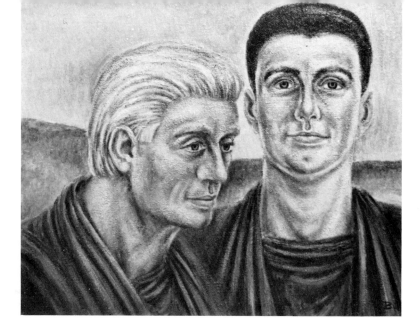

Above, Rob's double portrait of Ruburt and Joseph. This represents Jane's and Rob's Whole Selves, the sum of their reincarnational personalities. *(Robert Butts)* Below, Jane and Rob in the same pose for comparison. *(Rich Conz)*

452nd Session December 2/68 9:17 PM Monday

GOOD EVENING.

Good evening, Seth.

NOW. CHILDREN BUILD HOUSES OF CARDS AND KNOCK THEM DOWN. YOU DO NOT WORRY ABOUT THE CHILD'S DEVELOPMENT, FOR YOU REALIZE THAT HE WILL LEARN BETTER.

YOU MAY EVEN SMILE AT THE CHILD'S UTTER SENSE OF DESOLATION UNTIL HE FINALLY CONNECTS THE MOTION OF HIS OWN HAND WITH THE DESTRUCTION OF THE PAPER, CARDBOARD HOUSE THAT IS NOW GONE, AND IN HIS EYES GONE BEYOND REPAIR.

NOW, MANKIND BUILDS CIVILIZATIONS. HE HAS GONE BEYOND THE CHILD'S GAME. THE TOYS ARE REAL, AND YET BASICALLY THE ANALOGY HOLDS. I AM NOT CONDONING THOSE VIOLENCES THAT OCCUR. THE FACT IS THAT THEY CAN NEVER BE CONDONED, AND YET THEY MUST BE UNDERSTOOD FOR WHAT THEY ARE: MAN LEARNING THROUGH HIS OWN ERRORS. HE ALSO LEARNS BY HIS SUCCESSES, AND THERE ARE TIMES WHEN HE HOLDS HIS HAND, MOMENTS OF DELIBERATION, PERIODS OF CREATIVITY. (Pause.) IDENTITIES ⨉ TAKE MANY ROLES IN MANY LIVES.

THERE ARE PERIODS, CYCLES IF YOU PREFER, THROUGH WHICH SUCH IDENTITIES LIVE AND LEARN WITHIN YOUR SYSTEM. TO SOME EXTENT THEY ARE TAUGHT BY OTHERS, PRACTICE TEACHERS IF YOU PREFER. (Amused.)

(Today the newspaper carried the story of the violence attending the Democratic presidential convention in Chicago in 68, telling of the many clashes between police and various groups of demonstrators; and a guilty verdict re police behavior was rendered by an investigative commission. Jane and I had discussed the report at the supper table.)

THE RACE OF MAN IS FAR MORE THAN THE PHYSICAL RACE HOWEVER.

Page 4646 of the Seth Material, showing the start of Session 452. The full text of this session begins on the second page of the Appendix.

Jane Roberts with some of the fifty looseleaf notebooks of Seth Material that have been filled to date. (*Rich Conz*)

Seth calls dream-created personalities (such as my "black thing"), dual-hybrid constructions. In my case, the "expansion" he's speaking of occurred as I formed it with my own psychic energy. The "contraction" took place as I withdrew the main energy of my attention from it; but I could not take back the energy that I had given it that resulted in its existence. The creature continued to exist, but not in my dimension; it was set free on its own.

Still speaking of dreams, Seth says: *"Energy projected into any kind of construction,* psychic or physical, cannot be recalled, but must follow the laws of the particular form into which it has been for the moment molded. Therefore, when the dreamer contracts his multi-realistic objects backward, ending for himself the dream he has con-structed, he ends it for himself only. The reality of the dream continues."

The energy, as Seth explains it, can be transformed, but not annihilated.

Seth has answered many questions that were in Rob's mind, and are probably in your own. How is it that ordinary daily life seems much more real to us than any dream existence? And if such a uni-verse is valid, why doesn't it intrude on our daily life even more? At least we all more or less agree on what happens physically, but dreams are highly individual. How can there be any continuity to a dream universe? Within such a universe, how could anyone possibly agree with anyone else as to what was happening?

"First of all," Seth said, "the physical universe itself is a con-glomeration of diverse individualistic symbols, none of which means precisely the same thing to any two individuals, and in which even so-called basic qualities like color and placement in space cannot be relied upon. You merely focus upon the similarities. Telepathy could be called the glue that holds the physical universe in precarious position, so that you can agree on the existence and properties of objects. . . .

"So when you consider the dream world, you have the same sort of universe, only one constructed within a field that you cannot physi-cally perceive. But it has more continuity than the world you know, and there are similarities within it that are amazing to behold. . . .

"For one thing . . . those who know existence on the physical level now, have, because of certain cycles, lived before at approximately the same historical periods. They possess an inner familiarity, a cohesiveness that belonged to a more or less specific period and to periods before, where they inhabited the same sort of reality. Their dream experiences, then, are not so diverse as you might suppose. Certain symbols are constructed into realities in the dream system, then, in much the same manner that ideas are constructed into matter in the physical system.

"The same sort of psychic agreement holds the dream system together as holds the physical system together. If a man could actually focus upon those unrecognized elements in the physical universe upon which no agreements can be reached, if he could focus upon the dissimilarities rather than the similarities, then he would wonder what gave anyone the idea that there was even *one* physical object upon which man could agree.

"He would wonder what collective madness permitted man to select from a virtual infinity of chaos a mere handful of similarities and make of it a universe. So do you, viewing the seeming chaos of dream reality, wonder how I can say that it contains cohesiveness, actuality, and comparative permanence."

One reason, I think, that dreams seem so chaotic and meaningless at times is simply that we only remember dim fragments of them and forget the unifying factors. Another reason is that dreams have an intuitive, associative "logic" that has to be interpreted, and in which time, as we know it, has little meaning. According to Seth, some dreams are simple enough, dealing with unresolved present problems or events. Even in these, however, the dream event may also represent events from past lives.

Each dream object is actually double- or triple-decked, a symbol for other, deeper data. A dream involving reincarnational information, for example, may also serve to help us face a present-day problem by reminding us of other unused abilities inherent in our personalities. I've had two particularly vivid reincarnational dreams. One, occurring shortly after our sessions began, really frightened me because I was afraid that it might be precognitive, I dreamed that I was an old woman in a very poor hospital ward of some kind. I was dying of cancer and knew it, but wasn't a bit frightened. An old man beside me was also about to die. I told him not to worry, that I would be there to help him. Then I died, but there seemed to be no break in consciousness. I helped the old man out of his body and kept telling him that everything was all right.

We asked about the dream in the next Seth session. Seth told me that it referred to my death as a medium in Boston in the last century. He had given us some information about this life in previous sessions, and now he told me that I wouldn't again die of cancer (a mistake in tactics on his part, since he had long ago told me to give up cigarettes, and I haven't complied. He has never tried to bully me into giving up the habit, merely saying that it didn't help my overall health or development).

The other dream was even more vivid, and really enjoyable. I don't know when I've had such a great time—certainly not in waking life. On Seth's suggestion, I told myself before sleep that I would have a dream that would give me further information about my own reincarnational past. At this time I really didn't believe in reincarnation, but I said to Rob, "Well, what have I got to lose? I'll try it." Then I gave myself the suggestion several times and fell asleep.

In this dream Rob and I were both men in our late twenties and partners in the episode. I knew very well that we would "later" end up as Rob and Jane in this life, even though there was no physical resemblance. Rob, for example, was dark and swarthy, although now his skin and hair are both light. We wore long billowing trousers, bound tightly at the ankles, Turkish-style. I do not remember our names.

As the dream opened, we entered a large hall. A group of men, attired in the same costumes, sat on brightly colored pillows on the floor, roughly in a circle, with the center of the floor clear. I knew all of the men from a previous life in which I had been their leader, dying very young. These men had grown old, while I had been reborn. Now I had come back to fulfill a promise I had made to return. I was well aware that they would not recognize me in this body in which they had not known me.

I stated my case, while they listened politely. Their spokesman told

185

me that their dead leader had promised them that on his return he would perform one particular feat for which he was known to prove his identity. He asked me, then, to show by my actions that I was this personality, ready to take over his rightful position. Rob and I both smiled, having anticipated the test.

The center of the hall was vacant except for a few low tables. Rob-to-be asked that these be removed for the demonstration. This was done and the men came closer, squatting on the pillows. My partner stood behind me. I took several light bouncing footsteps that were somehow ceremonial, and then left my physical body. It slumped down to the floor, and my partner gently moved it to the side.

Then, in my astral body I went flying through the hall, which had a high-domed ceiling. Laughing at what I considered a great practical joke, I swung low above each man in turn and whisked off his turban. My partner handed me a feather—apparently he could see me clearly, and I could manipulate physical objects. Waving the feather through the air, I flew back and forth again several times so that, watching the feather, the men could follow my progress above them.

All the while my partner was laughing loudly, and I was having a tremendous time. Finally I returned to my body and stood up to the cries and shouts of recognition. The rest I hardly remember. I know women were brought to us, but, smiling, we waved them away, preferring to talk to our old comrades first. All of us had very dark skin.

Early in our sessions, Seth said that he once had a Turkish existence, but we have no information on one for us. We have all kinds of gaps to be filled in on our own past lives, however, because as long as I refused to accept reincarnation, I asked Rob not to ask for reincarnational material. Also, I became so upset when Seth gave such data that he probably thought it best to discontinue it for a while. When Seth is involved with a block of sessions on one subject, we hate to upset the continuity of the material by asking him to go into something else, and besides, we've learned that Seth eventually answers as many of our questions as possible.

The Turkish life was the only colorful past life I've had to my present knowledge. The Boston life was ordinary enough, according to what Seth said. I made no big splash as a medium, and gave sittings in order to help others and help pay the rent. I was quite undisciplined, however, and flighty—personality defects that I am trying to correct in this life. This dream, I believe, was to remind me that I had once been in a position of authority, and should not now be afraid of responsibility, or of my abilities. Seth insists that many people have dreams that give them information about past lives, but often they do not remember them simply because they do not realize the importance of dreams in general.

But what about that location, the Turkish hall? How real was it? How real are the places we seem to visit while we sleep? Here's what Seth has to say: "You think that you are conscious only when you are awake. You assume yourselves to be unconscious when you sleep. The dice are indeed loaded on the side of the waking mind. But pretend for a moment that you are looking at this situation from the other side.

"Pretend that you are in the dream state and concerned with the problem of waking consciousness and existence. From that viewpoint, the picture is entirely different, for you are indeed conscious while you sleep.

"The locations that you visit while dreaming are as real to you then as physical locations are to you now. Let us speak no more of a conscious or unconscious self. There is *one* self and it focuses its attention in various dimensions. In the waking state it focuses in physical reality. In the dream state it is focused within a different dimension.

"If you have little memory of dream locations when you are awake, you have little memory of 'physical' locations when you are in the dream state. When the physical body lies in bed, it is separated by a vast distance from the dream location in which the dreaming self may dwell. But this distance has nothing to do with space, for the dream location can exist simultaneously with the room in which the body sleeps.

"Dream locations are not superimposed upon, say, the bed and chest and chair. They exist composed of the very same atoms and molecules that in the waking state you perceive as bed and chest and chair. Objects, remember, are the results of your perception. From energy you form patterns which you then recognize as objects and use. But the objects are useless unless you are focused within the dimension for which they were specifically formed.

"In some dream states you form from these same atoms and molecules the environment in which you will operate. While dreaming you cannot find the bed or chest or chair; and awake you cannot find the dream location which was there only moments before."

This does not mean that we do not sometimes leave our bodies and travel in our dream or astral bodies to other physical locations. According to Seth we do so often, whether or not we remember. Some of my students, for example, have frequent out-of-body experiences from both the waking and the dream states, and on several such occasions we seem to have met in my living room.

Seth told us that this was possible long before I had any such experiences on my own and before I had read about them. But his ideas of the interrelationship between waking and dream reality are fascinating.

"I mentioned the Crucifixion, saying once that it was an actuality and a reality, although it did not take place in your [physical] time. It took place in the same sort of time in which a dream occurs and its reality was felt by generations. Not being a physical reality, it influenced the world of physical matter in a way that no purely physical event could.

"The Crucifixion was one of the realities that enriched both the universe of dreams and the universe of matter, and it originated in the universe of dreams. It was a main contribution of that system to your own, and could be physically compared to the emergence of a new planet within the physical universe."

Seth is *not* saying here that the Crucifixion was "just a dream." He is saying that though it did not occur *historically,* it did happen within another reality and emerged into history as an *idea* rather than a physical event—an idea that changed civilization. (According to Seth, of course, an idea *is* an event, whether physically materialized or not.)

Seth goes on to say: "The Ascension [of Christ] did not occur in time as you know it. It is also a contribution of the universe of dreams to your physical system, representing the knowledge that man is independent of physical matter. . . .

"Many concepts and practical inventions simply wait in the dream system in abeyance until some man accepts them as possibilities within the physical frame of reality. . . . Imagination is waking man's connection with the dream system. Imagination often reinstates dream data and applies it to particular circumstances or problems within daily life. . . .

"The dream universe, then, possesses concepts which will someday completely transform the history of the physical world, but a denial of such concepts as possibilities delays their emergence."

Some Seth sessions tell us precisely how we form dreams, what chemicals are built up during waking consciousness and then released in dream-making, and others deal with the electromagnetic composition of dream reality. But all through is the insistence upon what we would call, I suppose, the "objectivity" of dream life.

Seth gave us instructions first in dream recall. Following this, he told us how to awaken our critical faculties while we were dreaming, and how to project our consciousness out of our bodies, using a dream as a sort of launching pad. I was always delighted to try any experiments Seth suggested, and I still am. The resulting personal experience gave me subjective evidence of the validity of many of Seth's concepts; besides, I like to do things on my own.

Look at this projection from the dream state, for example. One morning after breakfast I lay down to try a dream projection. This simply means that I can sometimes recognize when I am dreaming, bring my normal "waking consciousness" into the dream situation, and then use it to project my consciousness elsewhere. When I got to this point that morning, I felt myself leave my body, knowing all the while that it was safe and comfortable in bed, with the door locked.

I traveled through the air so quickly that everything was a blur. Then I found myself on a strange city street. I was determined to find out where I was, so I walked around the block looking for street signs. The area was one of hotels and large shops. I saw two street names and finally decided to enter the lobby of one of the hotels.

189

Here I found a bookshop and walked over to the shelves to look around. There were three books by Jane Roberts on ESP, and at the time of the experience (1967), I'd written only one.

Startled, I looked around again. Everything seemed normal enough. Wherever I was, it was a physical place. Something made me look up. A young man was looking at me with a pleased, cat-caught-the-canary grin. He was one of the clerks, and I saw now that most of the clerks were quite young, and they were watching me.

I didn't know what to do or say. "Look, I'm really in an out-of-body state. This is an astral projection!" They'd never believe me. But what about the three books with my name on them and the clerk's knowing smile?

"Uh, I haven't seen these books before," I said.

"I should think not. Where you live, you haven't written them yet," the young man said. With this he started laughing, but in a friendly open manner, as did the others who now gathered around.

"Where am I?" I asked.

He told me and said, "But forget it. That is, you won't remember anyhow."

"Oh, yes, I will. I've trained myself."

"You just aren't that good at it yet," one of them said. And I really got angry. Whether I was astral-traveling or whatever, these people were really having a good laugh at my expense.

"Look," I said, "I'm in my astral body. My physical body is home in bed."

"We know that," the young man said.

The books caught my eye again. "Go ahead," he said, "memorize the titles. I'm sorry, but it won't do you any good. You won't remember." Now all of them smiled more sympathetically.

"I've already memorized two street names," I said. "Are you sure I'm going to write those books?"

"Here, you already have."

No matter what anyone said, I was determined to remember any specific material I could—names, street signs, or route numbers. Finally the clerk offered to take me on a tour, when I told him I was going to explore the place alone in any case. He was very nice. We chatted and he pointed out places of interest in the city even while he warned me that I wouldn't be able to remember them.

Then, without any warning, I felt myself pulled away. There was a terrific whooshing sound and I was back in my body. I really felt tricked. Usually its quite difficult to go right back to the same location, but I was so angry that I willed myself back. Not that it did me much good. I "landed" on the same corner, but the young man was nowhere to be found. Then I set out to find the hotel, and while I swear I walked the block three times and recognized the other buildings, I just couldn't find the hotel. Finally I returned to my body.

Naturally we asked Seth about the experience. He was giving us general information about the conditions we could expect to meet in projections from the dream state.

"There is form within dream reality," he said, "but form is first of all potential existing within psychic energy. The potential form exists long before its physical materialization. The house that you may live in within five years may not yet exist in your terms. It may not have been built yet, therefore physically you would not perceive it. Still, such a house does have form, and does exist within the Spacious Present.

"Now in certain levels of dream reality, forms such as this can be perceived. Within dream reality you can come into contact with many other kinds of phenomena with which usually you do not have to deal. With the projection experiments you have in mind, this information becomes highly practical. I would like to give you some idea, you see, of what to expect.

"When you are manipulating within physical reality, you have a fairly simple set of rules to serve you. Within dream reality there is greater freedom. The ego is not present. The waking consciousness, dear friends, is not the ego. The ego is only that portion of waking consciousness that deals with physical manipulation.

"Waking consciousness *can* be taken into the dream state; the ego cannot, as it would falter and cause immediate failure. In your experiments you will meet with various conditions, and until you learn control it may be difficult to distinguish between them. Some you can manipulate, some you cannot. Some dream locations will be of your own making, and others will be strange to you. They will belong to other dimensions of reality, but you may blunder into them.

"It is quite possible for a dreamer to visit other planetary systems, of the past, present, or future in your terms. Such visits are usually fragmentary and spontaneous. It is best that they remain so. Take advantage of them when they occur, but do not attempt such endeavors yet, however, as many difficulties are involved."

Whole blocks of sessions deal with the methods used and the conditions that can be met in projections of consciousness from the dream state. Seth says that he has personally assisted me in some of my own projection experiments, but that I have not been aware of his assistance. I've never dreamed of Seth, and I find this rather strange. I've often awakened, fully alert, in the middle of the night, suddenly conscious that I've been giving a kind of Seth session. I can hear Seth's words going through my head like signals. It's as if I'm tuning in on a radio broadcast that I'm not supposed to be hearing, because when I start to listen there is a clicking sound in my head, and the "station" turns off. On two occasions I heard enough to know what was being said and to whom the sessions were directed. Later the people involved told me that they dreamed that Seth was speaking to them through me on the same nights as my experiences. I had said nothing to them; they volunteered the information.

According to Seth, we do have shared dreams or mass dreams. These actually act as a stabilizing force in our daily lives. Are our dreams private? Apparently not nearly as private as we suppose. In the 254th session Seth had this to say: "In certain areas of mass, shared dreams, collective mankind deals with problems of his political and social structure. The solutions he reaches within dream reality are not always the same as those he accepts in the physical world.

"The dream solutions are held as ideals, however. Without mass dreams, for example, your United Nations would not exist. . . . At this stage of your development it is necessary that selectivity be used. If you were aware of the constant barrage of telepathic communications that do impinge upon you, it would be most difficult for you now to retain a sense of identity. Shared dreams, then, are also usually well beneath awareness. . . . As identity is strengthened through experience, it automatically expands itself to add further realities within which it can manipulate.

"When you dream of others, they know it. When they dream of you, you know it. There would be nothing to be gained, however, in conscious awareness of these conditions at this time."

In this session Seth also mentioned John F. Kennedy, and had some comments to make connecting racial problems with dreams. "As you know, many people dreamed of Jack Kennedy's death in advance. On one level the knowledge was available to the man himself. This does not mean that the death *had* to occur. It was a vivid possibility. It was also one of many solutions to several problems. While it was not the most suitable solution, it was the closest man could come at that particular time in physical reality. . . ."

Seth went on to say that the emotional intensity of a dream is very seldom recalled in its full strength. Then, briefly, he mentioned mass dreams as a way of bringing about historical change.

Those who are concerned about the present racial situation "dream individually and collectively of changing it. They act out in their dreams the various ways in which changeabouts could occur. *These dreams actually help bring about the resulting change that will then happen.* The very energy and direction of the dreams will help change the situation."

I could write several books dealing with dreams alone, as Seth explains them. According to the Seth Material, our psychic development and growth, learning processes and experience, are all involved with our dream life. In it we visit other levels of existence, and even gain needed skills. There are definite electromagnetic and chemical connections that unite our stages of consciousness at such times, and he goes into detail about them.

Through our dreams we change physical reality, and our physical daily experience alters our dream experience. There is constant interaction. Our consciousness is simply directed in a different kind of reality when we dream, a reality as vivid as waking life. We may forget our dreams, but they are always a part of us, even though we may not be aware of their entire reality.

According to Seth there are many other systems of reality in which we operate, all unknown to the waking ego. Not only are there universal systems composed of matter and antimatter, but there are an infinite variety of realities in between. Apparently there are also "probable realities," in which we follow paths we may have taken, but did not, in physical life.

Seth says: "The dream experience is felt directly by the inner self. Dreams have an electric actuality, as I told you. In this [electric actuality] they not only exist independently of the dreamer, but they have what you might call tangible form, though not in the form of matter as you are familiar with it."

Seth told us many times that all experience is electrically coded within our cells but not dependent upon them. And this also applies to dream experience. He goes on to say: "A man's thoughts and dreams are far more reaching than he knows. They exist in more dimensions; they affect worlds of which he is unaware. They are as concrete, in effect, as any building. They appear in many guises within many systems, and once created cannot be withdrawn. . . .

"The electric reality of a dream is decoded, so that its effects are experienced not only by the brain, but in the furthest reaches of the body. Dream experiences, long forgotten consciously, are forever contained as electrically coded data within the cells of the physical organism. . . . They exist within the cells [along with all an individual's experience] . . . The cells form about them. These electrically coded signals form counterparts of complete experience, and the pattern is then independent of physical reality."

In other words, our dreams attain a certain immortality of their own, along with our personalities. Seth makes this clear: "Each individual from birth forms his own counterpart from built-up, individual, continuous electrical signals that include his dreams, thoughts, desires, and experiences. At physical death his personality then exists detached from its physical form."

CHAPTER FIFTEEN:

Probable Selves
and
Probable Systems of Reality

————◆•◆————

In June of 1969 we were really startled when Seth told us that Rob might be visited by one of his "probable selves." At the time of the session, we didn't know what probable selves were, though Seth had used the term once or twice in the past. What *is* a probable self? According to Seth, each of us has counterparts in other systems of reality; not identical selves or twins, but other selves who are part of our entity, developing abilities in a different way than we are here.

These probable personalities are further removed from us than our reincarnational selves, more like distant relations who bear a family resemblance. According to the information we have so far, some of them have methods of perception different from ours.

In our system, for example, Rob is an artist. A few years ago he did some medical artwork and was amazed at his proficiency at it, and with the medical procedures and terminology, which were quite unfamiliar to him when he began. Each of Rob's sketches and paintings won prizes for the doctors for whom he did them. In this session, the 487th, Seth told Rob that in another system of reality, Rob has a probable self who is a doctor who paints as a hobby. This is why Rob took to the medical drawings so easily! (To the doctor, of course, Rob is a probable self.)

Seth told us quite a bit about this "man" that night, and described some of the methods he was using in an attempt to contact this reality. Seth said: "There are, in fact, infinite varieties of matter, existing in what *you* would call one space framework. Using the physical senses, of course, you can never perceive these other systems. Advanced training in the use of the Inner Senses can lead to such explorations, however. Your friend [probable self] is more advanced—his system is more advanced in this respect.

"In the same way that thoughts can be sent through space, so individual consciousness can be sent through systems of reality [other dimensions]. As a seed can fly through the air, so individual consciousness can travel through these systems, but it must be protected. Certain drugs can protect it. [All of this is the method used by Rob's probable self as he projects out of his probable system.]

"Now these drugs are like time capsules, cutting down stimuli for certain intervals, and then injecting stimulants as destination points are reached. The process is highly involved. The injections are made into the physical being, affecting the brain. Consciousness projects in an out-of-body experience. The physical brain is cushioned against shock, since in this case consciousness travels at such a fast pace that ordinarily contact between it and the body would be severed.

"Certain injections then given to the brain actually help consciousness outside of the brain and act as nourishment. This is simply one method that is being used, however. The drug allows for regulated periods of highly intensified consciousness, operating at peak levels, with all the mental faculties accelerated. Between these periods, however, there are periods of unconsciousness. These are of a protective nature.

"During the unconscious periods the drugs injected into the physical brain give increased nourishment to those areas of the brain involved in these ejections of consciousness. Therefore, even though your probable self is within reaching distance, so to speak, he is sometimes in these blackout-nourishment periods.

196

"In your time, the periods of high conscious activity would run approximately three days, followed by a day and a half to four days of inactivity, according to the circumstances. This involves the transfer of conscious energy from a home system to an alien one, and certain more or less automatic changes must be made from system to system, involving the use of brain waves, certain patterns being normal in different systems.

"There are other brain patterns, for example, than those discovered by your scientists. The drugs help in changing these patterns when it is necessary. If these brain patterns were not changed on entering and leaving a system, theoretically at least, the consciousness could become trapped within any given system: acceleration or deacceleration, you see, but mentally."

After the session, when Rob told me what Seth had been saying, we just sat looking at each other for a few minutes. *"Probably* you have a probable self," I said finally, with a laugh.

"It's not really a new idea," Rob said. "Scientists have theorized about a probable universe."

"But Seth's talking about an infinity of them, from what you tell me," I said. "And it's one thing to theorize about probable selves, and another to think that one of them might be going to contact you."

"I'm ready," Rob said; and he was. Over the next few weeks he did psychological time exercises suggested by Seth, and tried to be intuitively alert to anything out of the ordinary. In the meantime we had another session, and Rob had quite a few questions ready to ask Seth. According to what Seth told us, this probable self is a Dr. Pietra. He is an older man in his system of reality than Rob is in ours, and while he is engrossed in his painting, this interest is subordinated to his medical work.

"He is studying the use of painting in therapy," Seth said. "Not only working with patients and using art as therapy, but working with the idea that some paintings *in themselves* have a healing effect." Seth went on to say that "certain paintings can capture and direct the healing abilities of the viewer. . . . The painter's intent is embedded in his medium and in his painting."

"Does Dr. Pietra know I exist?" Rob asked.

197

"He knows of your hypothetical existence," Seth said. "He believes that he has a probable self, and he is endeavoring to visit this probable universe. He has no idea, however, that you might be expecting such a visit, or that you might be planning to meet him. . . . He has been working on the drug himself, along with two others.

"He will be able to manipulate in his own system while he is gone. Your state of mind and receptivity will be communicated to him and serve as a beckoning area that he will recognize. The sympathetic aspects of your personalities will serve to open clear channels between you. The passageway, you see, is not physical, of course, and yet molecular structure is to some extent involved."

"But will I see him physically?" Rob asked. "Granted we do make some kind of contact, will I know it consciously?"

"You should see him visually—either entirely objectified or in an unusually vivid inner image. But more than this, there should be an inner communication between you of a telepathic nature. He is also visually oriented, you understand. He may be able to show you images from his own system of reality. He may be able to take you there in a projection, and from that point you should be able to look into your own system, and in a series of flashes see your life and Ruburt's with greater clarity."

"But when will he be here in our terms?" Rob asked quickly, because it was almost time for the session to end.

"I believe that within seven hours he will be within your system, whether or not you perceive him. The drug may have the effect of coloring his image, so do not be surprised at a yellow or purplish tinge. For various reasons we cannot discuss this evening, the experiments are now being conducted over a period of some weeks, and they will not be tried again until your autumn. This has to do with the conductivity of cell structures, and your particular atmosphere during these periods."

This session was held June 9, 1969. Seth told Rob again that contact could be facilitated by the Psychological Time exercises. (These will be explained in the chapter dealing with the development of psychic abilities.) Rob did these exercises several times that week without making any contact with Dr. Pietra as far as he knew. On June 16 Seth surprised us by saying that near contact had been made twice.

"What happened was a very momentary merging of personality characteristics on deeper than conscious levels," Seth said. "Neither of you knew how to handle it. You were afraid of blurring your own identities, and rather frightened by some of the similarities within them. It was the similarities, however, that made even that [small] contact possible."

"When did this happen?" Rob asked.

"At a time when your thoughts veered off on a tangent. I believe you had a mental image of the inside portion of a human body, or a thought having to do with inner organs. This occurred as you picked up, on deeper levels, the presence of Dr. Pietra."

Rob *had* been working on portraits and human figures, so this data made sense to him. He didn't recall any strong inner image of the interior of a body, though; yet he said that he had been thinking of body interiors—something that I didn't know. Seth went on to say that fuller contact was still possible, "though Dr. Pietra's focus is not certain, and the intensity of his presence varies."

Seth also had a little more to say concerning the drugs that Pietra uses in his experiments. Apparently they insure that consciousness will not return to the physical brain too quickly. He also said that there were methods "by which the relative behavior and condition of the traveling consciousness is monitored at the other end. In case of any severe dangers, the consciousness is pulled back, but this is highly dangerous."

In case anyone is uncertain, this probable system of reality is as "real" as ours, according to Seth. To its inhabitants, it is composed of physical matter, and it is just one of an infinite number of systems or universes between matter and antimatter. The people in Pietra's system have hypothesized the existence of other probable universes, and Pietra is one of the first explorers, mostly because of his excellent medical background.

Such travel between probable systems is done through projection of consciousness out of the body, as was explained in the excerpts, but this seems to involve a welding of medicine, physics, and other disciplines. In other statements in the past, Seth told us that any far-ranging space travel within our own system would also involve mental rather than physical journeys.

If, as Seth maintains, we have probable selves and if, besides all this, we live various existences on this planet, what happens to the concept of a single soul?

Here I want to include excerpts from three sessions in which Seth explains the difference between a physical event and a probable one, and the relationship between us and probable systems of reality. (Remember, Rob and Dr. Pietra are each individuals. Seth explains this relationship by saying that the two are related, like distant cousins.) He begins with what I think is an excellent description of the whole self or entire identity as it is related to this and other existences.

From Session 231: The Self and Probable Realities

"Action is action whether or not you perceive it, and probable events are events whether or not you perceive them. Thoughts are also events, as are wishes and desires. The human system responds as fully to these as it does to physical events. In dreams, often portions of probable events are experienced in a semiconscious manner. This amounts to a bleed-through, and I use the term purposely, for your tape recorder can be used as an analogy.

"Imagine the whole self as composed of some master tape. Your recorder has four channels. We will give our recorder numberless channels. Each one represents a portion of the whole self, each existing in a different dimension, yet all a part of the whole self [or tape]. You see it would be ridiculous to say that Mono One on your tape was any more or less valid than Mono Two. Mono One could be compared to your present ego.

"We will now imagine these selves multiplied, for you have selves three, four, five, and six, and so forth. Now on your recorder you have a setting for stereo. This enables you to mix and combine harmoniously the elements of the various channels—simultaneously.

I am taking my time here so you get this clearly, because I do not often come through with the pure clarity of stereophonic.

"Your stereophonic setting can be compared to what we have termed the inner ego. Each of the selves experiences time in its own manner according to the nature of its perceptions. When the stereophonic channel is turned on, the selves then know their unity. Their various realities merge in the overall perceptions of the whole self.

"Until the whole self is thus able to perceive its own parts simultaneously, then these seemingly separate portions appear to themselves isolated and alone. There is communication between them, but they are not aware of it. The tape is the element common to all channels. Now the inner ego is the director, but the whole self (or soul) must know itself. It is not enough that the inner ego knows what is going on. Ultimately the inner ego must bring about comprehension on the parts of the simultaneous selves.

"Each portion of the whole self must become aware of the other parts. We are not dealing with anything as simple as a recorder, of course, for our tapes [selves] are constantly changing. . . ."

The Difference between Probable Events and Physical Events

"Take, for example, Event X. This probable event will be experienced by the various portions of the self in their own way. When it is experienced by your ego, it is a physical event. When it is perceived by other portions of the self, the ego does not know of it.

"It is actual all the same and is experienced in variation. The whole self perceives and is affected by probabilities, then, and perceives these as actions whether or not the ego has chosen to accept any given event as physical. The time sequence also varies. Past, present, and future are realities only to your ego.

"Now the inner ego, as you know, exists in the Spacious Present. The Spacious Present is the basic 'time' in which the whole self exists, but *the various portions of the self have their experiences in their own time systems.*

"It should be obvious that the psychological frameworks must be different when the time-experience is different. You can see for yourself the psychological variations that exist simply between the conscious and subconscious, for example. . . .

"The ego maintains much of its stability by looking backward into a 'past' and finding something of itself there. The portions of the self that deal in probabilities do not have experience with a 'past' to give them a sense of identity or continuity. Permanence, as the ego thinks of it, would be an alien concept to these portions of the self, and highly distasteful, adding up to rigidity.

"Flexibility is the key word here, a voluntary changing of the self as it is allowed to explore each probability. Experience is of a plastic nature. The basic sense of identity here is carried by what you could compare to the subconscious that you know. In other words, it is this portion of the psychological structure that carries the burden of identity, and it is the ego whose experiences are of a dreamlike nature."

From Session 232

"This system of probabilities is quite as real as the physical system, and you exist in it whether or not you realize it. You simply are not focused within it. You may become aware of it [or of one of your probable selves] while in the dream state occasionally. I have told you that dream images have a definite reality. So do probable events. They simply do not appear concrete to you.

"You may dream of holding an apple, for example, and awaken to find it gone. This does not mean that it did not exist, but in the waking state you do not perceive it. In the same way you do not perceive the actuality of probable events on a conscious basis. A portion of your whole self is quite involved in these probable events, however. The 'I' of your dreams can be legitimately compared to the self that experiences probable events. [That 'I' would consider itself fully conscious and view the waking 'I' as the probable self.]

"Let us consider the following. An individual finds himself with a choice of three actions. He chooses one and experiences it. The other two actions are experienced also, by the inner ego, but not in physical reality. . . . The results are then checked by the inner ego as an aid in other decision-making. The probable actions were definitely experienced, however, and such experience makes up the existence of the 'probable selves' just as dream actions make up the experience of the dreaming self. . . . There is a constant subconscious interchange of information between all layers of the whole self."

From Session 227

"The package of experience upon which you can focus is indeed composed of many small packages, but the whole package of reality is much larger than this. A portion of the self can and does experience events in an entirely different fashion [than the ego does] and this portion goes off on a different tangent. For when your conscious self perceives Event X, this other part of the self branches off, so to speak, into all the other probable events that could have been experienced by the ego.

"The ego must choose one event because of its limitations. But this other portion of the self can and does delve into what you could call Event X1, X2, X3, et cetera. It can pursue and experience all of these alternative events in the same amount of physical time that it takes for the ego to experience Event X alone.

"This is not as farfetched as it might seem. The shaking of a hand may be perceived by you as a simple action. You are not aware of the million small acts which make up this seemingly insignificant action. They exist nevertheless. It does not take you time to perceive them one by one. You perceive them in their completed fashion. Now this portion of the self experiences these probable events consciously, with as much rapidity as you subconsciously perceive the million small actions that make up the handshake."

From Session 227: Personality and Probabilities

"These portions of the self simply operate in a different dimension of reality, with different fields of activity. In this particular instance, compare the various portions of the whole self to the various members of a family: The man may work in the city. The woman may

203

work at their home in the country. Of three children, each may attend a different school. They are all members of the same family unit and operate out of the same house. There is no basic reason why any of the children could not spend his days at his father's office, but he would not be able to understand the events or activities there.

"I am trying to make the analogy clearer. The child would fit physically into the office building, you see. Physically speaking, there would be no barrier to keep him out, while admitting the father. The man could also enter the school, but there would be little purpose in such an arrangement.

"There is within the family a general realization of the experiences of its members, but these are secondhand except for those events shared by the family as a whole, as a unit. There is also a generalized intuitional knowledge on the part of any portion of the self as to the experiences of the other portions.

"Some events will be perceived by all layers of the self, however, though in their own fashion, and experienced as a unit. There are few of these but they are very vivid and they serve—as do the family's joint experiences—to reinforce the identity of the entire psychological structure.

"Again: probable events are as real as that one event chosen from them to be a physical experience. Take our Event X again. It is only one of numberless probable events. For its purposes, however, the conscious ego chooses Event X. But until this ego experiences the event, it is only one of all the other probable events, different in no way. It becomes actual in your reality only when it is experienced by the physical self. . . .

"These other probable events become just as 'real' within other dimensions. As a sideline, there are some interesting episodes when a severe psychological shock or deep sense of futility causes a short circuit so that one portion of the self begins to experience one of its other probable realities. I am thinking in particular of some cases of amnesia where the victim ends up suddenly in a different town with another name, occupation, and no memory of his own past. In some instances such an individual is experiencing a probable event, but he must experience it, you see, within his own time system."

Seth has given us more material than this, of course, on probable universes and events. He also discusses probabilities in connection with precognition and time. We haven't been able to make any conscious contact with Dr. Pietra. As I write this now, we are approaching the autumn months when Seth said contact would again be possible.

The thought of such contact is highly intriguing, and we cannot help but wonder what effect it would have, not only on Rob and Dr. Pietra, but on their separate systems of reality. Only Seth's assurances that contact is possible under certain conditions leads us to even consider it; the chances against such contact seem so high. We both feel that we need much more information and hard work, and look forward to further experiments along these lines through the years.

As you can see, many of the excerpts given in this chapter also throw light on the nature of personality. Because personality *is* multidimensional, it cannot be discussed under one heading alone, and in explaining it, Seth uses a method that is almost multidimensional itself. Not only what is said, but also what happens in sessions is important in this context. Soon I will describe a fairly recent and very significant development that demonstrates, far better than words, perhaps, the multidimensional aspects of personality.

Who or what are you? Do you feel lost in the face of all these ideas of entities and probable selves? Where do *you* fit in, as you know yourself? In the next chapter, devoted to Seth's ideas on personality, you will see that your identity as you know it is always retained.

CHAPTER
SIXTEEN:

The Multidimensional Personality

＊

Not too long ago, a young psychology professor called and asked me to speak to his class at the local college. It was a small group of about fifteen students, so I suggested that they come to my apartment instead. The man's attitude was apparent the minute he came in the door. Personally he wouldn't touch a medium with a ten-foot pole, but since they did exist and he knew of one, he felt duty-bound to "expose" his students to the phenomenon. And undoubtedly, he patted himself on the back for his broad-mindedness.

For two and a half hours I spoke on the potentials of human personality, and the necessity of recognizing, developing, and using them. To the best of my ability, I explained what telepathy, clairvoyance, and precognition were, and what experiments might be conducted to show them in operation. Finally I suggested an exercise to be done by the students, such as we sometimes use in my own classes. A target sketch was to be tacked on the inside of my door each day. The girls would try to "pick up" an impression of the target drawing and reproduce it. I would mail my drawings to the professor at the end of the allotted time, and he could judge the hits and misses for himself.

Carefully—I thought!—I explained that suggestion was very important, and asked the professor to have an objective attitude during the tests. But, as I later discovered through one of his students, his attitude was anything but objective and hardly scientific. He let the class know through his statements and general behavior that he thought such tests were beneath serious consideration. Oddly enough, the results weren't bad at all, but his attitude was so poor that only five girls took part in the experiment. I suggested that he try the experiment too, but he wouldn't; and his attitude discouraged enough students so that he could say, later, that the low number participating made tests results impossible to evaluate. He dismissed all of the hits made as coincidence.

The professor was intelligent, personable, earnest. Had we met under different circumstances, I probably would have liked him. But he didn't want to reconsider or evaluate his preconceived ideas of the nature of personality. He missed an opportunity to broaden his outlook, and, perhaps, to find the kind of evidence that would convince him that human personality was far less limited than he supposed.

This episode and a few similar ones have made me wary of such encounters with so-called objective academicians. But all psychologists aren't so narrow-minded and intellectually rigid. Last year one of my students was taking a psychology course in the local college night sessions, and with the professor's encouragement, she frequently discussed Seth and our ESP classes. My student wanted to do one of her required papers on the nature of personality as explained by Seth. She asked Seth if he would give a special session for this purpose. She wanted to record it and play it for the college class.

Seth agreed, and devoted one entire class to the session. He had some interesting things to say about his own reality, too. In a way, it is not the kind of in-depth discussion Seth would give in one of our private sessions, but it contains an excellent thumbnail description of his theories on personality, for those who have no previous knowledge of the Seth Material. For that reason, I'll use excerpts from it to open this chapter.

There were about ten of my regular students at the session. Seth was at his best: smiling, often breaking up serious material with a few light jokes or comments. Most of the time he spoke directly to the student who requested the session, or addressed the sixty members of her psychology class, who were not present. The whole session ran about six single-typed pages.

Seth began by saying: "Identity is not the same as personality. Personality represents only those aspects of identity that you are able to actualize within three-dimensional existence. . . . Personality may be molded by circumstances, in your terms, but identity *uses* the experiences and is not swept willy-nilly.

"It is true that there are no limitations to the self, and in one respect you can say that the self reaches out to encompass the environment. Current theories regarding the nature of personality do not take into consideration the existence of telepathy or clairvoyance or the fact of reincarnation. What you have, in effect, is a one-dimensional psychology. Identity operates in many dimensions, how-ever. . . ."

Then Seth addressed the members of the college class for whom the recording would be played. We all thought, later, that this session was hilarious in one way—a personality invisible in our terms, addressing an absent psychology class on the nature of personality! Yet Seth certainly knew what he was doing, for he used his own unorthodox method of communication as a case in point.

"You have here [in the session itself] a provocative demonstration of the nature of personality," he said. "For my personality is not Ruburt's, nor is his mine. I am not a secondary personality, for instance. I make no attempt to dominate Ruburt's life, nor indeed would I expect him to allow it. I do not represent any repressed portions of Ruburt's own being. As those here know, he is hardly the repressed type on his own!

"I have helped him, in that his own personality operates more effectively. He is able to use his own abilities more fully. But that is hardly a psychological crime. The facts are, dear psychology class and professor, that all of you are more than you know. Each of you exists in other realities and other dimensions, and the self that you call yourself is but a small portion of your entire identity.

"Now, in dreams you do have contact with other parts of yourself. This communication goes on constantly, but your ego is so focused upon physical reality and survival within it that you do not hear the inner voice. You must realize that what you are cannot be seen in a mirror. What you see in a mirror is but a dim reflection of your true reality.

"You do not see your ego in the mirror. You do not see your subconscious. You do not see the inner self in a mirror. These are but terms to express the part of you that cannot be seen or touched. But within the selves that you know is the prime identity, the whole inner self. This whole self has lived many lives. It has adopted many personalities. It is an energy essence personality, even as I am. The only difference is that I am not materialized within physical matter. You do not suddenly acquire a 'spirit' at death. You are one, now."

Then, smiling, Seth went further into the question of his own existence—and mine. He began by stating that he had always cautioned me to maintain a good balance between solitude and activity. Then he spoke to the professor of the psychology class:

"You may, if you wish, call me a subconscious production. I do not particularly enjoy such a designation, since it is not true. But if you do call me a subconscious extension of Ruburt's own personality, then you must agree that the subconscious is telepathic and clairvoyant, since I have shown telepathic and clairvoyant abilities. So, may I remind you, has Ruburt on his own. . . . However, unless you are willing to assign to the subconscious those abilities—and most of your colleagues do not—then I cannot be considered to have such a subconscious origin.

"If you *are* willing to concede the point, then I have other arguments. My memories are not the memories of a young woman. My mind is not a young woman's mind. I have been used to many occupations, and Ruburt has no memory of them. I am not a father image of Ruburt's, nor am I the male figure that lurks in the back of the female mind. Nor does our friend Ruburt have homosexual tendencies. I am simply an energy essence personality, no longer materialized in physical form.

"Personality and identity are not dependent upon physical form It

210

is only because you think they are that you find this sort of performance so strange. . . . You adopt a body as a space traveler wears a space suit, and for much the same reason."

The psychology class was as much interested in Seth's reality as in the nature of personality, as he well knew. Smiling, Seth said, "One other point: These sessions are scheduled, and therefore operate under certain controlled conditions. Ruburt's own personality is in no way threatened by them, and his ego has been carefully coddled and protected. It has not been shunted aside. Instead it has been taught new abilities. . . . I was not artificially 'brought to birth' through hypnosis. There was no artificial tampering of personality characteristics here. There was no hysteria. Ruburt allows me to use the nervous system under highly controlled conditions. I am not given a blanket permission to take over when I please, nor would I desire such an arrangement. I have other things to do."

As far as I can see, Seth's reference to hypnosis had to do with the "training" undergone by some mediums in which hypnosis is used to initiate and stabilize the trance state, and occasionally to call forth the communications of "control" personalities. This didn't happen in my case. The whole thing was spontaneous. Although I know how to use self-hypnosis now, having studied it in the past several years, I've never used it for a session.

Seth ended this discussion by outlining various ways to develop awareness of the inner self. This material will be given in a later chapter. My student played the tape during her next college class, and since it ran longer than the allotted time, the psychology professor and some of the students went to her house later to hear the whole tape and discuss it.

Seth's personality, of course, comes through on tape better than on the printed page, because his inflections and connotations are obvious. Also, we recorded a few moments of conversation, so that my normal voice could be compared with Seth's. Even the most lecturelike private session is always enlivened by Seth's gestures, and this is more marked when he is relating to a group.

Granted we survive death, what part of us survives? As Seth gave us more material on reincarnation and the inner self, we naturally wondered. Having a whole self may be great, but if my Jane Roberts self is engulfed by it after death, then to me that's not much of a survival. It's like saying that the little fish survives when it's eaten by a bigger one because it becomes part of it.

But according to Seth, no individuality is ever lost. It is always in existence. The tricky point here is that the self has no boundaries except those it accepts out of ignorance. Our individual consciousness grows, and out of its experience it forms different "personalities" or fragments of itself. These fragments—Jane Roberts is one of them—are entirely independent as to action and decision, yet the inner psychic components are constantly in communication with the whole self of which they are part. These "fragments" themselves grow, develop, and may form their own entities or "personality gestalts"—or, if you prefer, whole souls.

Seth says that even in this life, each of us has various egos; we only accept the idea of one ego as a sort of shorthand symbolism. The ego at any given time in this life is simply the part of us that "surfaces"; a group of characteristics that the inner self uses to solve various problems. Even the ego as we think of it changes constantly. For example, the Jane Roberts of now is different from the Jane Roberts of ten years ago, though "I" have not been conscious of any particular change of identity.

My own experiences convince me that I am more than my normal self, the self I refer to as "me." In getting clairvoyant information, for instance, some part of me knows what the Jane-part ordinarily does not. This portion of me communicates the knowledge to the Jane ego. I believe that this happens not only in the case of ESP, but also in connection with artistic inspiration: we tune into more knowledgeable portion of our own identities.

Of course, these abilities don't mean much unless you learn to use them and experience them for yourself. Early in our sessions Seth described what he calls the Inner Senses—inner methods of perception that expand normal consciousness and allow us to become aware of our own multidimensional existence. It was some time before we fully understood what these meant, and how we could use them, and we are still learning to use them more effectively.

As mentioned earlier, what Seth said to us in sessions was also backed up by what happened in them. As he spoke about latent potentials, we found ourselves discovering our own. To a large extent, then, our personal experiences corroborated Seth's theories. For example, Session 138 on March 8, 1965, is a case in point.

That night Seth was just beginning his material on personality as action. The ideas he presented are basic to his overall theories of identity, and since he deals with some of the characteristics of consciousness, they are also a basis for later material on the God concept.

At the time, we were having sessions in the bedroom, which is small, with one window looking out on the large yard. It was summer; hardly anyone knew of the sessions yet, and Seth's full voice, rising out on the nighttime air, would have raised questions we weren't ready to answer. As he has done since the beginning, Rob sat with pen and paper, taking verbatim notes. He often felt quite warm, since we closed the window to keep the sessions as private as possible, particularly since neighbors were often sitting in the yard. (The heat never bothers me when I'm in trance, although otherwise I'm very susceptible to it.)

Reading the excerpts, you can see that Seth did give hints as to what was to come. Some of you, reading between the lines, may even guess what was in store for us.

"Identity may be termed action which is conscious of itself. For the purposes of our discussion, the terms 'action' and 'identity' must be separated, but basically no such separation exists. An identity is also a dimension of existence, action within action, an unfolding of action upon itself—and through this interweaving of action with itself, through this re-action, an identity is formed.

"The energy of action, the workings of action within and upon itself, forms identity. Yet though identity is formed from action, action and identity cannot be separated. Identity, then, *is* action's effect upon itself. Without identity, action would be meaningless, for there would be nothing upon which action could act. Action must, by its very nature, of itself and its own workings, create identities. This applies from the most simple to the most complex.

"Once more, action is not a force from without that acts upon

213

matter. *Action is, instead, the inside vitality of the inner universe—it is the dilemma between inner vitality's desire and impetus to completely materialize itself, and its inability to completely do so.*

"This first dilemma results in action, and from action's own workings upon itself we have seen that identity was formed, and that these two are inseparable. Action is, therefore, a part of all structure. Action, having of itself and because of its nature formed identity, now also because of its nature would seem to destroy identity, since action must involve change, and any change seems to threaten identity.

"It is a mistaken notion, however, that identity is dependent upon stability. Identity, because of its characteristics, will continually seek stability, while stability is impossible. This is our second dilemma.

"It is this dilemma, between identity's constant attempts to maintain stability and action's inherent drive for change, that results in the imbalance, the exquisite creative by-product that is *consciousness of self.* For consciousness and existence do not result from delicate balances so much as they are made possible by lack of balances, so richly creative that there would be no reality were balance ever maintained.

"We have a series of creative strains. Identity must seek stability while action must seek change; yet identity could not exist without change, for it is the result of action and a part of it. Identities are never constant as you yourselves are not the same consciously or unconsciously from one moment to the next. Every action is a termination, as we discussed earlier. And yet without the termination, identity would cease to exist, for consciousness without action would cease to be conscious.

"Consciousness, therefore, is not a 'thing' in itself. It is a dimension of action, an almost miraculous state, made possible by what I choose to call a series of creative dilemmas.

"It should be fairly easy to see how the second dilemma evolved from the first. I have said that the second one resulted in—and constantly results in—consciousness of self. This is not ego consciousness. Consciousness of self is still consciousness directly connected with action. Ego consciousness is a state resulting from the third

214

creative dilemma, which happens when consciousness of self attempts to separate itself from action. Since this is obviously impossible, since no consciousness or identity can exist without action, we have the third dilemma.

"Again: consciousness of self involves a consciousness of self within—and as a part of—action. Ego consciousness, on the other hand, involves a state in which consciousness of self attempts to divorce self from action—an attempt on the part of consciousness to perceive action as an object . . . and to perceive action as initiated by the ego as a result, rather than as a cause, of ego's own existence.

"These three dilemmas represent three areas of reality within which inner vitality can experience itself. And here also we have the reason why inner vitality can never achieve complete materialization. The very action involved in vitality's attempt to materialize itself adds to the inner dimension of vitality itself.

"Action [inner vitality] can never complete itself. Materializing in any form whatsoever, it at once multiplies the possibilities of further materialization. At the same time, because inner vitality is self-generating, only a minute fraction of it is needed to seed a universe.

"In line with the statement made earlier that action necessarily changes that which it acts upon [which is basically itself], then it follows that the action involved in our sessions changes the nature of the sessions. I have spoken often of consciousness as the direction in which a self focuses. Action implies infinite possibilities of focus."

As Seth delivered the material you have just read, I had a series of continuing experiences that were new to me. I couldn't tell Rob about them until our breaks, of course, and indeed, they are nearly impossible to describe. The nearest I can come is to say that as this information was being given verbally to Rob, it was given to me in a different way also. I seemed to be inside "action," drifting through various dimensions.

I *felt* what Seth was saying, as if the words were translated into subjective experience. It was more like being swept along into something else than being, say, negated. My ego wasn't lost, but became part of the concepts Seth was talking about. I was inside them, looking out.

Toward the end of the session, Rob asked Seth if he'd explain what was happening. Seth said: "Ruburt is experiencing action gestalts. Like every other consciousness, he *is* action; but this evening he is experiencing action, to some small degree, without the ego's usual attempt to separate itself [from action].

"I mentioned, in our last discussion, that this material would be the basis for future sessions. It is true that another dimension has been added to the sessions, and I hope to instruct Ruburt along the lines of more direct perception as we continue. I told you that such developments could be expected. These are natural unfoldings and will continue according to their own nature and in their own time. I expect that this latest development will involve still another."

This sort of thing began to happen frequently in sessions. Later we took it for granted, I guess, without realizing what an impression it made on us the first time. My experiences usually parallel whatever information Seth is giving. According to Seth, this involves the use of the Inner Senses, and my experiences are meant to point up the existence of these abilities not only in me, but as the latent capabilities of each personality.

Seth says that the physical body and its senses are specialized equipment to allow us to live in physical reality. To perceive other realities, we have to use the Inner Senses—methods of perception that belong to the inner self and operate whether or not we have a physical form. Seth calls the universe as we know it a "camouflage" system, since physical matter is simply the form that vitality—action—takes within it. Other realities are also camouflage systems, and within them consciousness also has specialized equipment tailored to their peculiar characteristics. But the Inner Senses allow us to see beneath the camouflage.

These Inner Senses belong to the whole selves of which we are part. Each whole self helps and inspires its personalities. Starting with the personality as we usually think of it, "there is, after the operating ego, a layer of personal subconscious material. Beneath this is racial material dealing with the species as a whole. Beneath this, undistorted and yours for the asking, is the knowledge inherent in the inner self, pertaining to reality as a whole, its laws, principles, and composition.

"Here you will find the innate knowledge concerning the creation of the camouflage universe as you know it, the mechanics involved, and much of the material I have given you. You will find the ways and means by which the inner self, existing in the climate of psychological reality, helps create the various planes of existence, constructs outer senses to project and perceive these, and the ways by which reincarnations take place within various systems. Here you will find your own answers as to how the inner self transforms energy for its own purposes, changes its form, and adopts other realities."

Quite a mouthful! What Seth is saying is that each of us can reach the inner self, that the Inner Senses help us to perceive other than three-dimensional reality, and that we can get to this knowledge with determination and training. We start with ourselves and travel through our own subjective experience, working from the ego inward. The physical senses help us to perceive the exterior reality that we know. The Inner Senses let us perceive the inner ones.

To some extent Rob and I have experienced most of these Inner Senses to some degree. Take a fairly simple one—Psychological Time. Seth says, "From within its framework you will see that physical time is as dreamlike as you once thought inner time was. You will discover your whole selves, peeping inward and outward at the same 'time,' and find that all time is one time, and all divisions, illusions."

When we do "Psy-Time," as Rob and I call it, our experiences seem to take place outside of the usual time framework. It's like shifting gears, so that perception happens in a different context. Psy-Time is the "time" I travel in when I'm projecting, for example. When I went to California in the episode mentioned in Chapter 9, over six thousand miles were covered in a half hour. Obviously, in normal time, this would be impossible.

A deeper appreciation of this subject requires more information about the real nature of time, however; because according to Seth the inner self operates not within time as we know it, but through perceptions that largely ignore time as we know it.

The question comes up, then: How can we ignore time? What is there about ourselves, or time, that we can disconnect one from the other? Some of you may not be interested in such questions, but others will feel cheated if they are left unanswered. Seth does not ignore such issues, and I'm closing this chapter with a few excerpts in which he considers them. Here Seth partially explains the nature of time, and shows why we are basically free of it.

From Session 224: The Personality and Time

"The past exists as a series of electromagnetic connections held in the physical brain and in the nonphysical mind. These electromagnetic connections can be changed. . . .

"The future consists of a series of electromagnetic connections in the mind and brain also, and this is the only reality that you are justified in giving the present.

"In other words, the past and present are real to the same extent. On occasion the past can become more 'real' than the present, and in such cases past actions are reacted to in what you call the present. You take it for granted that present action can change the future, but present actions can also change the past.

"The past is no more objective or independent from the perceiver than is the present. These electromagnetic connections that compose the past were largely made by the individual perceiver, and the perceiver is always a participator.

"The connections, therefore, can be changed, and such changes are far from uncommon. They happen spontaneously on a subconscious basis. The past is seldom what you remember it to be, for you have already rearranged it from the instant of any given event. The past is being constantly re-created by each individual as attitudes and associations change. This is an actual re-creation, not a symbolic one. The child is indeed still within the man, but he is not the child that 'was.' For even the child within the man constantly changes.

"Difficulties arise, in fact, when such alterations do not occur automatically. Severe neurosis is often caused precisely because the individual has *not* changed his past. Once more, the only reality that can be assigned to the past is that granted to the symbols and associations and images that exist electromagnetically within the physical brain and nonphysical mind.

"I am speaking in your terms now, and this should be understood, as I am simplifying conditions considerably. A change of attitude, a new association, or any of innumerable other actions will automatically set up new electromagnetic connections and break others.

"Every action changes every other action—we go back to our ABC's. Therefore, every action in your present affects those actions you call past. Ripples from a thrown stone go out in *all* directions, and I am going out rather far on the limb myself right here. Remembering what you know of the nature of time, you realize that the apparent boundaries between past, present, and future are only illusions caused by the amount of action you can physically perceive.

"Therefore, it is possible to react in the past to an event that has not yet occurred, to be influenced by your own future. It is also possible for an individual to react in the past to an event in the future which may never occur in your terms.

"I am sure you remember the couple you saw at York Beach [This episode was described in Chapter 2]?"

"Yes," Rob said, looking up.

"Now this couple represented a sort of time-projection, for literally you could have become what they were. This existed in that present as a probability. You perceived that portion of the probable future and reacted to it, and the possible transformation of yourselves into those images did not occur. Because past, present, and future exist simultaneously, there is no reason why you cannot react to an event whether or not it happens to fall within the small field of reality in which you usually observe and participate.

"On a subconscious level, you react to many events that have not yet occurred as far as your egotistical awareness is concerned. Such reactions are carefully screened out and not admitted to consciousness. The ego finds such instances distracting and annoying, and when forced to admit their validity, will resort to the most farfetched rationalizations to explain them.

"The inner self can, indeed, perceive events that will occur after physical death. It never was imprisoned by ego time. Its perceptions are merely inhibited by the ego. The inner self can perceive events that will occur to itself after death, and those in which it is not involved.

219

"In all of these instances, however, there are uncertainties, for probable events can be seen as clearly as events that will physically happen. No event is predestined. Any given event can be changed not only before and during but *after* its occurrence. Again, I am *not* speaking symbolically, and I realize that I am leaving myself open to strong criticisms that certainly cannot be answered in this one evening.

"There are, for example, limitations set here that must be clearly stated, but within these limitations you will find that events can be changed and are constantly changed, regardless of the apparent point of their original happening.

"All of this applies unless, of course, an individual is taken completely out of the physical time system. A murdered man will not be returned whole and intact to physical life [though he may return as a 'spirit,' believing he is still alive].

"In summation: the individual is hardly at the mercy of past events, for he changes them constantly. He is hardly at the mercy of future events, for he changes these not only before but after their happening.

"Again: the past is as real as the future, no more or no less. For the past exists only as a pattern of electromagnetic currents within the mind and brain, and these constantly change. . . . An individual's future actions are not dependent upon a concrete finished past, for such a past never existed."

We were to discover that these ideas were not just theoretical. In the following chapter I'll tell you of one of the strangest experiences of my life—one in which I was swept out of the world of time and space and then, just as suddenly, thrown back into it again.

CHAPTER
SEVENTEEN:

A "Future" Seth—Origin of the Sessions

By now I was used to Seth. The sessions, so strange at first, were a familiar part of our lives. There was a lot I didn't understand—there still is—so I hoped to develop my abilities more fully and to learn more. But I thought that the Seth sessions themselves would more or less remain the same. Looking back now at the earlier material, I can see that I should have known better.

One night in April of 1968, we settled down for our usual Monday night session, unaware that anything new was about to happen. I sat in my rocker. Rob sat on the couch as usual, taking notes. According to Rob, Seth's voice was unusually powerful that night. My opened eyes were very dark, and Seth seemed to be watching Rob rather closely.

Seth began the session, our 406th, by telling Rob the direction the material would take in following years. "You have been given a sketchy outline, but we have time to fill it in," he said, smiling. "For that matter, the outline itself is scarcely completed. . . . We want to

221

deal with the nature of reality as it exists within your camouflage system and within other systems, and to study the overall characteristics that pertain to it, regardless of any given materialization.

"Some of this material will automatically answer many questions with which you have been concerned—problems with which your scientists have been dealing. We will discuss the interrelationship that exists between all systems of reality, including certain points of contact that include them all. These various points can be mathematically deduced, and will, in some future of yours, serve as contact points, taking the place of space travel in some cases."

This material ran several pages, as Seth discussed the future content of our sessions. Right after this we took our first break. Neither of us realized, even at this point, that the session would be any different from the usual. As soon as we resumed, however, I suddenly felt a powerful surge of energy flow through me, so that inside it "I" seemed almost lost and swept away.

I couldn't tell Rob what I was experiencing, of course, but he began to suspect that something was happening. Seth became very emphatic, watching Rob closely for one thing. For another, Seth began to stress each word.

"If you keep these channels open and free, you will get material that is as undistorted as possible," he said. "Ruburt's range is an excellent one, and the plane of reality in which I have my existence is far beyond those to which persons in the physical system usually have access. . . . You and he must see to it that Ruburt does not color his experiences through reading material that is distorted. This [kind of material] has its purposes, and it does do some good, explaining reality in terms that people can understand, for the props and fantasies are familiar ones. There is no necessity for them here, however." He continued, suggesting that I stay away from books that "deal exclusively with conventional religious subjects, interpreting reality in those limited terms."

At this point, Rob became aware of the new and rather odd energy in Seth's voice as his delivery grew more powerful. My open eyes were very dark. Rob began to look up whenever he could snatch a moment from note-taking.

Seth said, "We will make an effort in the future to give you both

222

some direct experience in concepts. These experiments will run along with, and closely follow, the vocalized expression of the concepts involved. They will give you some small glimmering of the unfortunate but necessary loss of meaning that occurs when any concept must be communicated in physical terms. This will be a different kind of in-depth learning, a rather unique and original development that will be as devoid as possible of stereotyped symbols, which are usually almost automatically superimposed on such experiences. Do you understand?"

"Yes," Rob said, but he spoke almost automatically; the delivery had quickened, and he was having trouble keeping up with the notes. Later we were to read that above paragraph over many times when—as you'll see shortly—I found myself almost "in over my head."

Seth's voice continued to get stronger. "I am the Seth that I say that I am, but I am also more. The Seth personality that is part of me is the portion that can most clearly communicate with you. Do you follow me?"

Rob nodded. "Yes," he said again.

"The Seth portion of me has been intimately connected with you both, and so, in that respect, have I. This is closely related to the definition of a personality energy essence, from which, of course, all personalities spring."

The voice became even more powerful. Rob thought of asking Seth to slow down, but he wasn't sure what was happening, and thought it best not to interrupt.

"There is a peculiar corner within Ruburt's personality, also deflected into your own, that allows him rather clear access to informational channels most difficult to reach from your system. During this session, and at this moment, the contact is particularly good. There is also access to energy far beyond that which is usually experienced. Ruburt sensed this in the past, and feared to open these channels until he felt himself suitably ready.

"There exists what could almost be compared to a psychological and psychic warp in dimensions, and that corner of Ruburt's personality is an apex point at which communication and contact can take place."

Then, to Rob's surprise, Seth told him to end the session. Rob was

223

to follow the procedure given, recently, to end my trance. (Just lately I had begun going into particularly deep trances compared to earlier ones, and Seth had suggested that Rob call my name three times.) Seth said, "This evening you have reached somewhat beyond the personality by which I usually make myself known to you. Even if I continue to speak, end the trance."

Rob called me several times, getting no response. Then he touched my shoulder and I jumped rather violently. This interrupted the trance state. I didn't know what was going on either. The powerful energy kept flowing through me. If I stood up I felt as if I'd go flying through the wall, propelled by this force. My head felt huge, as if my ears were out several feet. This last sensation wasn't new; I'd had it in some Psy-Time experiences. But trying to contain that energy was something else.

I shook my head, "Wow. If I ever had any doubts . . . whatever's going on, it's not coming from me, not from my own personality." Later in my own notes I wrote, ". . . tremendous energy seemed to flow through me, with the definite certainty—thank God—that this was coming from beyond me, and was automatically translated into words at my end. I feel this is as significant a development —almost—as the original Seth session. The sense of contact was undeniably there. The feeling I had was that I really was in touch with some all encompassing reality."

The next Wednesday night I was somewhat hesitant as session time approached. We began at the dot of nine, but instantly Rob knew that this wasn't going to be a "normal" session. For one thing, the voice was different. It was much more like my own voice, yet it wasn't mine. Seth's deep tones, his gestures and characteristic way of using words—these were absent.

The voice was much softer than usual. Rob had to listen closely to get all the words. "The development in the last session was latent from our first session, but it was a development that could or could not have occurred. Had it not, then many important future developments would have been blocked. The points where the [Seth] voice was loudest and most powerful—these points often represented openings through which the development could occur. For various reasons, however, that method was not used. The energy would have been diverted from the voice in which it had already been built up, you see."

The voice became lighter, almost lilting. "The laws of the inner universe [which had been given to us by Seth] are not laws in some book. They are attempts to explain in words the nature of inner reality. I must disentangle concepts, unravel them, in order to explain them, and much is necessarily lost in the process.

"I intend to implement this material whenever possible by helping both of you achieve subjective experiences that will fill out the words for you. These will vary according to conditions but are much more possible now, after the sessions' latest development.

"Each simple law of the inner universe that I have given you is in actuality a small inadequate statement in single-dimensional terms, yet it is more than most are given, and the best approximation that can be made of the basic facts beneath any existence, the best statement that can be made under the circumstances with which we must work. As words would give small hint of the reality of color or sound to someone who did not experience these, so words can only give insight into the nature of reality. I hope through the addition of subjective experiences of various kinds to give you the feel of concepts when possible.

"The Inner Senses, to some extent, will allow you to perceive the reality of inner existence, and in this new development Ruburt is using these in a more effective manner than before. There are some changes in the way connections are made. This gives Ruburt a feeling of strangeness."

I'm only giving excerpts here, but through these passages the voice became even more lilting and neuter. Finally it stabilized: high, clear, distant, and unemotional.

"The Seth personality has been an intermediary and a legitimate one. The information already given to you regarding the nature of personality gestalts should make this development seem a fitting one. Seth is what I am, yet I am more than Seth is. Seth is, however, independent, and continues to develop as I do. In the Spacious Present we both exist.

225

"Some material he can present to you more clearly than I." Rob looked up sharply this time. If Seth wasn't speaking, who was?

"While I was the source of the material [in the last sessions], Seth, as you think of him, was at times a silent partner, helping Ruburt make the proper translations, while stepping aside in a personal manner. Earlier [in previous sessions] Seth interpreted material from me so that Ruburt could receive it.

"You may rest. Seth will always be an element in these sessions as you know him. He is the connective between us, and he has been a part of me that I have sent out to you. He has participated willingly."

Here we had a break and I came out of trance easily enough. This also gave me the opportunity to tell Rob something that happened just before the session started. I got the feeling that a cone came down just over my head. I didn't think that an actual physical cone was there, but the idea of shape was definite. The wide end was about the size of my head, with the narrow part on top like a pyramid.

Since then, I've had this cone effect often, always in this kind of a session. Right after the session resumed, I began to feel that tremendous energy again as the new voice spoke. "You have always been in contact with me, but you were only able to 'see' a portion of me. Keep in mind that all names are arbitrary, and we use them merely for your convenience. Basically, Seth's name or mine isn't important. Individuality is important and continues in ways you do not suspect.

"In the most important way, and in the only basic way, I am Seth, dispensing with certain characteristics which are mine, which I used to contact you. The Seth personality, again, is legitimate and independent and is a part of my identity. Seth is learning as I am.

"Simply as an analogy, you could call me a future Seth, Seth in a 'higher' stage of development. This is not to be taken literally, however, since both of us are fully independent and exist simultaneously.

"There are reasons why these particular connections have been made. There are events that unite us and that have served as turning points in the development of our various personalities. In some strange manner, what I am now is linked to what you are.

"There are points of contact having nothing to do with time, as

226

you know it, that are significant to all personalities; origins of new energy that are sometimes brought into existence because of the strong latent psychic capacities within individual selves. At these points, whole conglomerations of new self-units come into being, their origin sparked, as given in the last sentence. They then disperse and go their own ways, but the mutual origin and the strength of that initial psychic birth remain."

(In here I had visual inner images as of stars being born—an attempt, I thought, to put the data into recognizable visual terms.)

"These [personalities] may develop in entirely different fashions and in various dimensions, but a strong sympathetic attraction exists between them. There is a point of contact where knowledge can be communicated from these various dimensions, and for too many reasons to give you now, Ruburt is in proper coordinates for such communication to take place.

"This communication, while taking place in your time, is nevertheless responsible in other dimensions for what you would call future developments in your own personalities which you can, in turn, contact. I look back on you as the selves from which I sprang, yet I am more than the sum of what you will be when you are finished with the dimensions and times that I have known.

"For I have sprung entirely away from you and would be alien in your terms. That you can even contact me is a most remarkable development. Yet had you not been able to contact me, I would not be what I am."

Here the voice was very distant, high and clear, so unlike the usual Seth voice that Rob was still rather taken back. "I am more, however, than this portion of me that you contact, for it is only one portion of me that experienced that reality. It is highly important, then, that this material not be distorted, for most communications take place on far different levels than this—[levels] so closely connected with your own system that even the most 'undistorted' data is highly distorted because the communicators themselves do not realize that they create the realities which they then describe.

"I have done my best to give you an understanding as a basis for future sessions. Seth as you knew him will also be Seth as you know him, for whether or not I speak as myself or through him, he is still the intermediary and the connection between us. More, he will still appear as you have known him. There are necessary emotional elements that are uniquely his own.

"My personality structure is far different—very rewarding to me but unfamiliar to you. . . . I do not want you to feel that I have taken away a friend. I am also a friend. In many ways I am the same friend. Other portions of me are concerned elsewhere, for I am aware of my own existence in other dimensions and keep track of them and direct my many selves."

When the session was over, Rob and I sat up talking. "It's crazy," I said. "When we have a usual Seth session, I sort of feel Seth take over, though I don't like that term. With this personality, though, I go somewhere, out of myself, and seem to make contact with it in some nowhere, leaving my body empty. I don't know how I get there, wherever it is, or how I get back."

Rob nodded. Both of us felt almost sad, in one way. I think we were afraid that our regular Seth sessions were over, and that the new ones would take their place. "Besides," Rob said, "what do we call this new personality?" We knew it was meaningless basically, but we felt we needed a name, a label. And how exactly was this new personality different from Seth? What could it do that Seth couldn't? "I wish it were more masculine or feminine," I said. "A neuter personality seems so strange."

Some of our questions were answered in the next session, our 419th on June 8, 1968. Just before the session started I began to get the pyramid effect again. I grinned, somewhat embarrassed, moving so that I sat directly beneath where I felt the pyramid had come down. Then the session started. A friend, Pat Norelli, attended.

"I have told you who we are. We are Seth, and whenever we have spoken we have been known as Seth. The entity had its beginning before the emergence of your time. It was instrumental, with many other entities, in the early formation of energy into physical form. We are not alone in this endeavor, for through your centuries other entities like us have also appeared and spoken.

"Our entity is composed of multitudinous selves with their own identities, many of whom have worked in this behalf. Their messages will always be basically the same, though the times and circumstances of their communications may differ and be colored accordingly.

"We taught man to speak before the tongue knew syllables. We adopt whatever personality characteristics seem pertinent, for in our own reality we have a bank of complete inner selves, and we are all Seth. We attempt to translate realities into terms that you can comprehend. We change our face and form, but we are always the one. Many of us have not been born in flesh, as I have not been. In one way we have seeded ourselves through endless universes.

"Physically you would find me a mass smaller than a brown nut, for my energy is so highly concentrated. It exists in intensified mass . . . perhaps like one infinite cell existing in endless dimensions at once and reaching out from its own reality to all others.

"Yet in such a small mass, these intensities contain memories and experiences electromagnetically coiled one within the other through which I can travel—even as I can travel through other selves which I have known and which are a portion of my identity, and yet which are so beautifully unpredetermined, for you do not exist as completed personalities within my memory, but you grow within my memory.

"You grow through my memory as a tree grows up through space, and my memory changes as you change. My memory of you includes your probable selves, and all of these coordinates exist simultaneously in a point that takes up no space. . . .

"I told you that Ruburt's personality acts like a warp in dimensions. In certain coordinates it exists at particular points that serve as entryways. The personality in general is formed from components existing in many realities and is an apex point. A window cannot see through itself, but you can see through a window. So Ruburt's personality . . . is transparent in that respect."

The next session showed us how different this new development could be. It also nearly scared me out of my wits, at least for a few moments. More than this, however, it opened our eyes to new possibilities of experience and demonstrated yet another phenomenon that could occur within the session framework.

Our friend, Phil—the salesman I spoke of earlier—dropped in

that evening; we began at 9 P.M. as usual. Seth spoke to Phil about some business matters and answered several questions that had been on Phil's mind. During our rest period, however, I felt the now familiar pyramid effect, and when we resumed, the other personality began to speak.

The transition from Seth's deep voice and lively gestures was very startling to Phil, who hadn't heard the other personality speak before. Now my body was almost puppetlike, and my face was devoid of expression. Just before the voice began to speak, I felt my consciousness drawn up through the invisible pyramid like a draft up a flue. There was no indication that anything else was about to happen, however.

The voice said: "You are like children with a game, and you think that the game is played by everyone. Physical life is not the rule. Identity and consciousness existed long before your earth was formed. You see physical bodies and suppose that any personality must appear in physical terms. Consciousness is the force behind matter, and it forms many other realities besides the physical one. It is only because your own viewpoint is presently so limited that it seems to you that physical reality is the rule and mode of existence.

"The source and power of your present consciousness has never been physical, and where I am, many are not even aware that such a physical system exists. The physical system is an illusion, but you must accept it and from its viewpoint try to understand the realities that exist beyond it. The illusions are real since they exist. Your [reality] is simply not one that I have pursued, and one of the purposes of my participation in these sessions is to acquaint the one called Ruburt with inner travel. He must leave the physical system, and in so doing set up habits and paths that can be used to advantage."

No one thought anything in particular about that last statement until later that night. The voice continued for a short time and I encountered some difficulty "getting back." I felt suspended in darkness somewhere far above, but I was also aware that Seth was close by. A few minutes passed. Suddenly Seth came through, loud and clear. The contrast between the two personalities was so marked that even Rob was startled. Seth started to joke. "Now that 'Big Brother' has had his say, I will bring our Ruburt back to you."

230

I came out of trance easily enough once Seth came through. We sat chatting for a few moments and then the session resumed, letting me in for one of the most remarkable experiences of my life. This is rather difficult to describe, so first I'll quote what the "other" voice was saying.

"The inner portions of your own identity and reality are not known to you, for you cannot objectify them, and therefore you do not perceive them. So much of your energy is used in these physical productions that you cannot afford to perceive any reality but your own. Again, like children playing with blocks, your focus of attention is upon physical blocks.

"Other shapes and forms that you could perceive, you do not. Even in explaining other realities to you, I must use the words 'shapes' and 'forms' or you would not understand me. You have your mathematics from us; a shadow of true mathematics, for here again you have insisted upon hemming-in realities. Your idea of progress is building larger blocks. Yet none of us would think of kicking aside your block constructions in ire, or telling you to put aside your children's toys, though one day you will do so.

"Later, in your time, all of you will look down into the physical system like giants peering through small windows at the others now in your position and smile. But you will not want to stay, nor crawl through the small enclosures. . . . We protect such systems. Our basic and ancient knowledge and energy automatically reaches out to nourish all systems that grow—"

Here I screamed and started shaking violently. Rob thought that my heavy rocker was about to tip over. Rob and Phil leaped to their feet, Phil knocking his glass of beer to the floor in the process. Rob rubbed my hands and tried to get me out of trance.

This time I'm quoting from my own notes, made later that evening:

When the personality compared physical reality with children's blocks, he made a remark about individuals returning in our future to peer into physical reality like giants squinting down to watch children play with blocks upon the floor. (As the voice spoke, my eyes were closed, of course, and I don't remember what the voice said, but have checked Rob's verbatim notes of the session.) In

231

here someplace, suddenly I saw a giant's face peer into our living room, its face filling up the entire window.

The next moment my own body, the room and everything in it began to grow to tremendous size. My body became massive. I could feel the organs inside me grow. At the same time all the furniture—everything—got larger and larger. It seemed as if the room now was huge enough to cover all of the city. Yet everything expanded in proportion, retaining its usual shape.

I didn't feel *as if* this were happening. To me it *was* happening, literally. I simply panicked and started yelling. It took Rob some minutes to get me out of trance, but by then I was ashamed of myself. I felt like a real coward.

Rob was worried about me and wondered if I should continue with the session, but by now I was really embarrassed at making such a fuss, and I knew that the experience was significant. I went back into trance, but very soon I was to break off again.

Here are a few quotes from Rob's notes just before the session resumed:

> I hoped this was the end of the session, but it was obvious that Jane wanted to continue, or at least was willing to continue, in spite of the unsettling experience. I tried to talk her out of it, but her eyes kept closing. . . .
>
> "I'm on my way up to the other guy" she said. "I just passed Seth and he joked with me, something about a *massive* experience."
>
> "Why don't you just come back down?" I asked.
>
> "I don't know how to," she said.
>
> 10:55. Jane resumed in the now familiar high, distant, very formal voice.

"The blocks of physical reality appear very real to you when you dwell within their perspective. Your Ruburt experienced a transmigration of systems. It was not meant to be unpleasant. This was his subjective interpretation. First he was involved in a microscopic adventure. Consciousness does not take up space—you must understand this. Then he reentered your own system of physical blocks, and by contrast that system then appeared huge and monstrous.

"When we make contact, his consciousness and personality in

concentrated form make a journey—in your terms, like a speck in space—the consciousness reduced to its essence. And from his experience we let him fall back into the physical system. The children's blocks then became massive by contrast . . . this was an experience in concepts."

During the above monologue my subjective experiences continued. Again, I wasn't aware of what the voice was saying, and only afterward did I realize that my experiences paralleled the meaning of the passages. Here are a few quotes from my notes:

I started to feel the microscopic nature of our physical universe, comparatively speaking . . . this is most difficult to put into words. There was a momentary sense of desolation accompanying this—my own, I think. I'm always aware of the pyramid shape above me just before this personality speaks. Usually I "go up through" it. This time, though, at the narrow end far above me I saw the same giant head, peering down at me and the room as through a microscope. If the room and everything in it was going to shrink as realistically as it had expanded earlier—and it was, I could tell—I just wasn't ready for the experience.

I tried to find my voice to tell Rob I wanted to end the session, but the other personality was using it. Through all of this I use the word "I," but "I" was so a part of the action that it was difficult to separate myself from it. Now, wanting out, I tried again to use my own voice.

This time I "found myself," pulled myself together, and found my vocal chords while the other personality paused for a moment. It was just about here that I saw the giant face peering down through the pyramid above me. In the earlier episode, I'd screamed involuntarily. In the second, I found that there were ways of "finding" my own voice, and ending the experience. With Seth such a question never arose. There was no pressure put upon me by the other personality to continue the experience . . . but I had to learn how to terminate it myself when I wanted to.

I don't believe the other personality understood that the experience was unpleasant for me, or for that matter, that such terms had any meaning for it. Information was being given in certain terms

—period—as far as it was concerned. I don't even know if it was aware of my reactions.

Very startling though, the whole thing. If a psychologist wants to say simply that the whole thing was hallucination, then he would have to admit that it was hardly random, but well directed, to a point and for a purpose. The merging of myself with the action in the expansion episode was frightening at first. All in all I guess I reacted well enough and brought the thing to an end in the second episode when I decided I'd had enough for one night. I wasn't just tossed willy-nilly the second time, and I broke the trance in anticipation of the experiences I knew were coming. So I did learn from the first episode.

That session was well over a year ago. Our usual Seth sessions still continue, and only now and then does this other personality speak. We refer to it as Seth Two. Often these sessions involve me in some kind of subjective experience, though now I am learning how to handle myself when this happens. Once during a rest period, for example, Rob wondered what it was like to be nonphysical. When the session resumed, I felt myself seemingly suspended, fully alert and aware—but bodiless—in space. I had no form as far as I knew, but I possessed complete freedom of motion—something like conscious air. This time I wasn't frightened, realizing that we were getting an answer to Rob's question. During this experience, the emotionless, lilting, distant voice explained what nonphysical existence was like.

The difference in the two personalities was particularly apparent in a recent ESP class session in which Seth was at his jovial best, showing personal interest in each student. As usual during such times, my face was extremely animated, and Seth's characteristic gestures were quite noticeable. After speaking to each student individually for a moment, Seth said with a touch of humor: "I come here, I hope, as an 'endearing' personality, with characteristics to which you can relate.

"Now, these characteristics are mine, and I am who I say I am. And yet the Seth that you know is but a small portion of my reality . . . the part that has been physical, and can understand your problems.

"But beyond that self there is another self and still another self of which I am fully aware. And to that self, physical reality is like a breath of smoke in air . . . and that self does not need the characteristics that you know and think of as mine."

The voice had been vibrant and full, booming and loud. Then there was a pause. And for the first time the other personality came through in class. All of Seth's gestures and mannerisms vanished. Instantly that high, distant, asexual voice began to speak. It is almost musical, without inflection, like single notes. "And that self tells you that there is a reality beyond human reality and experience that cannot be verbal nor translated in human terms. . . .

"Although this type of experience may seem cold to you, it is a clear and crystal-like existence in which no time is needed for experience . . . in which the inner self condenses all human knowledge that has been received through various existences and reincarnations . . . for all this has been coded and exists indelibly. You also exist now within this reality. . . .

"Know that within your physical atoms now the origins of all consciousness still sing and that all the human characteristics by which you know yourselves still exist. . . .

"So I am the Seth that is beyond the Seth that you know. And in me the knowledge and vitality of that Seth still rings. In your terms, I am a future Seth, but the terms are meaningless to me.

"We gave you mental images and upon these images you learned to form the world that you know. We gave you the pattern by which your physical selves are formed. We gave you the patterns, intricate, involved, and blessed, from which you form the reality of each physical thing you know.

"The most minute cell within your brain has been made from patterns of consciousness which we have given you. The entire webwork was initiated by us. We taught you to form the reality that you know."

CHAPTER EIGHTEEN:

The God Concept—
The Creation
—The Three Christs

Simply stated, this is one of the thumbnail passages that explain Seth's concept of God:

"He is not human in your terms, though he passed through human stages; and here the Buddhist myth comes closest to approximating reality. He is not one individual, but an energy gestalt.

"If you remember what I said about the way in which the universe expands, that it has nothing to do with space, then you may perhaps dimly perceive the existence of a psychic pyramid of interrelated, ever-expanding consciousness that creates, simultaneously and instantaneously, universes and individuals that are given—through the gifts of personal perspective—duration, psychic comprehension, intelligence, and eternal validity.

"This absolute, ever-expanding, instantaneous psychic gestalt, which you may call God if you prefer, is so secure in its existence that it can constantly break itself down and rebuild itself.

"Its energy is so unbelievable that it does indeed form all universes; and because its energy is within and behind all universes, systems, and fields, it is indeed aware of each sparrow that falls, for it *is* each sparrow that falls."

As mentioned earlier, however, the Seth Material does not ignore deeper questions having to do with the "beginning" of consciousness and of reality. I really think that this particular material can hold its own with the best metaphysical writings of our time. For this reason I am continuing this chapter with excerpts from sessions 426, 427, and 428, where Seth began with a fuller explanation of space, time, and probable realities and then led us, step by step, into a discussion of God.

"Your idea of space and time is determined by your neurological structure.

"The camouflage is so craftily executed and created by the inner self that you must, of necessity, focus your attention in the physical reality which has been created. The psychedelic drugs alter the neurological workings, and therefore can give some slight glimpses into other realities.

"These realities exist, of course, whether or not you perceive them. Actually 'time' exists as the pulses leap the nerve ends. You must then experience lapses, as this is not a simultaneous procedure. Past, present, and future appear highly convincing and logical when there must be a lapse between each perceived experience.

"There is no such lapse in many other personality structures. Events are simultaneously perceived. Reactions are also nearly instantaneous in your terms. Growth and challenge are provided not in terms of achievement or development in time, but instead in terms of intensities. Such a personality is able not only to react to and appreciate Event A, say, in your present time, but to experience and understand Event A in all of its ramifications and probabilities.

"Obviously such personalities need far more than the neurological systems with which you are presently equipped. Your own neurological system is physical, but it is based upon your own inner capabilities as of 'now.' It is the materialization of an inner psychic framework. Many other personality structures do not need a *materialized* perceptive framework such as this, but an inner psychic organization is always present.

"Your time—past, present, and future—as you conceive it, would be experienced entirely as present to many of these personalities. However, your past, present, and future would be experienced entirely as past to still other personality structures.

"Imagine past, present, and future then as a single-line delineation of experience in your terms; the line, however, continuing indefinitely. Other personality structures from other dimensions could then, theoretically, observe it from an infinity of viewpoints. However, there is much more than this. The single line [representing physical experience] is merely the surface thread along which you seem to travel. It is all of the thread that you perceive, so when you envision other dimensions you are forced to think in terms of observers far above the thread, looking down upon it from any given viewpoint.

"In actuality, following the image through, and strictly as an analogy, there would also be an infinite number of threads both above and below your own, all part of one inconceivably miraculous webwork. Yet each thread would not be one-dimensional but of many dimensions, and conceivably, if you knew how, there would be ways of leapfrogging from one thread to the other. You would not be forced to follow any particular thread in a single-line fashion.

"Now, there are personalities developed enough to do this. Each act of leaping, so to speak, forms a new thread. Following through with our analogy, imagine yourself Self A. We will start you off in physical reality on Thread A, though you have already traversed many other threads to get where you are.

"Without shortcuts or even average progression, any such Self A would travel Thread A along the narrow line toward infinity. At some point, however, Thread A would turn into Thread B. In the same manner, Thread B would turn into Thread C and so forth. At some inconceivable point, all of the threads would be traversed. Now on Thread A, Self A would not be aware, in his present, of the 'future' selves on the other threads. Only by meeting one of these other selves can he become aware of the nature of this strange structure through which he is traveling.

"There is, however, a self, who has already traveled these routes, of whom the other selves are but part. This self, in dreams and dissociated conditions, communicates with the various 'ascending' selves. As this self grows in value fulfillment, he can become aware of these travelers on other threads, who would seem to him to be future selves.

"All of this sounds complicated, but only because we must deal with words. I hope that intuitively you will be able to understand it. In the 'meantime,' the overall self is forming new threads of activity, you see. The frameworks that it leaves 'behind' can be used by others.

"The purpose is, quite simply, *being* as opposed to nonbeing. I am telling you what I know, and there is much I do not know. I know that help must be given one to the other, and that extension and expansion are aids to being.

"Now—and this will seem like a contradiction in terms—*there is nonbeing*. It is a state, not of nothingness, but a state in which probabilities and possibilities are known and anticipated but blocked from expression.

"Dimly, through what you would call history, hardly remembered, there was such a state. It was a state of agony in which the powers of creativity and existence were known, but the ways to produce them were not known.

"This is the lesson that *All That Is* had to learn, and that could not be taught. This is the agony from which creativity originally was drawn, and its reflection is still seen."

Seth uses the word "God" sparingly, usually when speaking to students who are used to thinking in theological terms. As a rule, he speaks of "All That Is" or "Primary Energy Gestalts."

"Some of this discussion is bound to be distorted, because I must explain it to you in terms of time as you understand it. So I will speak, for your benefit, of some indescribably distant past in which these events occurred.

"*All That Is* retains memory of that state, and it serves as a constant impetus—in your terms—toward renewed creativity. Each self, as a part of *All That Is,* therefore also retains memory of that state. It is for this reason that each minute consciousness is endowed with the impetus toward survival, change, development, and creativity. It is not enough that *All That Is,* as a primary consciousness gestalt, desires further being, but that each portion of It also carries this determination

"Yet the agony itself was used as a means, and the agony itself served as an impetus, strong enough so that *All That Is* initiated within Itself the means *to be*.

"If—and this is impossible—all portions but the most minute last 'unit' of *All That Is* were destroyed, *All That Is* would continue, for within the smallest portion is the innate knowledge of the whole. *All That Is* protects Itself, therefore, and all that It has and is and will create.

"When I speak of *All That Is*, you must understand my position within It. *All That Is* knows no other. This does not mean that there may not be more to know. It does not know whether or not other psychic gestalts like It may exist. It is not aware of them if they do exist. It is constantly searching. It knows that something else existed before Its own primary dilemma when It could not express Itself.

"It is conceivable, then, that It has evolved, in your terms, so long ago that It has forgotten Its origin, that It has developed from still another Primary which has—again, in your terms—long since gone Its way. So there are answers that I cannot give you, for they are not known anywhere in the system in which we have our existence. We do know that within this system of our *All That Is*, creation continues and developments are never still. We can deduce that on still other layers of which we are unaware, the same is true.

"The first state of agonized search for expression may have represented the birth throes of *All That Is* as we know It. Pretend, then, that you possessed within yourself the knowledge of all the world's masterpieces in sculpture and art, that they pulsed as realities within you, but that you had no physical apparatus, no knowledge of how to achieve them, that there was neither rock nor pigment nor source of any of these, and you ached with the yearning to produce them. This, on an infinitesimally small scale, will perhaps give you, as an artist [this was addressed to Rob, of course], some idea of the agony and impetus that was felt.

"Desire, wish, and expectation rule all actions and are the basis for all realities. Within *All That Is*, therefore, the wish, desire, and expectation of creativity existed before all other actuality. The strength and vitality of these desires and expectations then became in

241

your terms so insupportable that *All That Is* was driven to find the means to produce them.

"In other words, *All That Is* existed in a state of being, but without the means to find expression for Its being. This was the state of agony of which I spoke. Yet it is doubtful that without this 'period' of contracted yearning, *All That Is* could concentrate Its energy sufficiently enough to create the realities that existed in probable suspension within It.

"The agony and the desire to create represented Its proof of Its own reality. The feelings, in other words, were adequate proof to *All That Is* that It was.

"At first, in your terms, all of probable reality existed as nebulous dreams within the consciousness of *All That Is*. Later, the unspecific nature of these 'dreams' grew more particular and vivid. The dreams became recognizable one from the other until they drew the conscious notice of *All That Is*. And with curiosity and yearning, *All That Is* paid more attention to Its own dreams.

"It then purposely gave them more and more detail, and yearned toward this diversity and grew to love that which was not yet separate from itself. It gave consciousness and imagination to personalities while they still were but within Its dreams. They also yearned to be actual.

"Potential individuals, in your terms, had consciousness before the beginning or any beginning as you know it, then. They clamored to be released into actuality, and *All That Is,* in unspeakable sympathy, sought within Itself for the means.

"In Its massive imagination, It understood the cosmic multiplication of consciousness that could not occur within that framework. Actuality was necessary if these probabilities were to be given birth. *All That Is* saw, then, an infinity of probable, conscious individuals, and foresaw all possible developments, but they were locked within It until It found the means.

"This was in your terms a primary cosmic dilemma, and one with which It wrestled until *All That It Was* was completely involved and enveloped within that cosmic problem.

242

"Had It not solved it, *All That Is* would have faced insanity, and there would have been, literally, a reality without reason and a universe run wild.

"The pressure came from two sources: from the conscious but still probable individual selves who found themselves alive in a God's dream, and from the God who yearned to release them.

"On the other hand, you could say that the pressure existed simply on the part of the God since the creation existed within Its dream, but such tremendous power resides in such primary pyramid gestalts that even their dreams are endowed with vitality and reality.

"This, then, is the dilemma of any primary pyramid gestalt: It creates reality. It also recognized within each consciousness the massive potential that existed. The means, then, came to It. It must release the creatures and probabilities from Its dream.

"To do so would give them actuality. However, it also meant 'losing' a portion of Its own consciousness, for it was within that portion that they were held in bondage. *All That Is* had to let go. While It thought of these individuals as Its creations, It held them as a part of Itself and refused them actuality.

"To let them go was to 'lose' that portion of Itself that had created them. Already It could scarcely keep up with the myriad probabilities that began to emerge from each separate consciousness. With love and longing It let go that portion of Itself, and they were free. The psychic energy exploded in a flash of creation.

"*All That Is,* therefore, 'lost' a portion of Itself in that creative endeavor. *All That Is* loves all that It has created down to the least, for It realizes the dearness and uniqueness of each consciousness which has been wrest from such a state and at such a price. It is triumphant and joyful at each development taken by each consciousness, for this is an added triumph against that first state, and It revels and takes joy in the slightest creative act of each of Its issues.

"It, of Itself and from that state, has given life to infinities of possibilities. From its agony, It found the way to burst forth in freedom, through expression, and in so doing gave existence to individualized consciousness. Therefore is It rightfully jubilant. Yet all

243

individuals remember their source, and now dream of *All That Is* as *All That Is* once dreamed of them. And they yearn toward that immense source . . . and yearn to set It free and give It actuality through their own creations.

"The motivating force is still *All That Is*, but individuality is no illusion. Now in the same way do you give freedom to the personality fragments within your own dreams and for the same reason. And you create for the same reason, and within each of you is the memory of that primal agony—that urge to create and free all probable consciousness into actuality.

"I have been sent to help you, and others have been sent through the centuries of your time, for as you develop you also form new dimensions, and *you* will help others.

"These connections between you and *All That Is* can never be severed, and Its awareness is so delicate and focused that Its attention is indeed directed with a prime creator's love to each consciousness.

"This session needs reading many times, for there are implications not at first obvious."

In other words, the whole frame of reality according to Seth includes far more than reincarnation and development within the physical system that we know. We have many sessions dealing with the nature of other realities, and sessions on "cosmology" that can't be included in this book because of the space requirements. One of the most important points, I think, is that God is not static Himself. Whole blocks of Seth material discuss the potentials and makeup of consciousness as it is manifested in molecules, man, and pyramid energy gestalts. All of these are intimately connected in a cosmological web of activity. But as Seth says, "Even this overall pyramid gestalt is not static. Most of your God concepts deal with a static God, and here is one of your main theological difficulties. The awareness and experience of this gestalt constantly changes and grows. There is no static God. When you say, 'This is God,' then God is already something else. I am using the term 'God' for simplicity's sake.

"All portions of *All That Is* are constantly changing, enfolding and unfolding. *All That Is*, seeking to know Itself, constantly creates new versions of Itself. For this seeking Itself is a creative activity and the core of all action.

"Entities, being action, always shift and change. There is nothing arbitrary about their boundaries. Some personalities can be a part of more than one entity. Like fish, they can swim in other streams. Within them is the knowledge of all of their relationships.

"Any personality can become an entity on its own. This involves a highly developed knowledge of the use of energy and its intensities. As atoms have mobility, so do psychological structures.

"Consciousness, seeking to know itself, therefore knows you. You, as a consciousness, seek to know yourself and become aware of your self as a distinct individual portion of *All That Is*. You not only draw upon this overall energy but you do so automatically since your existence is dependent upon It.

"There is no personal God-individual in Christian terms," Seth says, "and yet you do have access to a portion of *All That Is*, a portion highly attuned to you. . . . There is a portion of *All That Is* directed and focused within each individual, residing within each consciousness. Each consciousness is, therefore, cherished and individually protected. This portion of overall consciousness is individualized within you.

"The personality of God as generally conceived is a one-dimensional concept based upon man's small knowledge of his own psychology. What you prefer to think of as God is, again, an energy gestalt or pyramid consciousness. It is aware of itself as being, for instance, you, Joseph. It is aware of itself as the smallest seed. . . . This portion of *All That Is* that is aware of itself as you, that is focused within your existence, can be called upon for help when necessary.

"This portion is also aware of itself as something more than you. *This portion that knows itself as you, and as more than you, is the personal God, you see*. Again: this gestalt, this portion of *All That Is*, looks out for ʏour interests and may be called upon in a personal manner.

"Prayer contains its own answer, and if there is no white-haired

245

kind old father-God to hear, then there is instead the initial and ever-expanding energy that forms everything that is and of which each human being is a part.

"This psychic gestalt may sound impersonal to you, but since its energy forms your person, how can this be?

"If you prefer to call this supreme psychic gestalt God, then you must not attempt to objectify him, for he is the nuclei of your cells and more intimate than your breath."

In another session, Seth explained it this way: "You are cocreators. What you call God is the sum of all consciousness, and yet the whole is more than the sum of Its parts. God is more than the sum of all personalities, and yet all personalities are what He is.

"There is constant creation. There is within you a force that knew how to grow you from a fetus to a grown adult. This force is part of the innate knowledge within all consciousness, and it is a part of the God within you.

"The responsibility for your life and your world is indeed yours. It has not been forced upon you by some outside agency. You form your own dreams, and you form your own physical reality. The world is what you are. It is the physical materialization of the inner selves which have formed it." But if God cannot be objectified, what about Christ? Seth says that he did not exist as one historic personage. "When the race is in deepest stress and faced with great problems, it will call forth someone like Christ. It will seek out and indeed from itself produce the very personalities necessary to give it strength. . . .

"There were three men whose lives became confused in history and merged, and whose composite history became known as the life of Christ. . . . Each was highly gifted psychically, knew of his role, and accepted it willingly. The three men were a part of one entity, gaining physical existence in one time. They were not born on the same date, however. There are reasons why the entity did not return as one person. For one thing, the full consciousness of an entity would be too strong for one physical vehicle. For another, the entity wanted a more diversified environment than could otherwise be provided.

"The entity was born once as John the Baptist, and then he was born in two other forms. One of these contained the personality that most stories of Christ refer to. . . . I will tell you about the other personality at a later time. There was constant communication between these three portions of one entity, though they were born and buried at different dates. The race called up these personalities from its own psychic bank, from the pool of individualized consciousness that was available to it."

After the assassination of Martin Luther King, Jr., my students in class were quite upset, and like many people throughout the country and probably the world, we began to discuss the meaning of violence. In the middle of our conversation, Seth came through:

"You have been given free will. Within you there are blueprints; you know what you are to achieve as individuals and as people, as a race, as a species. You can choose to ignore the blueprints. Now: Using your free will, you have made physical reality something quite different than what was intended. You have allowed the ego to become overly developed and overly specialized. In many respects, you are in a dream. It is you who have made the dream too vivid. You were to work out problems and challenges, but you were always to be aware of your own inner reality, and of your nonphysical existence. To a large extent you have lost contact with this. You have focused so strongly upon physical reality that it becomes the only reality that you know.

"When you kill a man, you believe that you kill him forever. Murder is, therefore, a crime and must be dealt with—because you have created it. Death does not exist in those terms.

"In the dawn of physical existence, in the dawn before history began, men knew that death was merely a change of form. No God created the crime of murder, and no God created sorrow or pain. . . . Again, because you believe that you can murder a man and end his consciousness forever, then murder exists within your reality and must be dealt with. . . . The assassin of Dr. King believes that he has blotted out a living consciousness for all eternity. . . . But your errors and mistakes, luckily enough, are not real and do not affect reality, for Dr. King still lives."

My class is small but students range in age from sixteen to sixty. One evening we were discussing student riots. Carl and Sue are both in their early twenties. They had been upholding ideas of nonviolence and peace. The older adults began complaining about the rioters with some bitterness, however, until Sue said with some heat: "Well, I'm against violence, too. But sometimes it's justified—"

She hardly got the words out of her mouth before Seth interrupted her. Everyone jumped. In the heat of the discussion, Seth and ESP in general had been forgotten. Now Seth's voice really boomed out. "There is never any justification for violence. There is no justification for hatred. There is no justification for murder. Those who indulge in violence for whatever reason are themselves changed, and the purity of their purpose adulterated.

"I have told you that if you do not like the state of your world, it is yourselves that you must change, individually and en masse. This is the only way that change will be effected." Here Seth stared at Carl and said, "If your generation or any generation effects a change, this is the only way it will be done. What I am telling you has been said before through the centuries. It is up to you [nodding at Sue and Carl] as to whether or not you will listen.

"It is wrong to curse a flower and wrong to curse a man. It is wrong not to hold any man in honor, and it is wrong to ridicule any man. You must honor yourselves and see within yourselves the spirit of eternal vitality. If you do not do this, then you destroy what you touch. And you must honor each other individual also, because in him is the spark of eternal vitality.

"When you curse another, you curse yourselves, and the curse returns to you. When you are violent, the violence returns. . . . I speak to you because yours is the opportunity [to better world conditions] and yours is the time. Do not fall into the old ways that will lead you precisely into the world that you fear.

"When every young man refuses to go to war, you will have peace. As long as you fight for gain and greed, there will be no peace. As long as one person commits acts of violence for the sake of peace, you will have war. Unfortunately it is difficult to imagine that all the young men in all of the countries will refuse to go to war at the same time. And so you must work out the violence that violence has wrought. Within the next hundred years that time may come. Remember, you do not defend any idea with violence.

"There is no man who hates but that that hatred is reflected outward and made physical. And there is no man who loves but that that love is reflected outward and made physical."

CHAPTER NINETEEN:

The Inner Senses— What They Are and How to Use Them

In a recent class session, Seth said: "If you would momentarily put aside the selves you take for granted, you could experience your own multidimensional reality. These are not just fine words that mean nothing. I do not harp to you about theory simply because I want to spout theory, but because I want you to put these ideas into practice."

"Precisely what steps do you want us to follow?" one of the students asked.

"First, you must try to understand the nature of reality. To some small extent I have begun to explain this in the Seth Material. The five hundred and some-odd sessions we have barely represent an outline, but they are enough to start with. The ideas, in themselves, will make you think. I have told you that there are Inner Senses as well as physical ones. These will enable you to perceive reality as it exists independently of the physical world. You must learn to recognize, develop, and use these Inner Senses. The methods are given in the material. But you cannot utilize the material until you understand it.

"The material itself is—if you'll forgive the term—cleverly ex-ecuted; so that as you grapple to understand it, you are already begin-ning to use abilities beyond those that you take for granted.

"You must, first of all, cease identifying yourself completely with your ego, and realize that you can perceive more than your ego per-ceives. You must demand more of yourself than you ever have before. The material is not for those who would deceive themselves with pretty, packaged, ribboned truths that are parceled out and cut apart so that you can digest them. That sort of material serves a need, but our material demands that you intellectually and intuitively expand."

One student had a guest with her, Mary, who wrinkled up her forehead when Seth finished speaking. "But if we 'momentarily put aside' the ego," she said to me, "won't we be unconscious?"

I didn't have a chance to answer. Seth answered for me—his way. "You are an identity," he said. "Pretend that you hold a flashlight, and the flashlight is consciousness. You can turn this light in many directions, but instead you are in the habit of directing it along one certain path, and you have forgotten that there are other paths.

"All you have to do is swing the flashlight in other directions. When you shift it, the path upon which you have been focusing will momentarily appear dark, but other realities and images will become available to you, and there is nothing to prevent you from swinging the flashlight back to the earlier position."

Seth has used several analogies to explain this point. He said in another class session: "You have more than one conscious mind. We want you to change the channels of your awareness. . . . If you consider the conscious mind that you usually use as one door, then you stand at the threshold of this mind and look out into physical reality. But there are other doors . . . you have other conscious selves. . . .

"You are not expected to become unconscious, then. There is no need to feel that when you block out the ordinary conscious mind, there is only blankness. It is true that when you close one conscious mind—door—there may be a moment of disorientation before you open another.

252

"It is also true that you may need to learn the methods by which you can perceive other realities, simply because you are not used to manipulating these other conscious portions of yourself. But these portions are as critical—and even as intellectual—as valid and as real as the consciousness with which you are ordinarily familiar."

Seth insists that there is only one way to learn what consciousness is: by studying and exploring our own awareness, by changing the focus of our attention and using our own consciousness in as many ways as possible. He says: "When you look into yourself, the very effort involved extends the limitations of your consciousness, expands it, and allows the egotistical self to use abilities that it often does not realize it possesses."

The Inner Senses are not important because they release clairvoyant or telepathic abilities, but because they reveal to us our own independence from physical matter, and let us recognize our unique, individual multidimensional identity. Properly utilized, they also show us the miracle of physical existence and our place in it. We can live a wiser, more productive, happier physical life because we begin to understand why we are here, individually and as a people.

The Inner Senses help us use telepathic abilities, for example. This doesn't mean that we will always be able to "read minds." It means that in family, business, or social contacts, we will be intuitively aware of what the other person is saying to us: we will know what is beneath words. We will also use words better ourselves to communicate our inner feelings since we will know what those feelings are. We will not be afraid of them or feel the need to cover them up.

At times, we can "read minds"—though that is a popular term, leaving much to be desired. But to use the Inner Senses properly, they must be used smoothly, often blending one into the other. It is often difficult to know whether we are receiving clairvoyant or telepathic information, for example. Not that it matters. Using the Inner Senses, we simply increase our entire range of perceptions.

As I write this, I am picking up all sorts of information about my environment, but I am hardly aware of doing so. Certainly I don't consciously separate visual and auditory data unless I stop to think of it, though I know I receive the information through different senses.

253

All of the physical senses operate at once to give us our picture of reality. We use the Inner Senses the same way, constantly, far beneath usual conscious notice. In order to explain them, we must describe them separately, though their effects are felt together.

Seth began to list and explain them early in our sessions, starting in February 1964, and we are still learning to use them. I will list them as he did, and give a few excerpts from his descriptions.

INNER VIBRATIONAL TOUCH

"Think of the Inner Senses as paths leading to an inner reality. The first sense involves perception of a direct nature—instant cognition through what I can only describe as inner vibrational touch. Imagine a man standing on a typical street of houses and grass and trees. This sense would permit him to feel the basic sensations felt by each of the trees about him. His consciousness would expand to contain the experience of what it is to be a tree—any or all of the trees. He would feel the experience of *being* anything he chose within his field of notice: people, insects, blades of grass. He would not lose consciousness of who he was, but would perceive these sensations somewhat in the same way that you now feel heat and cold."

This sense is much like empathy, but far more vital. (Seth says that we can't experience these Inner Senses in their full intensity now, because our nervous systems can't handle that much stimuli.) It's difficult to categorize experiences of this kind, but I think that I was using inner vibrational touch in the following instance:

One night while Bill and Peg Gallagher were visiting us, a neighbor also came to call. Polly was a rather emotional young woman, and she asked me if I could "pick up" any impressions about her. I refused, saying that I was tired. Actually I felt that she was "highly charged," unpleasantly so, and I didn't want to get involved. Apparently my curiosity got the best of me. I switched to my Inner Senses to find out what was wrong—but without realizing that I was doing so. (In the use of the Inner Senses, like anything else, we have to learn discrimination and discretion.)

Almost instantly I saw the young woman back in 1950, as a teen-

254

ager. She was in a hospital bed, having labor pains. I felt them, in my living room. The experience was exceptionally vivid, and the pain quite real. I saw an older woman and a young man in the hospital room and was able to describe them. Polly identified the people as a former husband and his mother, but denied having a child, though she said that a girl friend delivered an illegitimate daughter that same year.

At first the pain frightened me so that I just blurted out what was happening; I didn't mean to embarrass Polly. Later I felt foolish and angry at myself, wondering if the pain episode was some kind of subconscious dramatization. Two years later Polly left town. Before she went, she called to tell me that the episode was quite legitimate. The child had been her own, and my description of the room tallied with her hospital room. Naturally, she didn't want anyone to know about the child, who had been put up for adoption (and it was none of my business anyway). She had been brooding about the birth the night she visited us, because she had just heard from the baby's father for the first time in years. Probably this is why I "tuned in" to the episode. In this case I used inner vibrational touch to become aware of her feelings.

Generally, though, this first Inner Sense can be extremely valuable, leading to expansion of experience, greater understanding, and compassion. Using it, with practice, you can feel the living emotional element of any living thing, rejoicing in its vitality. It does not diminish individuality, and it does not imply psychic invasion. We are not to be psychic Peeping Toms, but should use these abilities only to help others or, joyfully, as we use muscles and bones. The intent is important, but I don't believe that you *can* use these senses wrongfully in any basic way; if you aren't ready to utilize them properly, your own personality will see to it that you don't use them consciously at all.

PSYCHOLOGICAL TIME

"Psychological Time is a natural pathway that was meant to give an easy route of access from the inner world to the outer, and back again, though you do not use it as such. Psychological Time originally enabled man to live in the inner and outer worlds with relative ease. . . . As you develop in your use of it, you will be able to rest within its framework while you are consciously awake. It adds duration to your normal time. From its framework you will see that physical time is as dreamlike as you once thought inner time was. You will discover your whole selves, peeping inward and outward simultaneously, and know that all divisions are illusion."

Actually, in practice, Psychological Time leads to development of the other Inner Senses. In Psy-Time, as we call it, you simply turn your focus of attention inward. Sit or lie quietly alone and close your eyes. Pretend that there is a world within as vivid and real as the physical one. Turn off your physical senses. If you want, imagine that they have dials and you flip them off, one by one. Then imagine that the Inner Senses have another set of dials. Imaginatively, turn them on. This is one method of beginning.

You may, instead, just lie quietly and concentrate on a dark screen until images or lights appear on it. Do not concentrate on worries or daily trivia that may arise as soon as you block out physical distractions. If such thoughts do come to the foreground of attention, then you are not ready to proceed. First you must get rid of them.

Since we can't concentrate fully on two things at once, you may focus your attention on the screen again or on any imaginary image— this will banish the annoying worries. Or you may pretend that the worries themselves have images and then "see" these vanishing away.

At a certain point you will feel alert and conscious but very light. Within your mind you may see bright lights. You may hear sounds or voices. Some may be telepathic or clairvoyant messages. Some may simply be subconscious pictures. As you practice, you will learn to tell one from the other.

Gradually as you progress, you will feel apart from time as we know it during the exercise. You may have various kinds of subjective experiences, from extrasensory episodes to simple periods of inspiration and direction. I sometimes have out-of-body travels, for instance, during Psy-Time. This sense leads to refreshment, relaxation, and peace. It can be used in many ways, for different purposes. Most of

256

my students now utilize this sense quite well, and use it as a preliminary to other experiences.

PERCEPTION OF PAST, PRESENT, AND FUTURE

"If you will remember our imaginary man as he stands upon a street, you will recall that I spoke of his feeling all of the unitary essences of each living thing within his range, using the first Inner Sense. Using this third sense, this experience would be expanded. If he so chose, he would also feel the past amd future essence of each living thing within his range."

Remember, according to Seth these Inner Senses are used by the whole self constantly. Since past, present, and future have no basic reality, this sense allows us to see through the apparent time barriers. We are seeing things as they really are. Any precognitive experience would entail use of this Inner Sense. It is often used spontaneously when Psy-Time is practiced.

THE CONCEPTUAL SENSE

"The fourth Inner Sense involves direct cognition of a concept in much more than intellectual terms. It involves experiencing a concept completely. Concepts have what we will call electrical and chemical composition [as thoughts do]. The molecules and ions of the consciousness change into [those of] the concept, which is then directly experienced. You cannot truly understand or appreciate any living thing unless you can *become* that thing.

"You can best achieve some approximation of an idea by using Psychological Time [as a preliminary]. Sit in a quiet room. When an idea comes to you, do not play with it intellectually, but reach out to it intuitively. Do not be afraid of unfamiliar physical sensations. With practice and to a limited degree, you will find that you can 'become' the idea. You will be inside it, looking out—not looking in.

"Concepts such as I am referring to reach beyond your ideas of time and space. If you become proficient in the use of the third Inner Sense [perception of past, present, and future] when cognition is more or less spontaneous, then you can utilize the conceptual sense with more freedom. Any true concept has its origins outside of your camouflage system and continues beyond it. Unless you use the Inner Senses in this manner, you will only receive a glimmering of a concept, regardless of its simplicity."

I was using this sense, I believe, in the episode described in Chapter 17, experiencing a concept that could not be expressed adequately in words, when everything in the room seemed to grow to tremendous size.

COGNITION OF KNOWLEDGEABLE ESSENCE

"Remember that these Inner Senses operate as a whole, working together smoothly, and that to some degree the divisions between them are arbitrary on my part. This fifth sense differs from the fourth [conceptual sense] in that it does not involve cognition of a concept. It is similar to the fourth sense in that it is free from past, present, and future, and involves an intimate becoming, or transformation of self into something else.

"This is difficult to explain. You attempt to understand a friend by using your physical senses. Use of this fifth sense would enable you to enter into your friend. In its fullest sense, it is not available to you within your system. It does not imply that one entity can control another. It involves direct instantaneous cognition of the essence of living 'tissue.' I use the word 'tissue' with caution and ask you not to think of it necessarily in terms of flesh.

"All entities are in one way or another enclosed within themselves, yet also connected to others. Using this sense, you penetrate through the capsule that encloses the self. This Inner Sense, like all others, is being used constantly by the inner self, but very little of the data received is sifted through to the subconscious or ego. Without the use of this sense, however, no man would ever come close to understanding another." This sense is a stronger version of inner vibrational touch.

INNATE KNOWLEDGE OF BASIC REALITY

"This is an extremely rudimentary sense. It is concerned with the entity's innate working knowledge of the basic vitality of the uni-

258

verse, without which no manipulations of vitality would be possible—as, for example, you could not stand up straight without first having an innate sense of balance.

"Without this sixth sense and its constant use by the inner self, you could not construct the physical camouflage universe. You can compare this sense with instinct, as you think of it, although it is concerned with the innate knowledge of the entire universe. Particular data about specific areas of reality are given to a living organism to make manipulation within that area possible. The inner self has at its command complete knowledge, but only portions are used by an organism. A spider, spinning its web, is using this sense in almost its purest form. The spider has no intellect or ego, and its activities are pure spontaneous uses of the Inner Senses, unhampered and uncamouflaged to a great extent. But inherent in the spider, as in man, is the complete comprehension of the universe as a whole."

Seth always maintains that the answers to our questions about reality lie within us. They reveal themselves to us when we turn our attention away from physical data and look inward; this is when the sixth Inner Sense comes into play. It also shows itself in inspirations, and episodes of spontaneous "knowing". Surely this sense suddenly came into operation during my experience with "cosmic consciousness" and was partially responsible for my "Idea Construction" manuscript. This sense gives rise to most experiences of a revelationary character.

The trouble is that we must somehow translate the data into terms that we can understand, explaining it verbally or with images—and distortions are bound to result. Some such experiences can't be expressed physically, yet the individual concerned is convinced of their validity.

Expansion or Contraction of the Tissue Capsule

"This sense operates in two ways. It can be an extension or enlargement of the self, a widening of its boundaries and of conscious comprehension. It can also be a pulling together of the self into an ever-smaller capsule that enables the self to enter other systems of reality. The tissue capsule surrounds each consciousness and is actually an energy field boundary, keeping the inner self's energy from seeping away.

"No consciousness exists in any system without this capsule enclosing it. These capsules have also been called astral bodies. The seventh Inner Sense allows for an expansion or contraction of this tissue capsule."

Rob and I have had some experience using this Inner Sense. So have several of my students. In Psy-Time this results in a peculiar "elephantiasis" feeling: I feel as if I am expanding and yet getting lighter and lighter in weight. The sensation can also arise just before an out-of-body experience. I have felt this in reverse in several sessions with the other personality, Seth Two.

DISENTANGLEMENT FROM CAMOUFLAGE

"Complete disentanglement from camouflage comes rarely within your system, although it is possible to achieve it, particularly in connection with Psychological Time. When Psychological Time is utilized to its fullest extent, then camouflage is lessened to an astounding degree. With disentanglement, the inner self disengages itself from one particular camouflage before it either adopts another set smoothly or dispenses with camouflage entirely. This is accomplished through what you might call a changing of frequencies or vibrations: a transformation of vitality from one particular pattern or aspect to another. In some ways, your dream world gives you a closer experience with basic inner reality than does your waking world, where the Inner Senses are so shielded from your awareness."

We've had very little conscious experience with this Inner Sense. Only in one small episode, mentioned earlier, when I felt bodiless and formless, like conscious air, have I ever approached using it.

DIFFUSION BY THE ENERGY PERSONALITY

"An energy personality who wishes to become a part of your system does so using this sense. The energy personality first diffuses himself into many parts. Since entry into your plane or system, as a member of it, cannot be made in any other manner, it must be made

260

in the simplest terms, and later built up—sperm, of course, being an entry in this respect. The energy of the personality must then be recombined."

What Seth is saying here is that the inner self uses this sense to initiate the birth of one of its personalities in physical life. It may also have a part to play in some mediumistic activities on the part of the surviving personality who wishes to communicate, and it may be used in out-of-body experiences that involve other than physical reality.

What is the point in learning to use the Inner Senses? Seth spoke about some of the benefits in the recorded session he gave for the college psychology class. He said, "You will not be swallowed by subjectivity. You will learn what reality is. . . . What is not understood is that self-investigation initiates states of consciousness with which you are usually not familiar. Now these can be used as investigative tools.

"In the sort of exploration of which I am speaking, the personality attempts to go within itself, to find its way through the veils of adopted characteristics to its own inner identity. . . . The inner core of the self has telepathic and clairvoyant abilities that greatly affect family relationships—and your civilization. Now you are not using them effectively. These are precisely those abilities that are needed now. If there is to be any hope of world communication, then each of you must understand where your potentials are as individual subjective creatures.

"Books cannot tell you this. Even if you discover, through psychoanalysis, where your neuroses lie, you are in very shallow water. You are still exploring the topmost levels of your personality, and you do not have the benefit of those altered states of consciousness that occur when you look into yourself in the manner I have prescribed.

"There is a condition of consciousness that is more awake than any you have ever known—a condition in which you are aware of your own waking and dreaming selves simultaneously. You can become fully awake while the body sleeps. You can extend the present limitations of your awareness."

What Seth is alluding to is that tne practice of Psy-Time does stretch normal consciousness. All kinds of previously inhibited inspirations, hunches, and helpful extrasensory information now come into conscious awareness. When you do Psy-Time regularly, you become alert to data that comes through the Inner Senses. You react to the data and learn to handle a larger amount of stimuli than before.

This intuitional alertness carries over into daily life and into the sleeping state. Through instructions given by Seth I've learned to come fully awake while dreaming, as mentioned earlier. In this state you recognize your dreams *as* dreams and can manipulate them more or less at will. You can leave your body safely sleeping, for a projection of consciousness. All of this involves work, however—at least on my part. You must learn, through experience, to maintain the proper level of consciousness, and there is always the possibility of falling back to the usual dream state.

These levels of consciousness are only preliminaries to another state that I have reached but seldom. In this state your intellect, intuitions, and entire being operate at a level that is really supranormal. Your senses are almost unbelievably acute. This state can occur whether you are normally awake, "awake" in the sleep condition, or in a trance. But you feel as if you have lived your life in a dream and are now awake. Momentarily you are aware of your multidimensional reality. Once you have had this experience, you never forget it.

These achievements begin with the simple practice of Psy-Time. They begin when you turn your focus of attention away from physical reality for a few moments a day. Each person will experience the Inner Senses in a different way, since perception of any kind is highly individual. It is extremely difficult to use the other Inner Senses without first using Psy-Time, however. In fact some of my students "turned on" their other Inner Senses spontaneously when doing Psy-Time. Some have used Psy-Time to receive information concerning their past lives; in this case, they used many of the Inner Senses together to search out the data they wanted.

Taken together, the Inner Senses will give each individual a picture of reality as it exists independently of physical matter, an image of the inner identity that is his own. They will automatically increase concentration and release abilities that will give daily life additional meaning, vitality, and purpose.

CHAPTER TWENTY:

Personal Evaluations— Who or What Is Seth?

As human beings we live suspended between life and death. We share this with the animals. It is a condition of our existence. But animals, as far as we know, do not anticipate their own death, or wonder about their status before birth. Their present is the moment.

We are aware of past, present, and future—a series of moments strung out, it seems, one before the other. What if this series is only part of a larger present, a more spacious "moment" of which we are unaware?

We would exist in this other dimension of time whether we knew it or not, of course, just as our cat exists in my four o'clock in the afternoon, without ever understanding what a clock is. In a way, the cat is more nearly right than I am, because clock-time is an artificial device, and he'll have nothing to do with it. Suppose, as Seth maintains, that past, present, and future are also artificial devices, divisions superimposed over a spacious moment in which all action is simultaneous.

Physically we can only handle so much data at once, since we are dependent in that respect upon our neurological structure. Each sensation we have received since our birth is still intact in the subconscious. We push such details "back" so that we can handle the present. We focus our attention upon a certain group of events—the "present" ones—and then drop them into the subconscious where they seem to fall away and become distant. If we could keep our attention on these past events and still concentrate on the present ones simultaneously, then our sense of present time would be immeasurably enlarged.

And what about the future? Perhaps it consists of events already in existence in this Spacious Present; events that we have conveniently decided not to contend with "as yet." According to Seth events are not concrete in any case, but plastic, and initially they are always mental. Some we form into physical realities, in which case we follow through with the process mentioned above. Others we do not handle at all in this dimension. They never even enter our past, present, or future reference.

Are we biologically unable to perceive any of these events, or do we have psychological blind spots as defense mechanisms to prevent our being overwhelmed by reality as it actually is? Our nervous systems allow us to perceive only so much; true, but beyond this limitation, my guess is that some psychological element causes us to block out much information that we could otherwise perceive.

If we could remove these blind spots and enlarge the focus of our attention, I think that we would become aware of these other events, and that telepathy, precognition, and clairvoyance would be normal, practical methods of obtaining information. In other words, I think that ESP abilities are natural ones that we have denied because they seem to contradict our ideas of reality.

I can hear quick emotional objections. "No, if we could do all that, we'd know when we were going to die!" But suppose we saw *beyond* the point of death, discovering to our surprise that we were still conscious—not only of ourselves as we "were" but of other portions of ourselves of which we had been unaware? Suppose in fact that Seth is correct: we only inhabit the flesh, existing within it but independent of it?

266

We identify with our bodies, as indeed the psychologists tell us that we must. But this identification is based upon the idea that without a body there is no self. It also supposes that all knowledge comes to us through the physical senses. Obviously, according to this idea, we couldn't perceive anything if we were out of our bodies. In fact, there would be no self to get out to begin with, since our consciousness would be the result of our body mechanisms. This is the orthodox view of many scientists and psychologists.

Organized religion professes to hold the opposite idea, that man's identity is independent of physical matter—after death. It often looks askance, however, at any investigations that might show man taking advantage of that independence *now*. While it preaches the survival of the soul, it is suspiciously uninterested in studying cases in which there seems to be communication between the quick and the "dead."

Yet I really believe that the facts are clear to anyone broad-minded enough to look into the field of parapsychology, or bold enough to do his own experimentation into the nature of consciousness. The facts should be clear to any person who has ever experienced a valid precognitive dream, clairvoyant event, or telepathic communication.

The facts of my experience—and that of others—are these. We are, to some extent, free of our physical bodies. We can see and feel and learn while our consciousness is separated from the physical form. We can perceive portions of the future. We do have access to information that does not come through the physical senses. If it wants to, science can take a hundred years to accept these ideas. In the meantime they are still facts. Hallucination is not involved, unless I am hallucinating now as I write this page, sip my coffee, and feel honest indignation that some of us would limit our abilities to protect limited concepts. Why should we take it for granted that concepts are right, if they contradict our experience?

Since the publication of my first ESP book, many people have written me to tell me of their own instances of telepathy, clairvoyance, precognition, or projection. Some confided experiences that they kept from their closest relatives. They knew such things weren't *supposed* to happen and were afraid that an extrasensory event cast doubts on their own mental or emotional stability.

In a way I was just as bad: I questioned myself and my experiences at every corner, and still do. But at least I didn't let outdated concepts dictate what portions of my own experience I could accept as real, and what portions I must reject. But if I had not been affected by such ideas, I could have accepted my initial psychic experiences more freely and examined them wholeheartedly. Instead, particularly in the beginning, I was as much appalled as delighted with each new development.

These experiences have taught me this: We *are* multidimensional personalities now—you and I and everyone else. I think that consciousness congregates just as atoms and molecules do; that there are clumps of consciousness just as there are clumps of matter; and that we are a part of these clumps, whether we know it or not. We know little about our own psychology and less about the nature of consciousness. To learn more we must be willing to examine our *own* consciousness, individually. In doing so, I'm convinced that we will discover a greater individuality, uniqueness, and sense of identity. In sticking so close to the confines of egotistical physically oriented awareness, we may be closing ourselves off from answers to our deepest questions, knowledge that can help us deal more intelligently with physical life.

My own work is such an investigation. I consider my psychic experiences, the Seth sessions, and my entire relationship with Seth as a learning adventure—a continuing one. I think that the Seth Material contains insights and information concerning the nature of reality that are sorely needed. The theories expand the meaning of individuality and challenge us to accept the larger self that both science and religion at various times have taught us to deny.

Above all, I am sure that Seth is my channel to revelational knowledge, and by this I mean knowledge that is revealed to the intuitive portions of the self rather than discovered by the reasoning faculties. Such revelational information is available to each of us, I believe, to some degree. From it springs the aspirations and achievements of our race. I think that revelational knowledge comes first in the form of intuitions, dreams, hunches, or experiences such as mine, and that the intellect then uses the information provided. Both are important.

As to who or what Seth is, his term "energy essence personality" seems as close to the answer as anyone can get. I don't believe he is a part of my subconscious, as that term is used by psychologists, or a secondary personality. I do think that we have a supraconscious that is as far "above" the normal self as the subconscious is "below" it, though Seth maintains there are no real levels to the self—the terms just make things simpler. I ascribe ESP abilities to this supraconscious and think that it has access to information regarding the nature of reality not normally available to the egotistical portions of the personality. It may be that Seth is the psychological personification of that supraconscious extension of my normal self.

If so, how independent would he be? The question can't be answered easily. Certainly he wouldn't be present within my personality structure as I know it. I don't believe, for example, that his presence would be disclosed by any psychological testing of my own personality. The inherent relationship would snap into focus during a session, however, when the supraconscious identity would take over.

The matter of Seth's sex also arises here. To me at least, the intuitive portions of most personalities seem to have a feminine rather than masculine cast. If Seth were just my higher intuitive self, I would expect him to be feminine or to be the pseudomasculine type of male character so frequently created by women writers. Usually males instantly recognize characters drawn in this manner as overly romantic. While Seth is not "blatantly" male, in his actions and speech he is more a man's man than the woman's man type. Men like him. While he is a teacher, he is not basically the stereotyped "spiritual guide" either. He is simply himself—which may, after all, be the badge of his own independent existence.

His effect upon others is immediate. Apparently he has considerable "presence." He reacts to others, and relates much better than I do to people from various walks of life. As the excerpts show, though, he has made it plain that the characteristics by which we know him are only a portion of his personality and those he finds most helpful in getting our attention and delivering the material.

Rob asked Seth once if he was always available to us for a session, and Seth's answer shows clearly that we have more than a simple one-to-one relationship. I trust the answers that we received and think that they are honest statements about a very complicated psychological connection.

"Now, as to my availability at your sessions, you are able, within the conditions we have set, and with my assistance, to call upon the elements of my personality with which you are acquainted. Sort of a vitalized fourth-dimensional letter or communication, in which, if you'll forgive the term, the medium is the message.

"In ways, Ruburt is turned into a vitalized telegram. When you send a communication or telegram, you merely send words. I send portions of myself. My entire essence need not always be involved. I need not be entirely focused within your dimension, in other words, but I am sufficiently focused to meet our appointments. The psychological bridge of which I have spoken serves us well, however, and this exists on Ruburt's part as well as my own.

"A certain portion of my reality is, therefore, available to you during appointed hours, and the bridgework is always available. Using it Ruburt can call upon me at other occasions. Using it, I may call upon you. This does not necessarily mean that such a call will always be met by an affirmative answer on either of our parts, or that contact will be made.

"It is as if there were two portions of a bridge, like a drawbridge, and these two portions must meet. [Earlier Seth had explained that this "psychological bridge" was constructed by both of us.] When you wish to contact me at other than [the] usual appointed times, I may or may not be easily available. Your own emotional need would be known to me, however. If that need was strong, I would of course answer it, even as you would not disregard the need of a friend. I am not automatically available, however, any more than you are."

We both know that some sessions seem more "immediate" than others, and now as Seth continued we saw why.

"I am, however, automatically a part of the message that I bring to you. At times I am 'here' more completely than in other sessions. These reasons often have to do with circumstances usually beyond normal control: electromagnetic conditions, psychological circumstances. These could be considered as atmospheric conditions through which I must travel.

"As I have told you, projection is involved to some extent, both on my part and Ruburt's. Your [Rob's] own presence is also important, whether or not you are present at any given session. . . . Now when you watch, say, educational television, you see the teacher, and he speaks. He may or may not actually be speaking at that time, for you may be watching a film. But the teacher exists whether or not he is speaking at that time, and his message is legitimate. So now see Ruburt as my television screen. . . . It makes no difference whether or not I am myself speaking within Ruburt now . . . or whether I did this last night in his sleep, and tonight is a film or playback.

"Again: the medium is the message in the Spacious Present," Seth said, smiling, "and whenever the time for the program arrives, I am here in your present, regardless of where I am in what *you* would term my present. . . . I may prepare my film in advance when Ruburt is not consciously aware of it. This does not imply that such a session is less legitimate."

Seth went on to say that I had given my permission for such an arrangement, and that much of our work went on while I was sleeping or otherwise engaged. "This does not mean that I use Ruburt as a puppet, and stuff his mouth with tapes as a recorder, that you are always listening to replays, or that emotionally I am not always with you in sessions. It means that in such multidimensional communications, more is involved than you suppose.

"The teacher is within the tape; the personality is condensed. Your question stems from the feeling that if I am here, I cannot be someplace else at the same time, or that all of my energies must be focused here if I am here. There are aspects of my identity with which you are not acquainted . . . though at a 'later' time you may be.

"All the channels are not yet working on this set, you see," Seth said humorously. "You know all of me that you are able to know at any given time in your terms. It would be relatively impossible for me to make my full reality clear to you, for your understanding would not contain it. Now, take a rest period. We would not want to blow a tube. . . ."

Obviously I've avoided calling Seth a spirit and leaving it at that. I don't like the phrase for one thing, and for another, I think that this is too easy an answer. In accepting one solution, we may be closing our minds to others that lie beneath. I am not saying that Seth is *just* a psychological structure allowing me to tune into revelational knowledge, nor denying that he has an independent existence. I do think that some kind of blending must take place in sessions between his personality and mine, and that this "psychological bridge" *itself* is a legitimate structure that must take place in any such communication. Seth is at his end, I am at mine. I agree with Seth here. I don't think it is a relatively simple matter of a medium just blacking out and acting like a telephone connection. I do think that Seth is part of another entity, and that he is something quite different from, say, a friend who has "survived" death.

I don't find these ideas contradictory. Seth could still be a part of an ancient entity, and Seth Two another portion more evolved in our terms. If physical life evolves, why not consciousness itself? I don't find it difficult to accept the possibility that we might be independent fragments of such entities or clumps of consciousness. And granting this, some kind of communication between us would be possible. We would be all formed from the same "mental stuff," whatever that stuff is. To us, however, such experiences *would* seem supranormal.

Seth Two said that certain portions of my personality acted as transparent windows into these other realities and consciousnesses. If so, many such "windows" must exist. Seth Two may have evolved almost beyond our understanding. The "distance" alone would make communication difficult, and a series of translators may be necessary —Seth may be one of them.

I have many questions myself. For example: How conscious is Seth when he is not speaking through me? If he is my window into other realities, am I *his* window into physical life? My idea is that Seth is fully conscious, but of—and in—other dimensions of existence. But this only leads to the question: What is nonphysical life like?

Seth has promised to write his own book, dictated during sessions, in which he will answer some of these questions: "In my book I will show the personality from the inside out, so to speak. . . . To some extent it will relate my own experiences, but I hope it will give a picture of the nature of reality as seen by someone who is not imprisoned within the three-dimensional system.

"The book would involve a study of mediumship, not from the viewpoint of the medium, but from the viewpoint of the personality for whom she speaks. It would involve an examination of your system of reality as it appears to me. . . .

"I would make clear the nature and conditions in which I now have my existence, and explain some of the reasons for the often contradictory statements made concerning life after death—statements received by various mediums in which quite different pictures of afterlife reality are received.

"Such a book would also include my methods of entry into your system and the sort of psychological bridge personality that results. Again: what you have in sessions is not my complete identity. There must be some sort of psychological structure present for me to use during my communications. At times, however, my identity comes through clearly enough so that, comparatively speaking, I can exist independently, as myself, without Ruburt's assistance.

"Such a book would have nothing to do with Ruburt's own writing, which would progress at its own rate. . . . The book would bear my name, but I would dedicate it to the both of you," he said with a broad smile.

"That's nice," Rob said dryly.

Naturally I do not claim that the material represents pure, undistorted knowledge. This question of distortion came up for perhaps the fiftieth time in the 463rd session. After I signed the contract for this book, our friend Peg Gallagher was doing a story about Seth for the local paper, and she attended a session to get material. After several joking remarks to Peg ("Someday I will interview *you*"), Seth began speaking about distortions.

"Now whether or not a medium is in a trance that is as deep as the Atlantic Ocean, the medium will not be a pure channel. The ego simply will be bypassed, but the other layers of the self, and the neurological structures particularly, will continue to operate as always. They will be altered by the perceptions that pass through them."

He went on to say that vocal communication is not the rule. It is not used by more advanced entities nor by less developed ones than ourselves. In order to make sense to our three-dimensional selves, information must be "squeezed" through—and this in itself causes some distortion.

"The words I speak to you transmit information, but the words are not the information, only the verbal carriers of it.

"Information can rarely flow like crystal-clear water, with the medium [as] a faucet to be turned off and on at will. It must be sifted through the layers of the medium's personality. The nervous system reacts to the data even as it translates it. Nothing is neutral in those terms. The information is received and translated, as it must be, into mechanisms which the nervous system can handle and interpret. Like any perception, the information then becomes a part of the nervous system's structure. It cannot be otherwise.

"Any perception instantly alters the electromagnetic and neurological systems of the perceiver. In your terms this is what a perception is: an alteration of neurological structure. The receiving mechanisms themselves change, and are changed by that which they perceive. I am speaking here of the physical nature of any perception.

"It is a logistic contradiction to imagine, with your physical structures, that any perception can be received without the perceiver's inner situation being altered. I am trying to make it as clear as possible—information automatically blends with, is intermingled with, and enmeshed with, the entire physically valid structure of the personality.

"Any perception is action and it changes that upon which it acts, and *in so doing, it is itself changed*. The slightest perception alters every atom within your body. This, in turn, sends out its ripples, so that as you know, the most minute action is felt everywhere."

Seth goes on to give examples of the various kinds of distortion that can occur in normal and extrasensory perception. "Now, Ruburt, or any individual in a low mood, might misinterpret information, overstating pessimistic elements. Persons given to the need for self-punishment will consistently misinterpret any perception in this manner."

As Seth continues to explain the nature of perception, it becomes obvious that physical perception itself shapes reality into certain forms. Even extrasensory perception must be translated into physical terms, if we are to be consciously aware of it. The Seth Material reveals what is beneath the normal reality that we know, but the very translation into words must necessarily distort the meaning.

Besides this, there are other variables. Seth is not static; he does not just methodically deliver the material as if we were recorders. He responds to questions, so that to some extent the questions put to him must, at times, cause him to change the particular way he discusses a particular subject.

Since he is responsive, he must be affected by his relationship to us (though perhaps not to the extent that we are affected by him!). There is no doubt that my own personality has grown as it accommodated itself to the Seth experience. I had to learn to handle more stimuli than ever before, and to maintain overall stability as I learned to develop latent abilities. This certainly involved strains and stresses as well as rewards: but none that couldn't be resolved with a sense of humor and some common sense. When I feel I need a rest, I take a break, which Seth respects with good grace.

With all Seth has told us about man's potentials, I must admit that we've wondered at times why the race isn't more developed morally and spiritually.

One night before our regular Wednesday session Rob and I were pretty upset over the state of the world in general. We sat talking and Rob wondered aloud why we behaved as we did. "What real sense or purpose is behind it all?" he said. "Granted some part of us knows what we're doing, still we seem hell-bent on destroying the planet, if not through war, then through pollution."

"I don't know," I said. I felt as bad as he did.

That was November 6, 1968, and starting that night we had a series of sessions dealing with the questions that were foremost in our minds. On that particular evening, our 446th session, the other personality, Seth Two, came through in that distant clear voice.

Among other things, Seth Two said: "The human race is a stage through which various forms of consciousness travel. . . . Before you can be allowed into systems of reality that are more extensive and open, you must first learn to handle energy and see, through physical materialization, the concrete result of thought and emotion. As a child forms mud pies from dirt, so you form your civilizations out of thoughts and emotions, and then see what you have created.

"When you leave the physical system after reincarnations, you have learned the lessons—and you are literally no longer a member of the human race, for you elect to leave it. Only the conscious self dwells within it in any case, and other portions of your identity dwell simultaneously within other training systems. In more advanced systems, thoughts and emotions are automatically and immediately translated into action, into whatever approximation of matter there exists. Therefore, the lessons must be taught and learned well.

"The responsibility for creation must be clearly understood. To some extent, you are in a soundproof and isolated room. Hate creates destruction in that 'room,' and until the lessons are learned, destruction follows destruction. . . .

"In the terms of other systems, that kind of destruction does not exist—but you *believe* that it does, and the agonies of the dying are sorely felt. A vivid nightmare is also sorely felt, but quickly over. It is not that you must be taught not to destroy, for destruction does not actually exist. It is that you must be taught and trained to create responsibly. Yours is a training system for emerging consciousness. . . .

"The training will serve you for existence in a variety of inter-related systems. If the sorrows and agonies within your system were not felt as real, the lessons would not be learned. The teachers within your system are those who are in their last reincarnation, and other personalities who have left the system but have been assigned to help those still within it. . . .

"You are dealing with the transformation of emotional energy into action and form. You then manipulate within the system which you have yourselves created, and by its effects learn where you have succeeded and failed. The system includes some fragment personalities who are entering for the 'first' time, as well as those in later reincarnations.

"Humanity dreams the same dream at once, and you have your mass world. The whole construction is like an educational play in which you are the producers as well as the actors. There is a play within a play within a play. There is no end to the 'within' of things. The dreamer dreams, and the dreamer within the dream dreams. But the dreams are not meaningless, and the actions within them are significant. The whole self is the observer and also a participator in the roles."

The Seth sessions are still continuing, twice a week. Seth's topics and range of conversation are widening and growing continually. If what we have so far is an "outline," then it is an outstanding one.

As Seth Two says: "It is not that your being exists in a lesser reality. It is that you have not learned to recognize the extent of the reality in which you do exist." I hope that this book and the Seth Material have given the reader some glimpse of his own multidimensional existence.

APPENDIX

In the foregoing chapters, I have taken excerpts from many sessions in order to present Seth's views on various topics. This appendix is included for those readers who would like a more complete look at individual sessions, and a clearer idea of the way in which the material was originally given.

For this reason I've chosen three full, though brief, sessions, and portions of several consecutive recent ones. This presentation shows Seth's way of weaving one subject through another as he inserts new discussions and information while building on past sessions, and points up his method of using Rob's and my own daily experiences as a launching pad for his own material.

The appendix includes several subjects not covered in the book proper. In one session, Seth discusses Jung's concept of the unconscious. In another, he presents some new material on the "original planetary system," and in answer to a friend's question, he begins an explanation of the perception of a fetus. These discussions show the current direction the Seth Material is taking as it constantly unfolds.

The sessions on the electromagnetic units that lie just beneath the range of matter have begun just now as I finish this book. Scientists have long wondered what physical matter "disappeared into," and Seth's EE units may well be the answer.

Except for punctuation, the Seth Material in this appendix is unedited, and Rob's notes have been included.

SESSION 452, DECEMBER 2, 1968, 9:17 P.M. MONDAY

Good evening.

(*"Good evening, Seth."*)

Now: Children build houses of cards and knock them down. You do not worry about the child's development, for you realize that he will learn better.

You may even smile at the child's utter sense of desolation until he finally connects the motion of his own hand with the destruction of the paper cardboard house that is now gone, and in his eyes, gone beyond repair.

Now, mankind builds civilizations. He has gone beyond the child's game. The toys are real, and yet basically the analogy holds. I am not condoning those violences that occur. The fact is that they can never be condoned, and yet they must be understood for what they are: man, learning through his own errors. He also learns by his successes, and there are times when he holds his hand, moments of deliberation, periods of creativity. (*Pause.*) Identities take many roles in many lives.

There are periods, cycles if you prefer, through which such identities live and learn again within your system. To some extent they are taught by others—practice teachers if you prefer. (*Amused.*)

(*Today the newspaper carried the story of the violence attending the Democratic presidential convention in Chicago in August 1968, telling of the many clashes between police and various groups of demonstrators; a guilty verdict re police behavior was rendered by an investigative commission. Jane and I had discussed the report at the supper table.*)

The *race* of man is far more than the physical race, however. You

280

see him in but one stage of development. When an individual leaves your system, it is for other systems. He has learned his ABC's, but that is all. There are exceptions—identities who choose to return and teach. They are not in the same league, so to speak, as those whose reincarnational cycles are not complete. They may return, even enduring violence, as a man might set up a school amid a jungle of savages.

Yet with all of this, there are advances made within your system itself. A nuclear weapon in the hands of the inhabitants of Middle-Age Europe would have been used almost immediately, and with nary a qualm, to wipe out all but Christendom. Christendom may well have perished along with the rest of the world, but this possibility would not have been considered, so narrow and evilly self-righteous were the governing powers at the time.

In those days neither did a sane, reasonable man give thought to sharing his wealth, or even consider the plight of the poorer classes. Not only was charity not given, its practical nature was not even considered. The archaic concept of God (*at that time*) nicely covered such matters. The poor were obviously sinful. Poverty was their penance, and it was considered a sacrilege to try to help those whom God had cursed. Animals were tortured in sport. Compassion for living things in males was regarded as a weakness to be plucked out. Women were scarcely thought of as human, except in very select circles.

The progression through the centuries would be far more noticeable if you knew all the facts. There is one aspect here that I have not previously mentioned: Man was not allowed to play with the more dangerous toys until certain evidence was given that he had gained some control. This does not mean that he could not have destroyed the world he knew. It simply meant that such destruction was not inevitable. You do not give a child a loaded gun if you are certain he is going to shoot himself or his neighbor.

Now: the weapons and destruction are the obvious things that you see. The counterparts are not so evident, and yet it is the counterparts that are important: the self-discipline learned, the control, the compassion that finally is aroused, and the final and last lesson learned—

281

the positive desire for creativity and love over destruction and hatred. When this is learned, the reincarnational cycle is finished.

There is a reason why these lessons must be learned in just this way. Elementally there is only creativity. Destruction is merely the changing of form. A cloudburst or a tornado knows nothing of destruction. This same energy encased within a human form is something else. There are different kinds of creativity, then, that must be learned, and a specialization in energy's focus and feelings that emerges—elemental energy becoming conscious of itself and aware of issues that did not exist for it "earlier"; millions of molecules momentarily united with living consciousness, filled with primal energy, now learning love and forming highly sensitive psychic patterns; electrical charges that now form emotions instead of clouds; the innocent chaos of undifferentiated personality that exists behind the highly specified and truly sophisticated mechanism of one thought. And all of this before an individual is born within your system! In terms of time, this is behind us all.

Little wonder that psychic battles wage. And yet beyond your system there are refinements impossible to describe and further developments more miraculous than those that have gone before. And through all of this, the entity formed from that massive chaos retains its identity and its knowledge of its "pasts" and continues to grow in creativity.

This is some of the most important material that I have given you, for you have wondered about the purpose (*of consciousness within this system*), and have been able often only to see one small speck of time and space.

The violence that you were both speaking of this evening opened up a chasm within each participator's soul, through which he glimpsed the dizzying origins that were behind his identity. There was the fear, then and afterward, of falling back into that "mindless" chasm.

Now a storm at times will fascinate many, and so will such a violence, but a highly destructive storm will find few going abroad in it. Each participator sensed the chaos to which he had direct access. (*Emphatic.*) He feared it even in his fascination, because he was bound to recognize that it would sweep him and his enemy into insanity or death.

Many of the participators have never known that they had access to such energy; therefore, the notion that it could be used creatively never entered their heads. Many of them felt tiny, alone, and powerless. Now the energy itself was exhilarating. For the first time, many of the participators realized intuitively that such energy was also the source of creativity. A good number of them will try various methods of reexperiencing this energy in order to release creative feelings they did not know they possessed. The energy, of course, was neutral. It was their use of it at the time that caused the destructive elements.

The energy that was liberated, however, has already changed your national scene and will continue to do so. Such massive liberations of energy will be used, but not in your lifetimes, to begin to unify the whole planet in peace. This will not happen before disasters also occur, but when it does happen it will represent the first time within the planet's history when there was peace with equality for all.

There have been various periods that were peaceful, but there was no equality. There have been countless other civilizations that have destroyed themselves in the planet's past, and before this, when another planet was approximately in earth's position. There were, however, civilizations that endured, that outlasted their planet, and went elsewhere.

Now you may take your break, and we shall continue.

(*10:09. Jane paused for a few moments, then resumed after I had thought she was out of trance and had called her name.*)

There were nine planets once, grouped like jewels around the sun. They were evenly spaced, one from the other, and they were evenly distributed outward from the sun. And this was the first system that knew the race of man. These were in your corner of the universe, but in your terms they would have seemed to have drifted off so far that none of your instruments could ever find them.

They exploded and were re-created many times—disappeared and returned. They would seem to pulsate. To you, they would seem to disappear for eons. To them, their existence was continuous. As atoms and molecules give your chairs a reality within your system

283

even though the atoms and molecules themselves come and go, so this planetary system still retains its identity. Your astronomers may perceive a ghost image of it at the edges of your universe, but only a reflection from a reality that you cannot perceive. Now take your break.

(*10:19. Jane left trance easily, eyes opening after a bit. She said she had been far out though and had a vision of the planets and sun.*)

(*I made a quick mental count of the planets we now know to be in our solar system, for a total of nine, the same total given by Seth. Naturally, Seth's data gave rise to many questions, but tonight wouldn't see them answered.*)

(*Just before break ended, Jane said, "I just got a whole chunk of thought from Seth." Resume at 10:31.*)

Now: existence uses form. When a planetary system is disrupted, in many cases entities who are attracted to it or consider it their home, simply change their form, regroup their forces, and—if they consider it worthwhile—put the house back in order. They enter, then, such forms as are available or make such forms as could survive. This has been done within your own system on several occasions. It is not *often* done, however, since with the materials at hand, often a complicated-enough structure cannot be formed in which consciousness can fully enough express itself.

There can be, in your terms, some loss of memory—complications that confuse the knowledge of origin. When the situation does occur, there is always a division of forces, some entities turning to form, and others not entering the process. These watch, keeping their memories and knowledge intact, and acting as directors against whose memories the new models are formed. Again: this has happened within your own system.

Many entities have no need for form, in your terms. But we will not be concerned with them this evening. This original system of which I have spoken will at least be theorized shortly, but the idea will not be taken seriously enough to cause any deep controversy.

The energy of this system was enormous, far greater than any you know, and the debris thrown off constantly from its pulsations gave birth to other systems. (*Long pause.*) We are struggling with Ruburt's vocabulary. (*Pause.*) The speed of its motion was also far greater than any you know, though it speeded up and slowed down in a cyclic manner.

(*Jane paused again. Her pace was slow in here and she used many gestures, drawing pictures in the air, frowning at times.*)

It possessed creatures of consciousness, but not as you know creatures. Energy, entities (*long pause*), continually transforming massive roytans . . .

(*Or perhaps roetans—my phonetic interpretation. I wasn't sure of the word Seth or Jane used and didn't press the point beyond one question which wasn't answered . . .*)

We are working with Ruburt's vocabulary.

(*"Do you mean roentgens?" I meant here the international unit of X rays.*)

They originated from themselves, massive units of energy that reacted automatically and in an explosive manner upon the form of the system. Their energy caused the behavior of the system.

There was a direct and instantaneous reaction between consciousness and matter, an outburst of electromagnetic power strong enough to seed a universe. Your universe is but one of many, and you perceive but a small portion of it. Now I will end the session unless you have questions.

(*"I'll have some later."*)

The evening's material has come to a natural breaking-off point, but we have also reached some subjects that we have not discussed in previous sessions, and tonight's session can serve as a preparation for later information. My heartiest good wishes to you both, and a fond good evening.

(*"Good evening, Seth."*)

(*10:52. Jane left trance quickly, though it had been deep. She felt a strong energy flow at session's end, she said.*)

SESSION 453, DECEMBER 4, 1968, 9:06 P.M. WEDNESDAY

(*Sue Mullin was a witness.*)

Good evening.

(*"Good evening, Seth."*)

Thank you for inviting me to your party.

(*"Okay."*)

Now: The planetary system of which we spoke in our last session was the first one within your universe, when you are speaking in terms of time. It is very difficult to explain to you that the universe that you see, the stars and planets that you view, are one-dimensional, comparatively speaking. You only perceive the portions of them that are apparent within your own system of reality.

The heavy hydrogen molecules had a large part to play in the birth of that (*earlier*) system. Consciousnes had first to create the void or the dimension in which the system could exist, and also to endow that void with all the probabilities for development that have come about in your time and are to come about. The void, in other terms, can therefore be compared to a mind, and who can predict what images or thoughts will be given birth there? There are, as I have told you, countless such systems, and yet within them all there is identity and direction.

This vast void, this infinite mind, came out of another that was greater than itself. (*Seth smiled.*) The possibilities that have come to reality within this universal system have each given birth to other systems and realities, as one tree bears a thousand seeds. You, yourselves, through your own mental actions, create realities of which you are unaware, and you give birth to more than physical children.

You do not understand the dimensions into which your own thoughts drop, for they continue their own existence, and others look up to them and view them like stars. I am telling you that your own thoughts and mental actions appear to the inhabitants of other systems like the stars and planets within your own; and *those* inhabitants do not perceive what lies within and behind the stars in their own heavens. Though they probe their own universe, they will not wander into your reality. They will only perceive the shape and form that your own mental acts—thoughts and dreams—take within their own system.

This last is material that we have not given you earlier, lest the implications lead you to feelings of insignificance. But you are not just receivers, you are also givers. As your own universe was formed by entities that you do not presently understand, so the discards of your own consciousness form realities for entities that are scarcely aware of your existence.

In this abundance nothing is meaningless nor wasted. There is interrelationship, intertwining realities, and connections that cannot be denied. I told you, for example, that dream reality consisted of more than you knew, and that the dream universe continued whether or not you perceived it. Within that context, those inhabitants dream—in turn—their own dreams, and form electromagnetic realities. You are not at the top nor at the bottom of the heap of consciousness, so to speak. You are not at the center, nor at the rim.

Instead, the inner self is intimately connected with each reality, though you are not aware of it; and the inner self can trace its own connections through the network of any existence and still keep its identity.

Remember, when we speak of the beginnings of your system, we speak only in consideration of your ideas of time. All, obviously, then exists at once. To your way of thinking, some lives are lived in a twinkling (*in various systems*), and others last for centuries. The perception of consciousness is not limited, however. I have told you, for example, that trees have their own consciousness. The consciousness of a tree is not as specifically focused as your own, yet to all intents and purposes, the tree is conscious of fifty years before its existence, and fifty years hence.

Its sense of identity spontaneously goes beyond the change of its own form. It has no ego to cut the "I" identification short. Creatures without the compartment of the ego can easily follow their own identity beyond any change of form. The inner self is aware of this integrity of identity, but the ego, focused so securely in physical reality, cannot afford this luxury.

Any consciousness is, therefore, innately aware of its basic identity. The inner self knows what is behind the physical stars and planets that the eye views, but the ego would be swept aside in panic at such realization.

The system spoken of earlier, the sun and original nine planets, in your terms have long ago passed into and formed other universal systems. The whole cosmic structure, however, was the materialization of one original thought, for the thought, the basic reality, must always exist before its representation. There was intelligence, therefore, within that first system. Now, you may take a break and we shall continue, and my heartiest wishes to our friend (*Sue*).

(*9:36. Jane came out of trance quickly, but said that the trance had been a good one. Seth came through rather stronger than usual and somewhat rapidly in a louder voice. Resume in the same manner at 9:44.*)

Now: again, each thought forms its own electromagnetic reality and is composed of energy which can never be dissipated, but only transformed. The subjective reality of one man, left alone in the universe, would emit enough energy to seed another. That sentence is not distorted.

You are going to have some extra sessions this weekend. I do not want to overdo Ruburt's resources, nor do I want to keep you strapped to the typewriter for three weeks. Therefore, this will be a very brief session, to supplement the material in our last session. I will still get the better of the bargain. (*Humorously.*) My heartiest good wishes to you all, then. I will remain awhile to enjoy your conversation.

(*"Good night, Seth."*)

(*9:48. It took Jane awhile to come out of trance. "I may be done, but I'm not back yet. I hate it when I'm half in and half out. It's like I'm in a cone. I can hear what's going on out there, but I still have to get out," she said.*)

(*By 9:55 we thought she was out of trance, but this proved to be an overestimation. Seth, or the trance state, lingered. Jane showed definite tendencies to go back into trance, notably a rolling up of the eyes, and I continually talked her out of it, gave her tea, etc.*)

(*One circumstance that kept her in this state came to my attention when she casually mentioned as she sat in the rocker, "Seth's still here. He's over to my right now," and she reached out with her arm. Seth, it seemed, occupied a space about five feet high, a "blob" of space into which I could step, just at the limit of Jane's reach, without*) *disturbing him. Seth's presence lingered into the evening as the three of us talked.)*

SESSION 503, SEPTEMBER 24, 1969, 9:32 P.M. WEDNESDAY

(About two pages of personal material was deleted here.)

(To resume: Sue Mullin, now Sue Watkins, one of Jane's ESP class members, left three questions last night for Seth to answer when possible. Here is question one: "When I project my consciousness out of my body, is my astral body pregnant because I am now pregnant physically? Does the astral body carry the astral counterpart of the fetus, or does the astral fetus remain in the physical body within the physical fetus?")

(I now asked Seth: "Can you say a little bit about Sue's first question, about the astral body of the fetus?" Jane had read Sue's questions some time earlier, but she didn't know I was going to ask any of the questions this evening.)

The fetus does have its own astral form. Now, this astral form belongs to the individual, the personality as it will be in this life. It is not the astral form that existed in a "previous" reincarnation. There are many complicated issues here and I will try to put them simply.

There is great energy connected with the fetus, for at no other time in physical life is so much energy utilized so purposefully and so well directed. It is this charge of energy of truly cosmic proportion that allows for the initial breakthrough into matter. The personality is busy transforming literally infinite data. Much of this work has already been done by the third month of pregnancy. As quickly as the new data forms the fetus and physical structure, the self from the previous reincarnation must begin to withdraw its hold. It enters briefly into this process (*of birth*) but it does not *become* the new individual.

It helps form the new individual, and then it must withdraw. The new self unit must be free and not hampered by the demands that could otherwise be put upon it. The new individual has a deeply buried memory of its past lives, but the personal consciousness of the

289

last reincarnated self must not be superimposed upon this new identity. The new personality, in its small astral body, does visit with other portions of the entire identity. It is even given lessons of a kind, but it is very much its own self.

(*"Does it project when Sue does, for instance?"*)

It may or may not. It does not have to. It may project to other areas entirely while Sue is somewhere else in her astral form. There is, at this time, however, a very strong connection between the two. On a deeper level, they are aware of their locations. The mother knows where the child is, even though she is not conscious of this. The mother may even go out after the child in a projection and bring it home.

Many natural abortions are caused when the new personality is having difficulty constructing the new form, projects to others for advice, and is advised not to return.

SESSION 504, SEPTEMBER 29, 1969, 9:17 P.M. MONDAY

Excerpt

I would like to add to the discussion we began in our last session. The fetus sees the physical environment. The cellular structure at that point responds to light, and activates latent abilities in the cellular structure of the mother's body. Quite literally, he sees through her body and with the aid of her body.

These are not sharp images, but he already begins to build up ideas of shape and form. It goes without saying, that the eyelids are also thus equipped. He can see through closed eyelids, in other words. He is aware of light and shadow, of shape and form, though he must learn to distinguish these portions from the available field of reality that you accept as objects, from the available field that you do not accept as objects.

He sees more than you do, or more than his mother does, because he does not yet realize that you only accept certain patterns and reject others. By the time he is born he has already learned to accept his parents' idea of what reality is. In a large sense he begins to train himself to focus only upon what you would call physical reality, though he still partially perceives other fields that you do not accept. He is only recognized and his wants satisfied, when he focuses in one particular reality. He learns quickly, then, to discard the others.

Now the fetus also hears, and the same thing applies here while within the womb. He hears sounds from the physical environment, but also sounds within the available range of reality that you do not accept. When the infant is born, he still hears these sounds and voices, but again, they do not answer his physical needs, nor bring milk when he cries, and gradually he discards them.

For some time he literally perceives many levels of reality at once, and part of what seems to be disorientation is simply the result of early confusion with so much data. According to the individual and the situation, the fetus may still be receiving messages from those he has known in the past. This adds to the confusion, and it is a matter of physical survival that he largely ignores these messages while he learns to focus in physical reality.

He is quite aware of temperature changes, for example, and the weather. He is in telepathic communication with animals and other people, and on a different level he is in a kind of communication with plants and other such consciousnesses. Plants will react quite sharply to an abortion. The fetus, however, will also react to the death of an animal in the family, and will be acquainted with the unconscious psychic relationships within the family long before it reaches the sixth month.

The plants in a house are also quite aware of the growing fetus; the plants will also pick up the fact that a member of the family is ill, often in advance of physical symptoms. They are that sensitive to the consciousness within cellular structure. Plants will also know whether a fetus is male or female.

(*Personal material, two pages, deleted.*)

(*Earlier this evening I'd mentioned to Jane my long-standing interest in Seth's statement, years ago, that all ESP perceptions have an electromagnetic basis. I was curious about this, because we'd read that no investigation has turned up any such electromagnetic relationship. Now I asked Seth about this.*)

I would rather tie this into our information on the fetus.

(*"Okay."*)

And in that way we can carry on both discussions.

(*"All right."*)

Now: there are electromagnetic structures, so to speak, that are presently beyond your (*scientific*) instruments, units that are the basic carriers of perception. They have a very brief "life" in your terms. Their size varies. Several units may combine, for example; many units may combine. To put this as simply as possible, it is not so much that they move through space, as that they *use* space to move through. There is a difference.

In a manner of speaking, thermal qualities are involved, and also laws of attraction and repulsion. The units charge the air through which they pass, and draw to them other units. The units are not stationary in the way that, say, a cell is stationary within the body. Even a cell only appears stationary. These units have no "home." They are built up in response to emotional intensity.

They are one form that emotional energy takes. They follow their own rules of attraction and repulsion. As a magnet, you see, will attract with its filaments, so these units attract their own kind and form patterns which then appear to you as perception.

Now: the fetus utilizes these units. So does any consciousness, including that of a plant. Cells are not just responsive to light because this is the order of things, but because an emotional desire to perceive light is present.

The desire appears on this other level in the form of these electromagnetic units, which then cause a light sensitivity. These units are freewheeling. They can be used in normal perception or what you call extrasensory perception. I will discuss their basic nature at a later session, and I would like to tie this in with the fetus, since the fetus is highly involved with perceptive mechanisms.

(*"Next session will be fine."*)

It is not that you cannot devise instruments to perceive these units. Your scientists are simply asking the wrong questions, and do not think in terms of such freewheeling structures.

Excerpt

Good evening.

(*"Good evening, Seth."*)

Now: These units of which we spoke earlier are basically animations rising from consciousness. I am speaking now of the consciousness within each physical particle regardless of its size—of molecular consciousness, cellular consciousness, as well as the larger gestalts of consciousness with which you are usually familiar. Because of Ruburt's limited scientific vocabulary, this is somewhat difficult to explain. Also some of the theories I will present to you in this discussion will be quite unfamiliar to you.

These emanations rise as naturally as breath, and there are other comparisons that can be made, in that there is a coming in and a going out, and transformation within the unit, as what is taken into the lungs, for example, is not the same thing that leaves on the exhale stroke. You could compare these units, simply for an analogy, to the invisible breath of consciousness. This analogy will not carry us far, but it will be enough initially to get the idea across. Breath is, of course, also a pulsation, and these units operate in a pulsating manner. They are emitted by the cells, for example, in plants, animals, rocks, and so forth. They would have color if you were able to perceive them physically.

They are electromagnetic, in your terms, following their own patterns of positive and negative charge, and following also certain laws of magnetism. In this instance, like definitely attracts like. The emanations are actually emotional tones. The varieties of tones, for all intents and purposes, are infinite.

The units are just beneath the range of physical matter. None are identical. However, there is a structure to them. This structure is beyond the range of electromagnetic qualities as your scientists think of them. Consciousnesses actually produces these emanations, and they are the basis for any kind of perception, both sensory in usual terms and extrasensory.

We are only beginning this discussion. Later you will see that I am

293

making it simple for you, but you will not understand it unless we start in this manner. I do intend to explain the structure of these units. Now, give us a moment.

These emanations can also appear as sounds, and you will be able to translate them into sounds long before your scientists discover their basic meaning. One of the reasons why they have not been discovered is precisely because they are so cleverly camouflaged within *all* structures. Being just beyond the range of matter, having a structure but a nonphysical one, and being of a pulsating nature, they can expand or contract. They can completely envelop, for example, a small cell, or retreat to the nucleus within. They combine qualities of a unit and a field, in other words.

There is another reason why they remain a secret from Western scientists. Intensity governs not only their activity and size, but the relative strength of their magnetic nature. They will draw other such units to them, for example, according to the intensity of the emotional tone of the particular consciousness at any given "point."

These units then obviously change constantly. If we must speak in terms of size, then they change in size constantly as they expand and contract. Theoretically there is no limit, you see, to their rate of contraction or expansion. They are also absorbent. They do give off thermal qualities, and these are the only hint that your scientists have received of them so far.

Their characteristics draw them toward constant interchange. Clumps of them (*Jane gestured; her delivery was quite emphatic and animated*) will be drawn together, literally sealed, only to drop away and disperse once more. They form—and their nature is behind—what is commonly known as air, and they use this to move through. The air, in other words, can be said to be formed by animations of these units.

I will try to clear this later, but the air is the result of these units' existence, formed by the interrelationship of the units in their positions and relative distance one from the other, and by what you could call the relative velocity of their motion. Air is what happens when these units are in motion, and it is in terms of weather that their electromagnetic effects appear most clearly to scientists, for example.

These units—let us discuss them as they are related to a rock. The rock is composed of atoms and molecules, each with their own consciousness. This forms a gestalt rock consciousness. These units are sent out indiscriminately by the various atoms and molecules, but portions of them are also directed by the overall rock consciousness. The units are sent out by the rock, informing the rock as to the nature of its changing environment: the angle of the sun and temperature changes, for example, as night falls; and even in the case of a rock, they change as the rock's loosely called emotional tone changes. As the units change, they alter the air about them which is the result of their own activity.

They constantly emanate out from the rock and return to it in a motion so swift it would seem simultaneous. The units meet with, and to some extent merge with, other units sent out, say, from foliage and all other objects. There is a constant blending, and also attraction and repulsion.

You may take your break, and we will continue.

(10:10. Jane's delivery was quite emphatic and animated throughout. Her trance state was good.)

(The rest of the session was devoted to Seth's interpretation of one of my dreams—Robert Butts.)

SESSION 506, OCTOBER 27, 1969, 9:40 P.M. MONDAY

(Sometime after 9 P.M. Jane and I sat to see if Seth would come through. I told Jane she needn't have a session, but she was willing enough, if Seth decided to. She has been working long hours on her book and has but a couple of chapters to rewrite.)

(Jane has had two recent, excellent and long sessions for her ESP class, however, featuring both Seth and Seth II, and including new material.)

Good evening.

("Good evening, Seth.")

Now: Ruburt need not worry that he has missed a few regular sessions. He has been exercising spontaneity, and paradoxically enough, it is upon spontaneity that the regularity of our sessions depends. Do you follow me?

("Yes.")

Now: the units about which I have been speaking do not have any specific, regular, preordained "life." They will not seem to follow many scientific principles. Since they are the intuitive force just beyond the range of matter, upon which matter is formed, they will not follow the laws of matter, although at times they may mimic the laws of matter.

It is almost impossible to detect an individual unit, for in its dance of activity it constantly becomes a part of other such units, expanding and contracting, pulsating and changing in intensity, in force, and *changing* polarity. This last is extremely important.

(*Pause, one of many.*)

With Ruburt's limited vocabulary, this is rather difficult to explain, but it would be *as if* the positions of your north and south poles changed constantly while maintaining the same relative distance from each other, and by their change in polarity upsetting the stability (*pause*) of the planet—except that because of the greater comparative strength at the *poles* of the units (*gestures, attempts to draw diagrams in the air*), a newer stability is almost immediately achieved after each shifting. Is that much clear?

("*Yes.*")

The shifting of polarity occurs in rhythm with changing emotional intensities, or emotional energies, if you prefer. The "initial" originating emotional energy that sets any given unit into motion, and forms it, then causes the unit to become a highly charged electromagnetic field with those characteristics of changing polarities just mentioned. The changing polarities are also caused by attraction and repulsion from other like units which may be attached or detached. There is a rhythm that underlies all of this changing polarity and changing intensities that occur constantly. But the rhythms have to do with the nature of emotional energy itself, and not with the laws of matter.

Without an understanding of these rhythms, the activity of the units would appear haphazard, chaotic, and there would seem to be nothing to hold the units together. Indeed, they seem to be flying apart at tremendous speeds. The "nucleus"—now using a cell analogy—if these units were cells, which they are not, then it would be as if the nucleus were constantly changing position, flying off in all directions, dragging the rest of the cell along with it. Do you follow the analogy?

("Yes.")

The units obviously are *within* the reality of all cells. Now: the initiation point is the basic part of the unit, as the nucleus is the important part of the cell. The initiation point is the originating, unique, individual, and specific emotional energy that forms any given unit. It becomes the entryway into physical matter.

It is the initial three-sided enclosure from which all matter must spring. The initial point forms the three sides about it. (*Gestures; pause.*) There is an explosive nature as the emotional energy is born. The three-sided effect, instantly formed, leads to an effect that is something like friction, but the effect causes (*more gestures*) the three sides to change position, so that you end up with a triangular effect, closed, with the initial point inside the triangle. Now, you understand this is not a physical form.

("Yes.")

The energy point, from here on, constantly changes the form of the unit, but the procedure I have just mentioned must first occur. The unit may become circular, for example. Now these intensities of emotional energy, forming the units, end up by transforming all available space into what they are. Certain intensities and certain positions of polarity between and among the units and great groupings of the units compress energy into solid form (*resulting in matter*). The emotional energy within the units is obviously the motivating factor, and you can see, then, why emotional energy can indeed shatter a physical object. You may take your break.

(*10:10. Jane came out of trance quickly enough, though it had been a good one. At times her delivery had been quite fast. She said she could feel Seth pushing at her to get her to let the material through as clearly as possible without distortion.*)

(*She also had some images while giving the material, though she could not remember them by break. Usually, she said, she forgets any images, or even whether or not she has had any, unless I specifically ask at once when a session is over or at break. Sometimes, she said, the same images will return to her when she reads a particular session; she then recognizes them.*)

(*Jane made it a point to mention that in regard to the switch in polarities of the units:* "This isn't only with the north and south switching, but opposites anywhere on the rim of the circle [*that was used as an analogy*], with east and west reversed, for instance.")

(*Resume 10:26.*)

Now: the intensity of the original emotional energy controls the activity, strength, stability, and relative size of the unit; the rate of its pulsation, and its power to attract and repel other units, as well as its ability to combine with other units.

The behavior of these units changes in the following manner. When a unit is in the act of combining with another, it aligns its components in a characteristic way. When it is separating itself from other units, it will align its components in a different way. The polarities change in each case, within the units. The unit will alter its polarities within itself, adapting the polarity-design of the unit to which it is being attracted; and it will change its polarity away from that design on breaking contact.

Take, for example, five thousand such units aligned together, formed together. They would, of course, be invisible. But if you could view them, each individual unit would have its poles lined up in the same manner. It would look like one single unit—say, it is of circular form—so it would appear like a small globe with the poles lined up as in your earth.

If this large unit were then attracted to another larger one, circular, with the poles running east and west, in your terms, then the first unit would change its own polarity, and all of the units within it would do the same. The energy point would be halfway between these poles, regardless of their position, and it (*the energy point*) forms the poles. They revolve, therefore, about the energy point. The energy point is indestructible basically.

Its intensity, however, can vary to amazing degrees, so that it could, relatively speaking, be too weak or fall back, not strong enough to form the basis for matter, but to project into another system, perhaps, where less intensity is required for "materialization."

These units may also gain so in intensity and strength that they form relatively permanent structures within your system because of the astonishing energy behind them. Your Stockridge—

(*Seth paused; Jane frowned as though groping for a word.*)

(*"Oak Ridge?"*)

No. (*Gesture.*) The remains of temples . . .

(*"Oh. Baalbek?"*)

These were places for studies concerning the stars. Observatories.

(*"Yes?" I thought I probably knew the word Seth/Jane was looking for, but I didn't have time to think and write notes.*)

The units so charged with intensive emotional energy formed patterns for matter that retained their strength. Now these units, while appearing within your system, may also have a reality outside it, propelling the emotional energy units *through* the world of matter entirely. These units, as I told you, are indestructible. They can, however, lose or gain power, fall back into intensities beneath matter, or go through matter, appearing *as* matter as they do so and projecting through your system.

We will deal with that portion of their activity separately. In such cases, however, they are in a point of transition obviously and in a state of becoming. You may take a break or end the session as you prefer.

(*"I guess we'd better end it."*)

I wanted to give you this material.

(*"It's very interesting."*)

It is only a beginning. I would disregard the analogies if you did not need them. A fond good evening.

(*"Good evening, Seth."*)

(*10:45. After we talked a bit, I deduced that Seth/Jane had been trying for the word "Stonehenge," meaning the ancient Druidic stone monoliths arranged in a circle in England, etc. Jane then said this was the word Seth had been trying to get her to say. She didn't know why it didn't come out while in trance, since she knows the word and what it stands for.*)

SESSION 509, NOVEMBER 24, 1969, 9:10 P.M. MONDAY

(*Today Jane had been reading* Experimental Psychology *by C. G. Jung, first American edition, published by Jung's heirs in 1968. We hadn't asked Seth to comment.*)

Good evening.

(*"Good evening, Seth."*)

Now: there is one large point, underestimated by all of your psychologists when they list the attributes or characteristics of consciousness. I am going to tie in this material with our discussion on our electromagnetic energy units, as there is a close connection.

Let us start with Jung. He presumes that consciousness must be organized about an ego structure. And what he calls the unconscious, not so egotistically organized, he, therefore, considers without consciousness—without consciousness of self. He makes a good point, saying that the normal ego cannot know unconscious material directly. He does not realize, however, nor do your other psychologists, what I have told you often—that there is an inner ego; and it is this inner ego that organizes what Jung would call unconscious material.

Again: when you are in a state that is not the usual waking one, when you have forsaken this daily self, you are, nevertheless, conscious and alert. You merely block out the memory from the waking ego. So when the attributes of consciousness are given, creativity is largely ignored. It is assigned, instead, primarily to the unconscious. My point is that the unconscious *is* conscious. Creativity is one of the most important attributes of consciousness, then. We will differentiate between normal ego consciousness and consciousness that only appears unconscious to that ego.

Now: the inner ego is the organizer of experience that Jung would call unconscious. The inner ego is another term for what we call the inner self. As the outer ego manipulates within the physical environment, so the inner ego or self organizes and manipulates with an inner reality. The inner ego creates that physical reality with which the outer ego then deals.

All the richly creative original work that is done by this inner self is not unconscious. It is purposeful, highly discriminating, performed by the inner conscious ego of which the exterior ego is but a shadow—and not, you see, the other way around. Jung's dark side of the self is the ego, not the unconscious. The complicated, infinitely varied, unbelievably rich tapestry of Jung's "unconscious" could hardly be *un*conscious. It is the product of an inner consciousness with far more sense of identity and purpose than the daily ego. It is the daily ego's ignorance and limited focus that makes it view so-called unconscious activity as chaotic.

The conscious ego rises, indeed, out of the "unconscious," but the unconscious, being the creator of the ego, is necessarily far more conscious than its offspring. The ego is simply not conscious enough to be able to contain the vast knowledge that belongs to the inner conscious self from which it springs.

It is this inner self, out of massive knowledge and the unlimited scope of its consciousness, that forms the physical world and provides stimuli to keep the outer ego constantly at the job of awareness. It is the inner self, here termed the inner ego, that organizes, initiates, projects, and controls the EE (*electromagnetic energy*) units of which we have been speaking, transforming energy into objects, into matter.

The energy of this inner self is used by it to form from itself—from inner experience—a material counterpart in which the outer ego then can act out its role. The outer ego then acts out a play that the inner self has written. This is not to say that the outer ego is a puppet. It is to say that the outer ego is far less conscious than the inner ego, that its perception is less, that it is far less stable though it makes great pretense of stability, that it springs from the inner self and is therefore less, rather than more, aware.

The outer ego is spoon-fed, being given only those feelings and emotions, only that data, that it can handle. This data is presented to it in a highly specialized manner, usually in terms of information picked up by the physical senses.

The inner self or ego is not only conscious, but conscious of itself, both as an individuality apart from others and as an individuality that is a part of all other consciousness. In your terms, it is continually aware, both of this apartness and unity-with. The outer ego is not continuously aware of anything. It frequently forgets itself. When it becomes swept up in a strong emotion it seems to lose itself; there is unity, then, but no sense of apartness. When it most vigorously maintains its sense of individuality, it is no longer aware of unity-with.

The inner ego is always aware of both aspects and is organized about its primary aspect which is creativity. It constantly translates the components of its gestalt into reality—either physical reality through the EE units I have mentioned, or into other realities equally as valid.

Now you may take your break and we shall continue.

(*During our break I wondered aloud if Jung had changed his ideas since his physical death.*)

(*Resume 10:05.*)

Now: the EE (*electromagnetic energy*) units are the forms that basic experience takes when directed by this inner self. These, then, form physical objects, physical matter. Matter, in other words, is the shape that basic experience takes when it intrudes into three-dimensional systems. Matter *is* the shape of your dreams. Your dreams, thoughts, and emotions are literally transformed into physical matter purposefully by this inner self.

The individual inner self, then, through constant massive effort of great creative intensity, cooperates with all other inner selves to form and maintain the physical reality that you know, so that physical reality is an offshoot or by-product of the highly conscious inner self.

Buildings appear to be made of rock or stone or steel. They appear fairly permanent to the physical senses. They are actually oscillating, ever-moving, highly charged gestalts of EE units (*"beneath," say, any atomic particles*), organized and maintained by the collective efforts on the part of inner selves. They (*the buildings*) *are* solidified emotions, solidified subjective states, given physical materialization.

The powers of consciousness are clearly not understood, then. Each individual has his part to play in projecting these EE units into physical actuality. Therefore, physical matter can be legitimately described as an extension of the self, as much as the physical body is a projection of the inner self.

It is obvious that the body grows up about the inner self, and that trees grow out of the ground, whereas buildings do not spring up like flowers of their own accord; so the inner self has various methods of creation and uses the EE units in different ways, as you shall see as we continue with the discussion.

Having determined upon physical reality as a dimension in which it will express itself, the inner self, first of all, takes care to form and maintain the physical basis upon which all else must depend—the properties of earth that can be called natural ones. The inner self has a vast and infinite reservoir from which to draw knowledge and experience. All kinds of choices are available, and the diversity of physical matter is a reflection of this deep source of variety.

With the natural structures formed and maintained, other secondary physical properties—secondary constructions—are projected. The deepest, most basic and abiding subjective experience is translated, however, into those natural elements: the ample landscape that sustains physical life. We will continue with this discussion at our next session.

Jung enlarged on some of his concepts shortly before he died. (*Leaning forward, humorously emphatic.*) He has changed a good many of them since then. Now you may take a break or end the session as you prefer.

(*"We'll take the break."*)

(*10:30 P.M. Jane said she thought the delivery had taken perhaps ten minutes instead of the twenty-five it had actually taken. Resume at 10:43.*)

We will shortly end the session. Suffice it to say, however, that in the future what I am telling you will be more generally known. Men will become familiar to some extent with their own inner identity, with other forms of their own consciousness.

Throughout the ages, some have recognized the fact that there is self-consciousness and purpose in certain dream and sleep states, and have maintained, even in waking life, the sense of continuity of this inner self. To such people it is no longer possible to identify completely with the ego consciousness. They are too obviously aware of themselves as more. When such knowledge is gained, the ego can accept it, for it finds to its surprise that it is not less conscious, but more, that its limitations are dissipated.

Now: it is not true—and I emphasize this strongly—that so-called unconscious material, given any freedom, will draw energy away from the egotistically organized self in a normal personality. Quite the contrary, the ego is replenished and rather directly. It is the fear that the "unconscious" is chaotic that causes psychologists to make such statements. There is also something in the nature of those who practice psychology: a fascination, in many cases, already predisposed to fear the "unconscious" in direct proportion to its attraction for them.

The ego maintains its stability, its seeming stability, and its health, from the constant subconscious and unconscious nourishment which it receives. Too much nourishment will not kill it. Do you follow me here?

("*Yes.*")

Only when such nourishment is for some reason cut off to a considerable degree is the ego threatened by starvation. We will have more to say concerning the ego's relationship with the "unconscious." In a healthy personality, the inner self easily projects all experience into EE units, where they are translated into actuality. Physical matter, therefore, acts as a feedback. Now we will end our session, unless you have questions.

("*I guess not. It's been very interesting.*")

My heartiest regards and a fond good evening to you both.

("*Did you like your pictures?*" *This refers to the photographs taken the night before this session, in our 508th session, by a photographer. The photographs will be used in Jane's book on the Seth Material.*)

I did indeed, and the young man who took them.

(*10:56*)

Index

thought as, 121–23
voice and, 49
Entities, 55, 156
  constant change by, 245
  three roles of, 155
Envelope tests, 68, 75–76, 79–88
Environment, influence of, 112
ESP, vi, 108
  author's book on, 4, 13–14, 43, 59–60,
    101, 190, 267
  electromagnetic basis of, 291–93
  envelope tests for, 68, 75–76, 79–88
  "Instream's" tests for, 68, 75, 77–78, 79,
    88–90, 92
  as natural ability, 266
  in Seth sessions, 52, 54
  See also Out-of-body experiences; Telepathy
ESP classes (author's), 1, 57, 104, 143–44,
  208, 234
Events, probable vs. physical, 201–2
Expansion or contraction of the tissue capsule,
  259–60

Fetus, astral form of, 289–92
Fifth dimension, 39, 45
"Fragment" personalities, see Personality
    fragments
Free will, 136, 247
Freedom, 167, 244
Freud, Sigmund, x
Friendships between planes, 47

Gallagher, Peg and Bill, 101–2, 254, 273
  experiments with, 71–74, 90–92
Garrett, Eileen, vii, viii-ix, 63
George, 94
God, 237–38
  as All That Is, 240–46
Guides, 142, 172

Health, see Illness
Hypnosis, 63–64
  of mediums, 211
  self-, 175

Ideas, see Thoughts
Illness and health, 159–75
  Mrs. Brian's, 107

Rob's, 9, 57–58
Seth on, 30, 58. 134–39, 161–75
Illusion, 98–101
Innate knowledge of basic reality, 258–59
Inner ego (inner self), 300–4
Inner Senses, 44, 118, 120, 196, 216–17, 225
  description of, 251–63
Inner vibrational touch, 254–55, 258
Internal visual data, 21
"Instream, Dr.," 63–68
  tests with, 68, 75, 77–78, 79, 88–90, 92

Jean, 146–47
Joanie, 159–64
Johnson, Raynor, on trance states, vi–vii
Jung, Carl, xi–xii
  Seth on, 299–300, 303

Kant, Immanuel, xi
Karma, 136
Kennedy, John F., dreams of, 193
King, Martin Luther, Jr., assassination of, 247

Leonard, Mrs. Osborne, vii
Linden, Jim and Ann, 126–33
Lowe, Rev., 143–45
Lydia, 145–46

Macdonell, Bill, 18–19, 33, 43, 106, 113–21
Materialization
  of personality fragments, 25–30
  of whole cosmic structure, 288
Matt, 152–55
Matter, 113–14
Maupassant, Guy de, x
Mediumship, v–ix
  hypnosis in, 211
  mental illness and, 52–53
  Seth on, 273–74
  trance depth and, 76–77
Mullin, Sue (Sue Watkins), 285, 289

National Hypnosis Symposium, 63–68
Negative thoughts, 164
Nonbeing, 240
Norelli, Pat, 228

Oakes, Sir Harry, 91